'England arise!'

"..FOR EVERY DAY I STAND OUTSIDE YOUR DOOR AND BID YOU WAKE!.."

'England arise!'

The Labour Party and popular politics in 1940s Britain

Steven Fielding,
Peter Thompson
and
Nick Tiratsoo

Manchester University Press
Manchester and New York
Distributed exclusively in the USA and Canada by St. Martin's Press

Published by Manchester University Press
Oxford Road, Manchester M13 9NR, UK
and Room 400, 175 Fifth Avenue, New York, NY 10010, USA

Distributed exclusively in the USA and Canada
by St Martin's Press, Inc., 175 Fifth Avenue, New York, NY 10010, USA

British Library Cataloguing-in-Publication Data
A catalogue record for this book is available from the British Library

Library of Congress Cataloging-in-Publication Data aplied for

ISBN   0 7190 3992 4 *hardback*
       0 7190 3993 2 *paperback*

First published 1995

99 98 97 96   10 9 8 7 6 5 4 3 2 1

Typeset in Great Britain
by Northern Phototypesetting Co Ltd, Bolton
Printed in Great Britain
by Bell & Bain Ltd, Glasgow

Contents

Illustrations and tables

Illustrations

Tables

Acknowledgements

This book would have been impossible without the help of those employed in a number of archives as well as various university and public libraries. We would like to express our particular gratitude to Stephen Bird and Andy Flynn at the Labour Party Archive in Manchester as well as Sarah Street and Martin Maw at the Conservative Party Archive in Oxford. The help of the staff of the following was also greatly appreciated: the British Film Institute Library, Birmingham Reference Library, the British Library of Political and Economic Science at the London School of Economics, Manchester Central Reference Library, the Modern Records Centre at the University of Warwick, the Public Record Office at Kew, Stockport Public Library and the Tom Harrisson Mass-Observation Archive at Sussex University.

Steven Fielding received financial assistance from the University of Salford Christopher Hale Fund.

The authors wish to acknowledge the permission of the Trustees of the Tom Harrisson Mass-Observation Archive for permission to quote material.

For their comments and help we would also like to thank the following individuals: Lindsay Abbot, Sandra Baum, Toby Haggith, Junichi Hasegawa, John Hodgkins, Hideo Ichihashi, Joan Keating, Frank Mort, Jim Obelkevich, Jim Tomlinson and Tatsuya Tsubaki. We also want to gratefully acknowledge the support and encouragement of our parents.

The authors would, finally, like to note their particular appreciation of the help given by Tony Mason to all three of them over the years.

In the second World war the British people came of age. This was a people's war. Not only were their needs considered. They themselves wanted to win. Future historians may see the war as a last struggle for the European balance of power or for the maintenance of Empire. This was not how it appeared to those who lived through it. The British people set out to destroy Hitler and National Socialism – 'Victory at all costs'. They succeeded. No English soldier who rode with the tanks into liberated Belgium or saw the German murder camps at Dachau or Buchenwald could doubt that the war had been a noble crusade. The British were the only people who went through both world wars from beginning to end. Yet they remained a peaceful and civilized people, tolerant, patient, and generous. Traditional values lost much of their force. Other values took their place. Imperial greatness was on the way out; the welfare state was on the way in. The British empire declined; the condition of the people improved. Few now sang 'Land of Hope and Glory'. Few even sang 'England Arise'. England had risen all the same.

A. J. P. Taylor, *English History, 1914–45*
(Oxford, 1965), p. 600

1

Introduction

This book examines the Labour Party's relationship with the British electorate from the late 1930s to the early 1950s. It follows Labour from the wilderness of the 'devil's decade', through the war, to six years of power under Attlee, and then final defeat by the Conservatives at the 1951 general election. The objective throughout is to provide a new perspective on events, challenging and adding to existing accounts. This introduction begins with a brief explanation as to why such revisionism has been felt necessary.

The current historiography of Labour in the middle decades of this century tends, unsurprisingly, to focus on the Party's period in office between 1945 and 1951.[1] Two broad interpretations have been offered. In the dominant view, the origins of Labour's ascent lie in Britain's decision to fight a 'people's war' against the Axis – a war involving all classes and both sexes. Co-opting the population in this way, it is argued, promoted a new sense of national purpose, and persuaded many of the need for social reconciliation. There could, in short, be no going back to the division and waste of the 1930s. Labour was the natural beneficiary of this mood and swept to power in 1945 on its back. Thereafter, the Party's performance was decisive and noteworthy: the picture presented is of a united administration, with a coherent programme, in step with public opinion, and as a result able to fashion new solutions both at home and abroad. Labour eventually fell, in this view, because it ran out of steam, but the ideas and spirit of the period were firmly enough established to live on, shaping the next thirty years of British history. The Attlee administration was, therefore, genuinely consensual. The country

desired change in 1945 and Labour was uniquely placed to provide it.[2]

Reacting against these somewhat benign assertions, some
marxist and feminist historians have continued to insist that the
1940s should be seen in a much more critical light. They share
the view that the war was an important catalyst but argue that
its impact was a good deal more directly political than the mainstream version suggests. Britain was fighting fascism, on the same
side as the Soviet Union, and this alone injected subversive perspectives. Furthermore, the mobilisation at home took place in a
way that boosted the role of the state and the confidence of ordinary people: it was the man from Whitehall and the woman in
the engineering factory that had ensured the smooth production
of weapons, not the capitalist plutocrat. Thus, by the end of the
war, the majority of people in Britain were radicalised and the
traditional class and gender hierarchies seemed to be crumbling.
Labour's victory in 1945 reflected this dramatic upsurge and suggested the beginning of a new order. However, what followed
provided only disappointment, since socialism, as Angus Calder
puts it, 'was not given rein, but was jerked back and confused'.
Labour contained some genuine socialists, but its leadership
believed in class collaboration and so soon became involved in
trying to re-stabilise capitalism and prosecute America's cold war.
A few reforms were enacted but these were deeply flawed, largely
because the Government mistrusted real popular involvement.
The National Health Service, which was allegedly bureaucratic
and managerial rather than democratic and participatory, illustrated the prevailing ethos. Within a relatively short period of
time, therefore, Attlee's administration was revealed, in Raymond
Williams's words, as 'an objectively quite reactionary government'. In these circumstances, it was inevitable that ordinary
people should feel betrayed, and, in the end, their disillusionment
proved so great that Labour was expelled from power. The whole
episode, to conclude, is most remarkable for the perfidy of the
Government and the diversity and richness of so-called 'sup-
pressed alternatives'.[3]

Both of these interpretations remain influential but in recent
years there has been a growing feeling that neither is wholly
credible. Critics of the consensus school have pointed out that
social-democratic ideas were hardly hegemonic either during the

1 Addressing the faithful. Clement Attlee facing delegates at the 1940
Labour Party Conference

war or afterwards. Discussion on subjects like education, welfare
reform, town planning and industrial policy usually involved disagreements between major participants.[4] Moreover, there has
been a general re-evaluation of the war's impact on British society, and many would now judge it far less disruptive of social
relations than was once imagined. Indeed, recent research on
some of the key developments that were supposed to have transformed attitudes – the evacuations, the employment of women in
factories, and army education – reveals that none acted straightforwardly in this way.[5]

A further criticism, which applies virtually across the board,
relates to the way in which popular political affiliations have been
typically presented. Statements about ordinary people's attitudes
and choices abound but many of these turn out, on close inspection, to be of dubious validity. In some left-wing historiography,
the working class of this period is simply assumed to have been

actually or potentially socialist because of its long experience of capitalist iniquity.[6] Little effort is expended on establishing the point. Thus, when the much quoted marxist political scientist Ralph Miliband set out to prove the Attlee Government's treachery, he saw no need to comment in any detail on the electorate's preferences: his case is established solely by a selective reading of Labour Party conference reports, bolstered by the odd reference to *Hansard*, the press and a small number of political biographies.[7] In more conventional accounts, the problem is that popular politics tends to be viewed only from the perspective of Westminster, and constructed from cabinet papers and ministerial diaries. This allows an appreciation of how those in power evaluated possibilities but it largely ignores some important other dimensions. Little is said about the party machines, as they existed either nationally or locally. Moreover, once again, the ordinary voters remain somewhat mysterious, present at election times in the psephological data but otherwise without a significant voice.

Of course, some would claim that they have circumvented these difficulties through the use of oral evidence and there is now quite a large radical and feminist literature of this type covering the war and after.[8] However, it is by no means clear that these accounts represent any real advance. Taped recollections are presented as if more authentic than conventional evidence but this ignores the fact that abnormal conditions – trauma or great excitement – structure memory in particular ways and make an 'innocent' verbal reconstruction of an event almost impossible. It may well be, therefore, that oral histories covering such a dramatic period as the 1940s are poor guides to what really happened. Tom Harrisson, a founder of the social research organisation, Mass-Observation, made this point some years ago when discussing the Blitz. He noted that those who had lived through the bombing rarely later recalled it with any degree of accuracy:

> For most surviving citizens the major effect has been (as often) in two opposite directions, both processes in 'reality obliteration': either to be unable to remember anything much (with no wish to do so), or, more usually, to see those nights as glorious. There is not much in between. But in between is where most of the unpub-

lished evidence points – the evidence, that is, written down and filed immediately, without any intention of publication.[9]

Given the extent of these problems, it seemed appropriate to construct a new account of Labour's fortunes in the 1940s using an approach that genuinely embraces the popular. The following chapters, therefore, attempt to develop what might be termed the social history of the period's mass politics. The key concern throughout, in other words, is with ordinary people's general views, their electoral choices and the range of factors that may have influenced both, not least the various campaigns conducted by the two main political parties.

In practical terms, this has meant examining a large range of sources, including the records of various institutions, material collected by Mass-Observation, an array of social surveys and the findings of Gallup and other polling organisations. One or two of these may be considered controversial, perhaps even unreliable. Mass-Observation, it has been suggested, was in part a social movement not a pure exercise in scientific investigation.[10] Opinion poll data, some argue, may give an unduly static impression of the public mood and mould complex viewpoints into simple answers. However, while there is something in each of these objections, none can be considered as finally invalidating. Most of those who collected information on social attitudes in the 1940s, whatever organisation they reported to, were aware of the need for objectivity and there was considerable discussion about techniques and methods.[11] Opinion pollsters, in particular, continued to be extremely concerned about accuracy and compiled what were, by today's standards, very large samples as a result.[12] Moreover, it should be noted that these sources have been deployed here in a way that tends to minimise risk: they are used to establish broad trends, almost always alongside other forms of evidence. In such circumstances, anxieties about methods of data collection seem of much less importance.

To complete these preliminary remarks, it remains only to indicate how what follows has been organised. The format is essentially chronological. Chapters 2 and 3 deal with the war and investigate, first, the general development of public attitudes and, next, the more specific question of political activity. Chapters 4, 5 and 6 focus on Labour's years in power, describing the Party's vision of socialism and then what happened when attempts were made to implement it. Chapter 7 examines why Labour was finally beaten by the Conservatives, while Chapter 8 provides a brief overview and conclusion, summarising the book's argument and explaining what this implies for the wider historiography. However, before any of these topics can be tackled, it will be necessary to return to the 1930s and outline where Labour stood in the final years of peace. The rest of this chapter forms such a prologue.

Looking at the political situation in the late 1930s, there were certainly good reasons for thinking that Labour was in a strong position. The Party had reached its nadir in 1931, of course, smitten by MacDonald's defection and an election disaster, but afterwards seemed to have gradually recovered. At the 1935 election, there had been no real possibility of defeating the Conservatives, but Labour's performance was nevertheless far better than four years previously, with 1.7 million more votes yielding three times as many MPs.[13] Subsequent by-election results confirmed the generally favourable trend. Sometimes success was spectacular. At Ipswich in February 1938, Labour overturned a government majority of more than 7,000, prompting its national agent to record: 'The election was fought by both political organisations very intensely and polling day excitement and tension will long be remembered'.[14] Moreover, the Party itself appeared to be in relatively good shape, very different from the divided and demoralised shell of 1932 and 1933. Membership had fallen from 2 million in 1930 to an interwar low of 1.9 million four years later but had then begun to revive, reaching 2.6 million in 1938.[15] Furthermore, activity levels looked impressive. The national organisation was promoting several big campaigns every year at the end of the 1930s, based on themes such as 'peace and security' and 'food and farming' and each involved much hard work. For example, the rural drive during the summer of 1938 comprised as many as 2,035 meetings in seventy-eight constituencies and the distribution of over four million leaflets.[16] Meanwhile, some local parties were also working to good effect. As many as 150 regularly produced their own newspaper, while many others canvassed and marketed literature, with the two million books and pamphlets sold in 1938 breaking all previous records.[17] All in all, there seemed to be a new confidence abroad.

Indeed, Labour could even boast that it was now supported by the country's biggest selling morning newspaper, since the relaunched *Daily Herald* had finally passed all of its more right-wing Fleet Street competitors.[18]

In these circumstances, there were some who had begun to predict that the Party was actually on the verge of power. A veteran constituency agent told the novelist and reporter Walter Greenwood in early 1939 that Labour's prospects were "'decidedly healthy'" because "'the pendulum is swinging our way again'". The Conservatives would have to hold an election some time before the end of 1940, and there was every chance that they could be beaten.[19] However, as those at the centre of Labour's organisation knew very well, it was easier to express such sentiments than actually justify them. For while enormous progress had undeniably been made since 1931, this was very different from saying that the Party would win the next general election. In fact, appraising Labour's chances in a realistic way revealed that much ground still needed to be made up. Too many problems within the Party's rank remained unresolved. More importantly, there was little sign of any pronounced leftward shift in the electorate, the kind of sea change that would really transform fortunes.

At Labour's headquarters, finance continued to be a central limiting constraint. Legislation passed in 1927 by the Conservatives had curtailed trade union contributions to the Party and created the conditions for a continuing imbalance in the yearly accounts.[20] A report by Labour's Finance and General Purposes Sub-Committee in 1938 complained: 'For over twelve years now the Party has been in constant financial difficulty. Annual deficits, often substantial, have recurred with great regularity'.[21] In this situation, there was always pressure to curtail spending and public work suffered as a consequence. Labour certainly ran big campaigns, as has been noted, but many of these used old fashioned techniques and outmoded publicity material. At a New Fabian Research Bureau gathering in 1936, one participant observed that the Party's methods reflected a time when there was no mass electorate. During a conference on 'selling socialism', held the following year, the tenor of criticism was even more pronounced. Most agreed with the contention of a *Daily Herald* journalist that Labour should conduct a wholesale review:

What were the present defects of party propaganda? It was too dif-
fuse and lacking in simple central ideas; tended to be gloomy and
out of touch with human interests, and was too obviously propaganda and often directed to the politically interested section of the
population only; it lacked a patriotic note.[22]

In the country at large, Labour's position was weakened by
other difficulties. Some local parties prospered but others appeared
to be stagnating. Apathy and decay were particularly remarked
upon in areas where Labour had made its earliest breakthroughs.
A report on West Ham at the end of the 1930s found that the
party there had virtually no public presence: 'The word "retired"
may be interpreted exactly, for labour in the borough has now
grown old and sleepy and has settled down to enjoy the recollec-
tion of its past achievements, and to do, politically, nothing'.[23] A
correspondent to Labour Organiser in the summer of 1938 noted a
similar trend in the coalfields:

> The miners' vote is solid.
> And yet there are two unsatisfactory features in most of these
> constituencies.
> In the first place, political, or rather Party, machinery is often of
> the poorest, or even absent altogether, and secondly, individual
> membership of a good and paying sort is most frequently conspicu-
> ous by its absence.[24]

Indeed, Labour's influence in such areas had sometimes degener-
ated into a form of clientism, divorced from any wider political
considerations. Visiting the north-west Monmouthshire townships
of Nantyglo and Blaina in 1937, the journalist Phillip Massey
described how such a relationship was almost all-pervasive:

> There seems to be little doubt that many Labour leaders owe much
> of their support to creating a personal sense of obligation ... and a
> common ground of criticism is that they will promise to 'see to
> things' for an individual, rather than challenge on the principle
> involved, thus creating a feeling of indebtedness.[25]

Elsewhere, the problem was not so much inactivity as division.
At the end of the 1930s, some on the left of the Party had begun
promoting the idea of a popular front to oppose fascism – a front
that would embrace Communists and Liberals – and this was

being vigorously resisted by the leadership and many ordinary members.[26] Much of the debate took place in left-wing periodicals but in some cases the tensions were also evident in local parties. A visitor to the East Willesden constituency organisation in 1938 found it riven by internal squabbling: 'A Communist could not oppose a Fascist more bitterly than they oppose each other within the Management Committee, and it is the seeming joy of their days for these two factions to oppose each other'.[27] A more general kind of debility stemmed from the typical gender hierarchy that existed in the Party.[28] Male members tended to dominate proceedings and internal elections, leaving their women comrades feeling excluded. Sometimes greater female participation was actively limited by direct discrimination but, more often than not, the impediment appeared to be less tangible, a matter of the prevailing ethos. An organiser in Rhondda West, active during 1937, noted that Labour women were loath to attend meetings at the Pentre Labour Club because of the unpleasant atmosphere. 'They have to pass through a corridor near the Bar', she explained, 'and very often there are men there drinking'.[29]

Turning to the question of influence with the electorate, it was evident that, here too, Labour's real position was a good deal weaker than some imagined. The Party's performance at the 1935 election was without doubt creditable but it could not be described as exceptional. Labour had done well in the poorer areas of Scotland and London, as well as in the coalfields. However, most of the rest of the country was solidly Conservative. G.D.H. and Margaret Cole noted, for example, that in 'the whole of South and East England, from Lincolnshire to Cornwall, but excluding London itself, the Conservatives and their "National" allies won 156 seats, whereas Labour won only 15, and the Liberals only 3'. What this showed was that Labour had failed with a large section of the working population – as the Coles described them, 'the huge army of clerks and typists, managers, shop assistants, garage hands, lorry drivers, attendants at cinemas, road houses, swimming pools and other places of amusement, hotel servants and restaurant workers and domestic servants'.[30] Nor was progress after 1935 really any more promising. Labour won some by-elections, it is true, but the average swing involved was nowhere near large enough to suggest victory at a general election.[31] Meanwhile, the situation at a local gov-

ernment level also remained unpromising. A Party document of
late 1938 described recent trends:

> Since 1934 we have been at a standstill outside London. In the
> County Boroughs we hold only a third of the Councillorships, and
> in the non-County Boroughs about a sixth. Although there are
> altogether about 9,400 Councillors' seats, our net gain since 1930
> has been under 300. During 1924–29 there was steady progress;
> during 1930–32 a severe setback; in 1933–34 a considerable
> recovery; and nothing much has happened since, despite increased
> efforts.[32]

What made this situation all the more dispiriting to Labour
strategists was the fact that it appeared to be essentially unalter-
able. For while some working-class electors enthused about the
Party's aims and a smaller number actively opposed them, the
majority were plainly uninterested, sometimes even oblivious. On
occasion, this was the result of poverty: unemployment and low
wages produced demoralisation and a cynicism about society.[33]
However, more often than not, it represented an active choice.
The normal working-class world centred on the family, the home
and recreation, and tended to be largely self-contained. It was
marked, as outsiders frequently observed, both by 'an absolute
stress on private life' and by a relative indifference to wider
issues.[34] In these conditions, all party politics could easily appear
to be simply irrelevant. Significantly, this attitude held firm even
during and after the Munich crisis of 1938.

The typical priorities in working-class culture were evident
throughout the life-cycle. Amongst adolescents, the emphasis was
usually on hedonistic enjoyment, but when looked at more closely, much of this could be seen as essentially about finding a part-
ner. The journalist H.V. Morton met a young and politically committed seamstress who complained that all her workmates did
was talk about the opposite sex: '"Girls are sloppy. It's men, men,
men all day long ... You ought to work in a factory and sit
besides the girls and eat your food in a canteen and go home in a
tram with them and you'd never want to hear the word 'men'
again"'.[35] Later, in married life, the key concern became the
home, with recreation still important but now necessarily
confined to the margins. Mass-Observation conducted exhaustive
research in Bolton during the late 1930s and concluded: 'On the

whole people care about their own homes, and their few personal dreams (security, a holiday week at orientalised Blackpool, a fortune in the Pools) and nothing else matters very much except the progress made by the town's famous football club'.[36] Occasionally, in the better-off suburbs of other cities, developments had gone a stage further, and the common aspirations could be seen crystallising into a definite life-style, based upon material possessions and driven by personal ambition. One radical writer visited a new East Midlands housing estate in 1939 and was shocked by its inhabitants' philistine and introverted sensibilities, remarking that 'Pope would be their poet, Coward their diversion, their own skins their god, respectability their religion'.[37]

In contrast to the energy that was invested in family and home, most ordinary people were only marginally interested in the outside world, whether it be the local neighbourhood or the nation as a whole. The number who took part in community activity of any kind was always small. The sociologist Ruth Durant surveyed a new residential development on the fringes of London at this time and reported: 'If ... we regard membership of local organisations as indicative of people's interests, it appears that the men and women on the Estate are more concerned with their family problems than with either communal recreation or traditional and modern creeds'.[38] Similar trends were also evident in longer established areas. South Wales had a strong tradition of proletarian activism but many of its key organisations, too, were suffering because of popular apathy. Massey investigated adult education at Nantyglo and Blaina and found that it had 'declined considerably as compared with pre-war days when there were less counter-attractions'.[39] Activists in the Welsh Co-operative Movement, meanwhile, frequently complained that while working-class families usually shopped in their stores, they would rarely help run them. One told the *Co-operative Review*: 'The percentage of members who take more than a passing interest in Co-operative affairs is lamentably low'.[40]

Events and organisations in the national arena usually provoked even less enthusiasm. Only about one-third of male workers and a sixth of their female counterparts belonged to trade unions and few of these could be counted as activists. The typical level of commitment was illustrated by the fact that some 64 per cent of union members in 1939 had not bothered to 'contract in' and thus help finance the Labour Party.[41] In fact, the way society operated tended to be not very well understood and so infrequently discussed. Mass-Observation analysed 15,000 conversations recorded in Bolton and discovered that on a normal day only 0.3 per cent were about politics.[42] Many working-class men, it is true, disliked those in authority and believed that 'they' were 'running the country for their own benefit', but such views were usually expressed without any particular political implication.[43] For the most part, the common feeling was that ordinary people should accept their lot and 'make the best of it'. Even practical issues bearing directly on working-class life provoked relatively little interest. An extra-mural lecturer at Durham University examined unemployment in the Newcastle area at the end of the 1930s and was shocked by the degree of public ignorance on the subject. He wrote:

> If we could send a questionnaire or examination paper around to the adult inhabitants of Tyneside asking them what proportion of their population was in 1938 in receipt of U[nemployment]. A[ssistance]. B[oard]. allowances, and how this proportion compared with that in other parts of England, we should receive undoubtedly very few answers at all, and very few of those would be correct.[44]

Not surprisingly, many of these general attitudes coloured feelings about the more specific question of party politics. A tiny proportion were members of the main organisations.[45] Amongst the majority, interest could flicker but it was rarely sustained and usually quite quickly dissipated given new conditions or the removal of key personalities. Ebbw Vale Labour women told a national organiser in 1937 that 'they were very concerned ... [about] the indifference ... creeping into the area, owing to the prosperity that the New [steel] works of Richard Thomas was bringing'.[46] In fact, politics had often become synonymous in the public mind with voting, but even this was often done in a way that suggested lack of enthusiasm. Many women were apparently content to leave the whole matter in the hands of their partners. '"My husband sees to all that"', according to Mass-Observation, was 'the characteristic female pre-war remark about voting intentions'.[47] Moreover, members of both sexes abstained in some numbers, especially at local contests. A survey of municipal elections, which focused on cities with populations of 50,000 and above in

1935, found that only about half of their electorates normally voted. Outside the big urban areas, abstentions were even more common. One writer noted in 1937 that Surrey County Council was 'in the unchallenged position of the German Reichstag', since at a recent election about three-quarters of its seats had not been contested.[48]

There were some, particularly on the left, who argued that these attitudes to politics were rapidly being transformed during 1938 and 1939 as a result of German aggression and British appeasement. Ordinary people, they believed, were disgusted by Chamberlain's foreign policy and had at last woken up to the reality of their subordination. Strong convictions could be seen emerging from the miasma of apathy.[49] However, as those with a better purchase on public opinion knew very well, such views were more than a little illusory.

Small numbers had, no doubt, been interested in politics by European events – the Spanish civil war and the Munich crisis, in particular. Nevertheless, for most people, developments abroad remained remote and incomprehensible. Mass-Observation reported that the normal reaction during 1938 and 1939 was one of 'bewilderment', adding: 'For those millions who do not understand maps and have no passport, the whole thing seems largely crazy'.[50] Other observers came to similar conclusions. A Carnegie Trust enquiry, based on a large sample of unemployed young adults, concluded that few had been touched by foreign affairs:

> The interviews during the crisis period of September 1938 were perhaps the most revealing. A number of men joined the Territorial Army, and some of them found work on Air Raid Precaution measures. Apart from these manifestations of crisis activity, it was difficult to discover any real concern at the possible outcome of the international situation. The state of apathy and indifference was not only true of the unemployed but was found to a certain extent amongst the employed. They understood politics only in terms of work and saw in the international difficulties a chance of getting some employment, even though that might be in the Army. Apart from this, there was an absence of concern which was disconcerting.[51]

Moreover, there was no real departure from this pattern at the by-elections of the period. In October 1938, shortly after Munich, the Master of Balliol, A.H. Lindsay, fought the Conservatives' Quintin Hogg at Oxford, and made the Government's foreign policy a major issue. However, there was little popular response. As a student of the contest remarked: 'One could not help being struck by the fact that electoral apathy ... functioned even in a campaign so important as [this]'.[52]

In fact, taking the situation as a whole, it was quite clear that the various crises had done little to stimulate political change, either by raising interest or by changing allegiances. Conservative dominance remained intact. Gallup enquired about the Prime Minister's performance on ten occasions in the year to October 1939 and found an average 58 per cent satisfied as against 42 per cent critical. On the broader question of which party should be in power, opinion was even more emphatic: asked in February 1939 who they would vote for in a general election, 54 per cent plumped for the Government and only 30 per cent for the opposition.[53] Meanwhile, those who supported radical alternatives were simply isolated. A sympathetic observer's description of a peace demonstration in Sheffield during early 1939 said much about the reality of popular preferences:

> The number of the processionists was disappointing; at the most there were only a thousand. The reaction of the Sheffield people was still more disappointing, for quite a few, in their ignorance laughed ... Why should people be so indifferent? ... It was a Saturday afternoon, and the city was filled with people, but they were not in the procession. My wife, more practical than me, supplied the answers to my questions. First, she said, that the men had been working hard all the week and couldn't be expected to get a thrill out of marching in a peace procession; secondly, the women had their shopping to do; and thirdly, most of the people who organise peace movements have little in common with ordinary working-class people.[54]

To conclude, there was little reason to suppose that Labour stood on the verge of a breakthrough at the end of the 1930s. The Party enjoyed a good deal of support in the working class but not nearly enough to threaten the Conservatives. In 1935, J.B. Priestley had written of his worries about the way public opinion was developing:

It is true that the English are kindly folk. But a good deal of what is praised as tolerance is merely indifference, based on a dwindling interest in politics and also a false feeling of security. It is not so much that these people are monuments of patience and kindness as that they do not really care about what is happening in public affairs.[55]

Four years later, despite the slide to war, the same mentality still tended to dominate. The next two chapters will look at how attitudes were modified once the fighting started.

Notes

1 For a useful overview of the historiography, see S. Burgess, '1945 Observed – A History of the Histories', *Contemporary Record*, 5:1 (1991), 155–70.

2 This view is best presented in P. Addison, *The Road to 1945* (London, 1975); P. Hennessy, *Never Again. Britain 1945–1951* (London, 1992); and K.O. Morgan, *Labour in Power, 1945–51* (Oxford, 1984).

3 The quotations in this paragraph come from A. Calder, 'Labour and the Second World War', in D. Rubinstein (ed), *People for the People* (London, 1973), p. 235 and R. Williams, *Politics and Letters. Interviews with New Left Review* (London, 1979), p. 71. Other studies which advance this interpretation are B. Campbell, *The Iron Ladies* (London, 1987); G. Elliott, *Labourism and the English Genius* (London, 1993); J. Fyrth (ed), *Labour's High Noon* (London, 1993); R. Miliband, *Parliamentary Socialism* (London, 1961); and J. Saville, *The Labour Movement in Britain* (London, 1988).

4 See, for example, S. Brooke, *Labour's War. The Labour Party during the Second World War* (Oxford, 1992); J. Hasegawa, *Replanning the Blitzed City Centre* (Buckingham, 1992); K. Jefferys, 'British Politics and Social Policy during the Second World War', *Historical Journal*, 30:1 (1987), 123–44; N. Tiratsoo, *Reconstruction, Affluence and Labour Politics: Coventry 1945–60* (London, 1990); and N. Tiratsoo and J. Tomlinson, *Industrial Efficiency and State Intervention: Labour 1939–51* (London, 1993).

5 See, for example, S.P. Mackenzie, *Politics and Military Morale* (Oxford, 1992) and various contributions in H.L. Smith (ed), *War and Social Change. British Society in the Second World War* (Manchester, 1986).

6 See, for example, E. Hobsbawm, 'The Forward March of Labour

Halted?' and 'Observations on the Debate', in M. Jacques and F. Mulhern (eds), *The Forward March of Labour Halted?* (London, 1981), pp. 1–19 and 167–82.

7 Miliband, *Parliamentary Socialism*, pp. 272–317.

8 For example, P. Ayres, *Women at War* (Birkenhead, 1988); P. Grafton, *You, You and You!* (London, 1981); and L. Verrill-Rhys and D. Beddoe, *Parachutes and Petticoats. Welsh Women Writing on the Second World War* (Dinas Powys, South Glamorgan, 1992).

9 T. Harrisson, *Living Through the Blitz* (Harmondsworth, 1978), p. 321.

10 P. Summerfield, 'Mass Observation: Social History or Social Movement?', *Journal of Contemporary History*, 20:3 (1985), 439–52.

11 For example, M. Abrams, *Social Surveys and Social Action* (London, 1951) and K. Box and G. Thomas, 'The Wartime Social Survey', *Journal of the Royal Statistical Society*, 107: 3–4 (1944), 151–89.

12 The News Chronicle and the British Institute of Public Opinion, *What Britain Thinks* (London, 1939); *Public Opinion*, 10 February 1950; and R. M. Worcester, *British Public Opinion. A Guide to the History and Methodology of Political Opinion Polling* (Oxford, 1991).

13 G.D.H. and M.I. Cole, *The Condition of Britain* (London, 1937), pp. 310–11.

14 Labour Party Archive, Manchester [hereafter LPA], NEC Minutes 23 February 1938, National Agent, 'By-Election Report', [n.d.], p. 3.

15 Labour Party, *Report of the Thirty-Eighth Annual Conference of the Labour Party* (London, 1939), p. 92.

16 *Ibid.*, p. 68.

17 Anon., 'Our Directory of Local Labour Newspapers', *Labour Organiser*, 18:199 (1938), 10-13; Anon. 'Our Directory ... Second List', *Labour Organiser*, 18:200 (1938), 34–5; and M. Hackett, 'Literature', *Labour Organiser*, 19:211 (1939), 10.

18 F. Williams, *Dangerous Estate. The Anatomy of Newspapers* (London, 1959), pp. 161–77.

19 W. Greenwood, *How the Other Man Lives* (London, n.d. but 1939), pp. 254–5.

20 The legislation placed the emphasis on trade unionists' 'contracting in'; previously they had 'contracted out' if they did not wish to pay. See M.A. Hamilton, *The Labour Party To-Day* (London, n.d. but 1939), pp. 59–61.

21 LPA, Finance and General Purposes Sub-Committee, 17 March 1938, 'Preliminary Memorandum on Increasing and Stabilising Normal

Party Income', February 1938, p. 1.

22 Fabian Society Archive, Nuffield College Oxford, J. 15/6, New Fabian Research Bureau, 'Weekend Conference', 18–19 January 1936, p. 9; and J. 16/6, New Fabian Research Bureau 'Report ...', 23–4 October 1937, p. 1.

23 E.D. Idle, *War Over West Ham* (London, 1943), p. 32.

24 Anon, 'The Problem in Mining Divisions', *Labour Organiser*, 18:206 (1938), 165.

25 P. Massey, 'Portrait of a Mining Town', *Fact*, 8 (1937), 42.

26 B. Pimlott, *Labour and the Left in the 1930s* (London, 1977), pp. 143–82.

27 LPA, NEC Minutes 6–7 September 1938, W. Stimpson, 'East Willesden Parliamentary By-Election ... Report', 26 August 1938, p. 2.

28 P.M. Graves, *Labour Women. Women in British Working-Class Politics 1918–1939* (Cambridge, 1994) examines this issue.

29 LPA, Mary Sutherland Papers, LP/WORG/37/339, E. Andrews, Report of a visit to Rhondda West, 27 July 1937.

30 Coles, *Condition of Britain*, pp. 412 and 418.

31 D. Butler, 'Trends in British By-Elections', *Journal of Politics*, 11:2 (1949), 401-5.

32 LPA, Labour Party Campaign Committee, 8 November 1938, Item 67.

33 See, for example, L.E. White, *Tenement Town* (London, 1946), pp. 17–18.

34 Mass-Observation, *The Pub and the People* (London, 1943), p. 5.

35 H.V. Morton, *Our Fellow Men* (London, 1936), p. 145.

36 Mass-Observation, *Pub and the People*, p. 19.

37 J. Hilton, *English Ways* (London, 1940), p. 79.

38 R. Durant, *Watling. A Survey of Life on a New Housing Estate* (London, 1939), p. 60.

39 Massey, 'Portrait', 50.

40 W.S. Collins, 'Saga of South Wales', *Co-operative Review*, 17:3 (1943), 43.

41 H.A. Clegg, *A History of British Trade Unions since 1889. Volume 3. 1934-1951* (Oxford, 1994), p. 430.

42 Mass-Observation, *War Begins At Home* (London, 1940), p. 148.

43 M.G. Dickson, 'The Factory Workers' Philosophy', *Sociological Review*, 28:3 (1936), 295–312.

44 D.M. Goodfellow, *Tyneside. The Social Facts* (Newcastle, 1942), p. 16.

45 See, for example, A. Lush, *The Young Adult* (Cardiff, 1941), p. 50.

46 LPA, Mary Sutherland Papers, LP/WORG/37/473, E. Andrews, Report on Visit to Ebbw Vale, 11 January 1937.

47 T. Harrisson, 'Appeals To Women', *Political Quarterly*, 13:3 (1942), 265.

48 E.C. Rhodes, 'Voting at Municipal Elections', *Political Quarterly*, 9:2 (1938), 271; and R. Sinclair, *Metropolitan Man* (London, 1937), p. 321.

49 See, for example, *Listener*, 8 December 1938.

50 *New Statesman*, 22 April 1939.

51 C. Cameron, A. Lush and G. Meard, *Preliminary Report on the 18+ Age Group Enquiry* (Edinburgh, 1940), p. 47.

52 S.F. Rae, 'The Oxford By-Election: A Study in the Straw-Vote Method', *Political Quarterly*, 10:2 (1939), 279.

53 G.H. Gallup, *The Gallup International Public Opinion Polls. Great Britain, 1937–75, Volume One* (New York, 1976), pp. 9, 11, 12, 13, 14, 16, 17, 18, 20, 21, and 23.

54 Hilton, *English Ways*, p. 31.

55 J.B. Priestley, 'Introduction', in I. Brown, *The Heart of England* (London, 1935), p. vi.

2

Popular attitudes in wartime

In 1945 commentators of every political hue were agreed that Labour's election victory was due, at least in part, to the conduct of the war effort. The 'people's war', it was alleged, had promoted a new sense of national purpose – transcending the divisions of class, gender, ethnicity and region that normally characterised British society. Since the crisis of Dunkirk in 1940 the nation was, in an oft-repeated wartime phrase, 'all in it together', united by a spirit of self-sacrifice.[1] Government policy only served to reinforce this feeling. Conscription, evacuation, rationing and communal air raid shelters were widely believed to have strengthened social cohesion. At the same time, many argued, all of these developments had a radical edge. Working-class families seemed to have grown more confident because of their immersion in the war effort and were now determined that there should be no return to the suffering of the 1930s. Attitudes among the better-off, too, were apparently changing as an increasing number became aware of how their poorer fellow citizens lived. Many in the middle class resolved to tackle the poverty, bad housing and disease which soured working-class life. The enthusiastic endorsement of Labour's reform programme in 1945, it was concluded, reflected the culmination of these trends, the common desire for a new Britain.

The following two chapters offer a reassessment of these common contemporary perceptions. Chapter 3 deals with the explicitly political aspects of the wartime situation, and describes both party activity and the pattern of popular loyalties. This chapter serves as an introduction to such a discussion by outlining the broader context. It looks at the way the conflict shaped experience and traces how ordinary people reacted to their altered circumstances. The object is to discover whether there was, indeed, a new and widely-held desire for change in 1945. For ease of exposition, the argument is divided into three parts. The first examines two key home front developments – evacuation and the Blitz – and asks to what extent either promoted social solidarity. The second concentrates on the alleged growth of popular radicalism and explores both military and industrial spheres to assess its real proportions. A final section summarises views on reconstruction – the way Britain was to be rebuilt after the Axis had been defeated.

The origins of the Government's evacuation scheme lay in contemporary anxieties about the character of modern warfare.[2] By the 1930s it was widely assumed that in any future war the civilian population of Britain's major towns and cities would be the target of enemy bombing. Evacuation – the removal of people from vulnerable urban centres to the safer countryside – would, it was believed, both minimise casualties and pre-empt any unofficial mass exodus which was bound to follow such air raids. The scheme, as it emerged in the winter of 1938-39, provided for the voluntary evacuation of some four million 'priority classes' – largely children, mothers with pre-school children, pregnant women and the disabled. They were to be billeted in private houses, an unavoidable consequence of the numbers involved. The country was divided into evacuation zones (from which the movement of priority classes would take place), reception zones (which would receive the evacuees) and neutral zones.

Mass evacuation began in the first week of September 1939 with the dispersal of some 1.45 million people – mainly mothers and children – to reception zones up and down the country.[3] Although involving markedly fewer than the three to four million anticipated, the scheme was still dogged by logistical problems. Evacuees were sent to the wrong place and local billeting officers frequently found themselves with parties of a different size or social composition than they had expected. On arrival, almost all were tired, hungry and homesick. Yet within days, many were reasonably settled in their new surroundings. However, the behaviour and condition of others was the subject of much controversy among both host families and the general public.[4] For evacuees were drawn disproportionately from the most deprived areas of Britain's cities. Many were, it was alleged, dirty, verminous and disease-ridden. The mothers were rude, feckless and irresponsible whilst the children were often bad mannered, ill-clothed and had little knowledge of toilet training. Nor was such behaviour apparently confined to the very poor. The Conservative industrialist Oliver Lyttleton remembered the thirty-one infants in his care as 'completely ignorant of the simplest rules of hygiene'; they apparently regarded the floors and carpets 'as suitable places upon which to relieve themselves'. He was, however, 'still more surprised when some of their parents arrived in motor cars to see them at the week-end'.[5]

By January 1940, nearly 90 per cent of evacuated mothers and children and almost half of the unaccompanied children had returned home.[6] Judged in terms of protecting the civilian population, the scheme was therefore something of a failure. Subsequent evacuations, most notably during the Blitz of 1940-41 (involving some 1.25 million people) and the flying-bomb attacks of mid-1944 (dispersing a further one million), were more successful. By the end of the war, just over four million city dwellers had spent some time in the relative safety of the British countryside. Many had, in fact, left home more than once, returning when the immediate danger appeared to have passed. A further two million had made their own arrangements – with friends, relatives or hotels – and received no help from the Government.[7]

From the perspective of centre-left social reformers, evacuation had produced unforeseen and positive side-effects. Most importantly, it had led to the rediscovery of poverty in Britain, as town met country and middle class met working class. Writing in 1940, the Fabian socialist Margaret Cole believed that the evacuation scheme had made 'the countryside and the comfortable classes suddenly and painfully aware, in their own persons, of the deep and shameful poverty which exists to-day in the rich cities of England'.[8] In a similar vein, the Women's Group on Public Welfare (which had close links with the Labour Party) saw evacuation as the 'window through which English town life was suddenly and vividly seen from a new angle'.[9] Sympathetic reviewers found their report, *Our Towns*, an inspiration for action.[10]

However, other contemporaries were far less convinced that wartime billeting had evoked such benign responses amongst the better-off. They argued that contact between the classes often reinforced division.[11] The common dangers and anxieties of war had certainly not diminished long-standing prejudices about the urban poor. Thus, many host families continued to believe that the condition of evacuee children reflected incompetence and laziness rather than social and economic deprivation. Mothers were blamed for their children's inadequate clothing and footwear even though they had no way of knowing about country conditions and needs.[12] The widespread incidence of bed wetting was ascribed to lax moral standards in spite of the fact that it usually reflected fear or loneliness.[13] Finally, the children's' frequent problem with head lice was also interpreted unsympathetically. Medical opinion explained the condition as a consequence of environmental factors like overcrowding. Yet this did not stop many in the reception areas from believing that it was a further sign of a needlessly unwholesome life-style.[14]

Nowhere were such class misunderstandings more apparent than in a whole range of seemingly trivial disputes around the home. The accommodation of the evacuee mother and child proved particularly problematic. One study discovered 'very little spirit of give and take' and concluded that such incompatibility was one of the main reasons for the high incidence of mothers and children returning home.[15] Similarly, a Fabian survey of billeting arrangements in the winter of 1939–40 found that both parties 'resented the curtailment of privacy in daily living, and were unavoidably critical of each other's standards of living, domestic skill and child management'. Meal times were often so fraught that they had to be staggered in order that both women could avoid sharing the kitchen at the same time.[16] As one evacuated mother explained to a member of the Women's Voluntary Services, '"I can't eat like them, although its very kind I'd give anything to be put with my own class"'.[17]

Such disagreements could happen in any home, yet contemporary investigation revealed that evacuees were almost always happiest when they resided with families of a similar social background.[18] Some working-class parents feared that their children might judge them harshly after exposure to middle-class mores. One London couple, for instance, insisted that their offspring be removed from the care of a middle-class family on the grounds that they were '"too uppish"'.[19] Indeed a major reason for the relative success of later evacuation schemes was that like were usually housed with like. After the first few months of the war the vast majority of host families were working-class. Although in part a reflection of a shift in official billeting policy, this was also a by-product of the increasing reluctance among the rural middle class to accommodate evacuees. The journal *Social Work* was not alone in noting the selfishness of 'Many owners of larger houses and farmers': 'In many cases it is the only thing country people have been asked to do for the war effort, and yet they have not been willing to do it'.[20]

The study of evacuation, therefore, questions the idea of developing social harmony. Much of rural Britain had been shocked by the exodus from the cities but the conclusions drawn were mixed and certainly not all charitable. Was a new cohesion any more observable in urban areas during the dramatic events of the Blitz? By common agreement the Blitz began in September 1940 and ended in May 1941.[21] During those nine months, German planes attacked many of the major conurbations, including London, Birmingham, Glasgow and Liverpool, as well as a number of important provincial cities – notably the ports of Bristol, Hull, Portsmouth, Plymouth and Southampton, together with industrial centres like Coventry and Sheffield. But by almost any measure, it was London – and particularly the predominantly working-class East End – which felt the full force of the enemy. The metropolis endured some seventy major night-time raids (more than all the other towns and cities of Britain combined) and over 60 per cent of the total tonnage of high explosive dropped. However, the Blitz was particular to London in one other important respect. With the exception of Liverpool, it was only in the capital that public shelters were used by significant numbers and with any regularity. Elsewhere, civilians 'trekked out' to the surrounding countryside or simply stayed at home.

Nevertheless, the experience of public shelters dominated much contemporary analysis of the Blitz. Any war correspondent could see the queues of anxious Londoners waiting to enter the tube stations before the nightly air raids. It was here, and in other communal shelters, that the image of a new collective solidarity was born: of cheery Cockneys 'all in it together', despite the bombs and the appalling and often insanitary conditions.[22] Within days of the first air attacks, the left-wing journalist Ritchie Calder had noted the extent to which previously antagonistic groups living in Stepney (East London) had bonded together, sharing food and much else under the same common danger.[23] It was held by many at this time that public shelters had, in the words of one social worker, 'increased "matey-ness"', and in the process broken down the '"keep yourself to yourself" attitude of Londoners'.[24] This upsurge in sociability was also evident among the many thousands involved in civil defence duties. For example, the comfortably-off London borough of Wimbledon had some 7,000 fire watchers and the editor of the local paper was in no doubt that such levels of civic participation were instrumental in eroding middle-class isolation. As he put it in March 1941:

> Time has gone by when a man could say he has lived all his life in one house without so much as knowing his neighbours' name. Almost every week people living in the same street meet and discuss fire fighting problems and fix up rotas of duty.
>
> But this neighbourly business has a lot more to it. The man who is doing his bit is keen on seeing that the other man is doing it, or wants to know the reason why.
>
> So, in the long run, these fire parties are starting points which will ensure that everyone is doing something to help the war effort. They will also break down an age old tradition of isolation and class consciousness.[25]

Away from the Conservative suburbs, those on the political left also saw the Blitz as something of an informal education in civics. Barbara Betts (later Castle) believed that it had awakened many to the responsibilities of local government, as the homeless came face to face with town hall bureaucracy in their attempt to find new accommodation or essential items of furniture.[26] Revisiting London's East End in March 1941, Ritchie Calder was struck by a new development in popular democracy – the shelter committee. These were informal bodies, directly elected by the inhabitants of communal shelters, which provided, after negotiation with the local authority, canteen facilities and entertainment. They even took responsibility for the cleanliness of the shelter, arguing that it was largely their own concern. Here, in deeds not words, was what a number of optimistic commentators hailed as the 'active citizen'. Once dominated by Communists, shelter committees were now, according to Calder, mainly drawn from 'people who have never found any kind of expression hitherto in active political or administrative work – the back street acquiescents'. In the crisis of the Blitz, he argued, this stratum was 'suddenly finding self-expression and self-confidence'.[27] The left-wing Labour weekly *Tribune* claimed that such committees could be found in 'nearly every tube station where people sleep'.[28]

If true, shelter committees still only represented a small proportion of Londoners. Official figures varied, but the first shelter census of metropolitan London, in November 1940, found just 4 per cent of the estimated population in the tubes, 9 per cent in other public shelters and a further 27 per cent in household shelters. No more than 160,000 spent any one night on the platforms of tube stations. In London, as in other urban centres, the majority of the population stayed at home, in their beds, under the stairs or elsewhere.[29] For most people the Blitz was a private, familial experience. Moreover, there is a large, and at the time unpublished, body of evidence which suggests that even for the minority who used communal shelters, social harmony was fragile and political participation limited.

Reviewing the material that he and his fellow Mass-Observers collected on shelter life, Tom Harrisson came to the conclusion that although strangers were drawn together, 'it would be a mistake to make too much of these temporary associations'. There were 'few signs of any keen urge to share once an immediate threat was past' and 'as many fresh disputes and frictions as new fellowships'.[30] Those frictions were amply evident in Stepney, for example, where ethnic and religious differences remained. Indeed, contrary to Ritchie Calder, shelter life may well have intensified pre-existing prejudices – perhaps unsurprisingly given the cramped and difficult conditions. The small West African and West Indian community of the area complained about discrimination, particularly from Jews, and inferior air raid accommodation.[31] East End anti-Semitism appeared to increase during the Blitz. According to a local and knowledgeable Catholic priest, these attitudes were largely the product of a rumour that Jews were either cowardly or selfish. Some, it was claimed, left for safer areas when the bombing became severe, while others were believed to have monopolised the tube shelters.[32]

The widespread identification with place, whether town, district or street, remained stubbornly intact throughout the period. Indeed, there is little evidence to suggest that the Blitz encouraged a wider sense of suffering, or common danger, beyond the known and familiar. At its most extreme there were occasions when public shelters were guarded by men with shotguns in an attempt to

ensure that only locals came in.[33] More generally, popular interest
appeared to be determined by the location of the previous night's
raid. A Mass-Observer serving in the Army was of the opinion that
his comrades were solely concerned for the safety of their own families. His diary entry for the 30 December 1940 ran as follows:

> I heard London had been badly bombed, so I asked several people
> with papers what had happened to London. They looked it up for
> me, but none of them had read about it, or bothered at all....Two of
> them asked: 'Why, has Lancs been bombed?' As I answered No, they
> replied, 'Oh, it's alright then', and changed the subject. It didn't
> interest them.[34]

For those directly involved, enemy bombing encouraged a preoccupation with the personal. Wider issues, like politics, seemed
increasingly irrelevant. Mass-Observation's 'news index' investigation – based on a twice weekly small sample survey of adults in
London and the provinces – demonstrated that public apathy grew
throughout the months of the Blitz. By the spring of 1941 between
33 and 39 per cent of those questioned were not following war
news; in heavily bombed Portsmouth, a lack of interest in outside
events was displayed by some 90 per cent of those questioned.[35] At
the largest of the communal shelters, 'Tilbury' in Whitechapel (East
London), where up to 10,000 people regularly spent the night, the
participatory citizens of the shelter committee were nowhere to be
seen. In their place, a number of often self-appointed 'shelter mar-
shals' took some pleasure from 'Little Hitlering' the inhabitants.
Some of those present had become involved in petty disagreements
but most found little to keep themselves occupied. A random survey
of activities at Tilbury revealed that the majority were sleeping or
simply 'doing nothing'.[36]

Taken together, therefore, this evidence qualifies the idea that the
war straightforwardly boosted social solidarity. Evacuation touched
many people but it did not necessarily encourage greater understanding. The impact of the Blitz was also mixed. The bombing
inspired great individual courage and heroism.[37] Nevertheless, the
experience rarely brought people together to the extent that some
imagined. As has been shown, family or neighbourhood loyalties
sometimes remained paramount even at moments of greatest
danger. The image of a people standing together in communal
defiance of the German bombs seems to be, in part, a myth.

The argument that the war increased popular radicalism rested upon a number of observations. Some pundits and journalists felt that the key changes occurred in the armed forces. To them, the conscript citizen-soldier was at the very forefront of a more general shift to the left. Elsewhere, the emphasis was on a new spirit of militancy in industry. Each of these contentions will now be examined in turn.

The claim that ordinary members of the armed forces were becoming more radical was advanced on many occasions during the war, not least by Tom Harrisson of Mass-Observation.[38] Outsiders were particularly struck by new techniques which were said to be transforming army education and thus promoting fresh attitudes. The key innovation, most agreed, was the creation of the Army Bureau of Current Affairs (ABCA), a body which later became legendary because of its alleged impact on the 1945 election result.[39]

ABCA's establishment in 1941 was an attempt to counter the widespread cynicism and ignorance of service personnel.[40] Following the fiasco of Dunkirk and other military defeats, those in authority were concerned about army morale. The general view was that most conscripts lacked the enthusiasm of their forefathers who had volunteered in 1914. Evidence collected by Mass-Observation in the first months of 1940 confirmed that few of those awaiting conscription saw war service in a patriotic or positive light.[41] Such high levels of cynicism were widely thought to impair fighting efficiency. The answer appeared to lie in a programme of compulsory citizenship education with the express intention of impressing upon the troops just what Britain was fighting for. This was a proposal which suited both the War Office – trying to cope with the morale problems of a citizen army – and a number of radical commentators concerned to inculcate democratic values in a war against fascism.[42]

ABCA was founded under the direction of W.E. Williams, an influential figure in the adult education movement and the driving force behind the Penguin Specials of the 1930s. Williams was one of a number of outside educational experts drafted into the Directorate of Army Education for the duration of the war. Under his guidance, ABCA produced a series of pamphlets entitled *Current Affairs* and *War*, with the express aim of providing background material for Army Education Corps officers, or more usually regimental officers, to lead compulsory weekly talks and discussions with the troops. A complementary initiative, called the 'British Way and Purpose', was introduced in the winter of 1942–43 and provided an extra compulsory hour of citizenship education.[43]

From its inception ABCA was mistrusted by those in authority. Opposition came, most famously, from Churchill, who felt that a successful army needed discipline not discussion.[44] Within the War Office and the Army Council there were many who shared the Prime Minister's misgivings.[45] ABCA in their eyes was little short of subversive left-wing propaganda. Such critics alleged that under Williams, and his like-minded followers in the Army Education Corps, the teaching of war aims – 'what we were fighting for' – had become the indoctrination of peace aims. Official anxiety was, of course, only matched by radical enthusiasm. Few on the left would have disagreed with Williams's assessment of ABCA's significance:

> A.B.C.A. is not only a safety-valve for the citizen-soldier's ignorance, bewilderment or indignation; it is becoming also the one and only place where he can hammer out his notions of the post-war world and where he can learn the rudiments of his obligation as a citizen.[46]

Comparisons with Cromwell's New Model Army were not uncommon.[47] Britain's conscript army, it was claimed, was one that discussed the future with enthusiasm and seriousness. As E.P. Thompson remembered of his experiences during the invasion of Italy, 'everywhere across Italy, on wall newspapers, in bivvies around our tanks, in supply depots the argument was going on'.[48]

Indeed, surveys of soldiers in convalescent centres, transit and training camps undertaken during the winter of 1943–44 revealed that around 60 per cent of all home units conducted ABCA sessions. However, the fact that such camps were away from the front with few rival attractions meant that these figures could easily give a rather misleading impression. Implementation overseas was less impressive. In North Africa, for example, only 30 per cent of units found regular time for ABCA.[49] Problems encountered included hostility from commanding officers and a shortage of instructors. Nevertheless, involvement in combat was usually the source of greatest disruption.[50] A typical case occurred during 1945 when Army Education Corps officers at Deolali in India reported: 'Men straight from the battlefields of Burma know little of Army education; ABCA and British Way and Purpose are scarcely even names to them'.[51]

Overall figures also revealed little about the manner in which ABCA discussions were actually carried out. Williams described an exemplary ABCA session as follows:

> Thirty odd soldiers ... are sitting in a semi-circle ... The platoon commander has opened the discussion which, this week, is on Town Planning ... The atmosphere is informal ... [the chairman] puts his own points without exploiting his rank or authority, and he takes special care to draw into the argument the inarticulate soldier ... Two processes are taking place on this occasion; the men are considering an important social topic ... and in the give-and-take of discussion they are learning the discipline of civilised argument.[52]

All too often, however, the 'discipline of civilised argument' consisted of listening to an inarticulate and ill-prepared officer grudgingly performing an official duty.[53] Moreover, for those who were interested, obtaining further reading could be problematic. One soldier described his unit library as consisting of 'out of date copies of *The Field, Punch* and *The Lady*, together with superannuated dumps of Edwardian bestsellers'.[54]

Reaction in the ranks to this situation varied. Some saw ABCA sessions as a chance to 'sit down and smoke for half an hour'; consequently whatever happened hardly registered.[55] Countless others treated the whole initiative with the same mixture of cynicism and distrust they reserved for anything official.[56] Service women, though less cynical, were, by all accounts, even more apathetic. Lecturers found themselves 'addressing rows of bent heads', since citizenship education often took place during the time when many women chose to sew or mend clothes.[57] On balance, interest in ABCA appears to have been concentrated among technical and administrative units. This reflected, in part, the relative ease of establishing regular discussion groups outside the combat zone, and the higher educational standards and prior trade union experience of these soldiers.[58] Other instances of forces' radicalism, like the Cairo Parliament, seem to have largely involved the same social types.[59] Such troops might best be characterised as belonging to the public-spirited middle class and the 'earnest minority' of the working class.[60] As a political agent put it in 1944, ABCA addressed 'the same few and same type that we get at any peace time public or political meeting'.[61]

ABCA's overall impact, to conclude, can easily be overestimated.

" Hurry up with that job. I'm waiting to get on your back again ! "

2   The enemy and the people. *Daily Herald* cartoonist Whitelaw's view of capitalist attitudes as the war drew to a close in the spring of 1945

An active, comparatively well educated minority certainly enjoyed army education and no doubt benefited from it. On the other hand, most saw the sessions as an irrelevance: being lectured at increased rather than alleviated boredom. There were few real signs of the idealised citizen-soldier.

The case for a radicalisation in industry depended on the simple observation that workers had begun to show a greater propensity to contest fundamental issues of control. Early in the war, all had worked as hard as possible to ensure the nation's survival. However, the production crisis of 1941–42 had changed relationships in industry. Employers were revealed as inefficient and selfish. Many workers, it was believed, would never accept their authority again. Meanwhile, organised labour had grown in stature and confidence, symbolised by the ascendancy of the former General Secretary of the Transport and General Workers' Union, Ernest

Bevin, at the Ministry of Labour. Given these developments, it was predicted that the approach of final victory in Europe would be accompanied by the growth of a new combative mood on the shop-floor. Workers had become more political about their jobs, it was asserted, and were now ready to strike against capitalist iniquity.[62]

At first sight, this argument seems quite plausible.[63] Table 1 collates some statistical data on the incidence of disputes and the number of working days lost for the years 1940–44.[64] It shows that though strikes and lock-outs effectively became illegal with the passing of Order 1305 in July 1940, industrial relations certainly became more fraught as the war progressed. Indeed, nearly four times as many working days were lost to strikes during 1944 as had been during 1940.

Table 1 *Strikes in wartime: number of disputes and working days lost (WDL), 1940-44*

Year	Total		Coalmining		Metals, Eng. and Ship.	
	No.	WDL 000s	No.	WDL 000s	No.	WDL 000s
1940	922	940	381	505	229	163
1941	1,251	1,079	470	335	472	556
1942	1,303	1,527	526	840	476	526
1943	1,785	1,808	843	889	612	635
1944	2,194	3,714	1,253	2,480	610	1,048

Source: H.A. Clegg, *A History of British Trade Unions since 1889. Volume III 1934-1951* (Oxford, 1994), p. 240; H.M.D. Parker, *Manpower* (London, 1957), p. 505.

Nevertheless, further reflection reveals that these overall figures require considerable qualification. In the main, wartime industrial disputes were short – the vast majority lasted under one week – and limited to individual firms or localities. Moreover, while strikes occurred in many sectors of the economy at one time or another, most of industry remained essentially peaceful. Three-quarters of all wartime strikes happened in just four trades – metals, engineering, coalmining and shipbuilding – and two of these had long histories of poor industrial relations.[65]

A final point concerns the motivations of those who went on strike. Some disputes were fought over issues of control. For example, the largest engineering conflict of 1942 hinged on calls for the reinstatement of two sacked shop stewards. However, across the wartime economy, the most common cause of grievance was earnings. Some 60 per cent of all stoppages in metals, engineering and shipbuilding between 1941 and 1944 were caused by wage disputes. In coal, the incidence of strikes and the number of working days lost were closely related to the timing of pay awards. Indeed despite Government (and often trade union) calls for wage restraint, there were many workers who saw full employment and continuous production as propitious conditions in which to pursue their wage claims.

As the war drew to a close it was clear that both sides of industry were looking to gain the upper hand. In December 1944, the Regional Industrial Relations Officer (RIRO) for Wales reported that:

> the general view ... expressed by several trade union officials is that any concessions which they can obtain should be striven for now, otherwise the opportune moment will pass and the struggle to maintain standards secured during the war will be a matter of much greater difficulty in the post-war period.[66]

Similarly, in Scotland, workers were also concerned that the 'fruits' of the war should not be lost in the peace. This was so much the case that any suggested changes by management were viewed as an attempt to 'revert to a normal peace-time basis, to the disadvantage of the employees'.[67] Thus, many were opposed – contra traditional trade union policy – to any reduction in wartime overtime earnings or production bonuses, regarding both as part of the weekly wage packet. In the spring of 1945 the Scottish RIRO made this point with some force, claiming that workers had developed 'an appetite for overtime earnings' at the very time the unions were attempting to obtain 'a further reduction in the normal working week'. He continued: 'Since longer hours normally mean employment for less numbers, this attitude towards overtime is one demonstration of personal interest rather than full employment being in mind at the moment'.[68]

In most cases, therefore, rank-and-file demands had little to do with challenging control. Political considerations came a poor second to bread and butter issues. Workers were largely concerned with protecting the material gains that the war situation had delivered, even if this meant jeopardising future employment prospects. As in the army, radicalism was confined to the few and disregarded by the many.

The final topic to be considered in this chapter is the public's attitude to reconstruction. Debate about Britain's future ebbed and flowed throughout the war. Moreover, different issues dominated at different times, as a variety of agencies struggled to impose their particular visions. Consequently, summarising the overall position remains difficult. However, some broad trends are discernible and these are outlined over the following pages.

To begin the discussion it is useful to examine popular reactions to various official pronouncements made about Britain's future. The Coalition Government was always wary about raising reconstruction issues since most ministers agreed with Churchill that the first task was to win the war.[69] Nevertheless, the need to maintain the nation's morale meant that the administration could not keep totally silent. Therefore, statements were released from time to time about possible future policies. On occasion, this actually led to fresh legislation being passed in Parliament. Many of these developments were followed with great interest by the public. Indeed, a superficial impression suggests that the people were hungry for change. However, closer examination reveals, once again, that the real situation was more complex than it initially appears.

The first great public debate on the Government's reconstruction aims occurred with the publication of the Beveridge Report in December 1942. Sir William Beveridge had been appointed to review the social security system and his final proposals recommended fundamental change – the adoption of comprehensive cradle-to-grave provision, paid for by a universal flat rate contribution. This provoked great popular interest. One day after the report had been issued, Mass-Observation found that 92 per cent of a random sample knew of its existence.[70] Some two weeks later, the British Institute of Public Opinion (BIPO) confirmed these findings using more scientific methods. A nationwide survey of the civilian population – taking due account of age, class and a number of other variables – established that 'an astonishing figure' of 95 per cent were aware of Beveridge.[71] In addition, 88 per cent thought it should be implemented by government. Popular enthusiasm was not simply the product of material calculation. About one-third of those in favour believed they would be no better off, perhaps even poorer, if Beveridge's proposals were adopted. Enthusiasm was particularly evident in the public-spirited middle-class, the professions and the civil service.

There was general approval for the main features of the report, notably old age pensions, unemployment benefit and free medical treatment. Detailed knowledge, however, rarely matched popular interest.[72] When asked, respondents usually had an opinion of what they considered was the appropriate level of pensions or unemployment benefit. Indeed many expressed dissatisfaction with existing welfare provision. Nevertheless, few had any idea of how structural reform might be organised.[73] The principle of universality, for example, was at the heart of the report. Yet BIPO found that a 'large number' had 'not grasped' the advantages of an insurance scheme based on the idea that everyone should contribute. Some 30 per cent of all socio-economic groups believed that an income limit should be fixed, excluding those whose earnings exceeded that maximum. Of this body, those less well off thought the rich did not need benefit; while those in the middle and upper income bracket did not want to contribute. Mass-Observation found similar evidence of middle-class self-interest: 29 per cent of those questioned were against Beveridge on the grounds that it would support the 'idle' poor.[74]

Despite majority public support, only 53 per cent of those questioned by BIPO in December 1942 thought the report would be implemented. Cynicism was widespread. A considerable number clearly felt Beveridge was 'too good to be true'. The debate on the report in the House of Commons in February 1943 only served to further depress those who wanted quick implementation. The attitude of Conservative ministers, most prominently Sir Kingsley Wood, convinced many that the Government was not serious about post-war social reform. By this point, Mass-Observation estimated that the proportion expecting all of Beveridge's proposals to become law had dropped from 49 to 34 per cent.[75] One month later, only 27 per cent of the public declared themselves satisfied with the administration's response against 47 per cent who were dissatisfied.[76]

A second bout of intense public discussion on official reconstruction proposals occurred in 1944. Interest was aroused by the Government's plans for education reform, culminating in the Education Act passed in August, and a White Paper on methods intended to secure full employment. These were crucial issues but popular reactions were, once again, far from straightforward.

General support for educational reform was certainly widespread.[77] Some two-thirds of those questioned by the Government's own social survey thought that changes in the educational system were essential – raising the school leaving age and a desire for greater equality of access were particularly popular. However, as with Beveridge, enthusiasm for reform was not matched by knowledge of detail. Six months after the 1944 Education Act had become law, only 45 per cent of a representative sample of nearly 2,000 adults had heard of any of its proposals. Of those claiming to know of its existence, barely one-third could mention a single change. Understanding of the Act was closely related to income and educational experience. Respondents with higher earnings and secondary or university education were more informed than those without. Thus, as the Social Survey remarked with some regret, 'ignorance' was 'especially marked in those sections of the population whom the new Act is most likely to benefit'.

The public's response to the Government's employment proposals revealed a similarly differentiated pattern. In June 1944, opinion poll enquiries found that 60 per cent of those questioned had heard of the recently released White Paper. On the other hand, only 21 per cent of this group felt that the recommendations would be effective.[78] In fact, memory continued to be the strongest influence on such attitudes. Job insecurity had been a central fact of working-class life in the 1920s and 1930s, and wartime full employment had done little to overcome fears that the future would be just like the past. Most of those who came into contact with workers recorded that they wanted employment stability but doubted whether it would ever occur.[79] Older factory employees worried that their jobs would go to younger men when they returned from the armed forces.[80] Meanwhile, soldiers were reputedly anxious for a quick demobilisation because they feared that peacetime jobs would be few and far between.[81] The widespread expectation was that a short post-war boom would be followed by a longer slump, whatever the Government might promise.[82]

Thus far, attention has been focused on the reception given to official pronouncements about reconstruction. However, the debate about Britain's future involved many more protagonists than just the Government and so it is sensible to conclude the discussion by examining whether these other organisations were any more successful at winning public confidence and support. For practical reasons, this is best achieved by focusing on one policy area – the question of how the nation's cities were to be rebuilt.

In professional circles, discussion of urban reconstruction began even while the Blitz was occurring.[83] Architects and planners agreed that they had been presented with a great chance for improvement. Before the war, British cities had too often been remarkable only for their traffic chaos, pollution and disfiguring slums. In future, they could be rebuilt on entirely new lines and in ways which would benefit all their inhabitants. There were to be not only 'homes fit for heroes' but also improved urban environments, providing light, clean air and better health. The key to turning those kind of objectives into reality lay with the people: they must become active in a new kind of democratic planning. As a pamphlet issued by the Architectural Press explained:

> When people get sentimental they quote 'Our England is a garden'. Our England is not a garden or if it is the rubbish heap has run amok. But it might almost be thought of as a large ... Estate: run at the request of the life-tenants by 600 more or less carefully elected stewards (still mostly Whigs at heart). A big chance has come the way of the people on the estate, the biggest in its history. We must learn what is required of us. And then we must act. First a Survey – then a plan of action – *and then the action.*[84]

This was a stirring message, which was repeated throughout the war in both the technical and popular press. What reactions did it provoke?

Popular interest in housing was certainly always intense during these years. From the summer of 1944 onwards opinion polls confirmed that most people viewed housing as the most urgent post-war problem.[85] This was hardly surprising given the impact of German bombing on British cities. About 3.75 million houses had been damaged or destroyed between 1940 and 1945, roughly two in every seven. In some areas the destruction was even more severe. In heavily bombed Plymouth, for example, some 25 per cent of the housing stock was uninhabitable for most of the war; while in Bermondsey (South London) only four houses in every hundred were untouched by the Blitz.[86] Overcrowding and a consequent lack of privacy was commonplace. Indeed, the housing shortage was so bad that many occupants refused to leave badly damaged homes for fear of being unable to find alternative accommodation.[87]

Interest in housing did not, however, necessarily infer concern with the wider issues of community or the built environment. Admittedly, 1940 and 1941 had seen an explosion of interest in planning as even a cursory glance at the press testifies. Yet, as the *Architects' Journal* regretfully noted, the public's enthusiasm for reconstruction during 1941 'seemed to wax and wane in proportion to the severity or lightness of enemy air-raids'.[88] By 1942 it was clear that most people had become tired with what was often interpreted as empty talk about the 'new Britain' to be built after the war. In his address to the Housing Centre in March of that year, Tom Harrisson commented at some length on this gap between the ideals of architects and town planners and the desires of ordinary people. What worried him most was the 'way that planners ... talked as if they were winning over the general public when really they were only winning over each other'.[89] During the next two years, this gloomy prognosis would be confirmed time and again by a series of surveys into popular attitudes towards future housing provision.[90]

These studies established that, for the majority, immediate needs took precedence over long-term planning. Private over public, home over community; these were the dominant features of most people's post-war vision. Central to popular concerns was the home. The war had destroyed lives and property and disrupted relationships.[91] Conscription had led to family separation – in both the forces and the factories. Couples commonly described their relationships in the following terms: '"five years married, but parted for four"'; '"happy, what we've had of it"'; '"it's been a honeymoon on the instalment system"'.[92] In such circumstances it was hardly surprising that re-building the home – and with it family life – should be at the top of most people's agenda.[93]

Home was, moreover, a place where sharing was to be a thing

of the past. Evidence from a variety of sources found that the public disliked sharing, whether it be with the evacuated, the billeted, or even their own relations.[94] One study of the views of women on the design of post-war houses concluded that privacy was widely seen 'as the first essential condition for happy family life'.[95] Similarly, Mass-Observation found, from over a thousand interviews in eleven towns and cities, that home was not simply a place in which to live, it was also somewhere to retreat from the outside world:

> Whatever people may think of their neighbours in the street or the people they meet shopping or going to town, they definitely like to have their home to themselves. Any idea of having to share a home, even to share a gateway or front-porch, is repugnant to a great many people, and this applies also to being overlooked, either while sitting in the garden or when in the house.[96]

These sentiments informed the public's response to questions about the design of homes and communal facilities. Thus, all surveys revealed that an overwhelming majority (often over 90 per cent) wished to live in houses rather than flats – and most also preferred a garden.[97] Yet, following the preference for privacy, few had definite opinions about the provision of communal facilities and town planning in general. For most, the neighbourhood consisted of little more than the pub, the church, the shops and the cinema. Where available, community centres were used by a minority of people and only for specific pursuits or hobbies rather than for meeting neighbours.[98] When pressed, it seems that most women wanted those amenities which provided assistance to the family while not endangering its independence. There was, therefore, some enthusiasm for health centres and maternity and child welfare clinics, and a marked antipathy towards communal laundries or restaurants. However, the wider aspects of common provision were regarded with, at best, indifference and, at worst, open hostility.[99]

Taken together, the evidence assembled in this chapter demonstrates that the war was less of a catalyst than some believed. A substantial number were drawn to radical conclusions because of their experiences during the conflict. A Ministry of Information enquiry of 1942 found that between 5 and 20 per cent of Britain's population had been seriously thinking about the country's future, with most favouring state-led solutions.[100] However, a majority of ordinary citizens did not share these interests or sentiments. Above all else, the war had been extremely disruptive and so there was a common desire that it should be followed by a period of normalcy. The priority was to re-establish home and work life on a civilian basis as quickly as possible. Wider questions seemed less pressing. Nobody wanted to return to the misery of the 1930s, and many had 'vague and nebulous' desires for a better post-war Britain, but this tended to be the extent of popular thinking about political abstractions.[101] Writing in 1943, at the height of the country's mobilisation, G.D.H. Cole noticed how few Britons were interested in politics. In army camps, queues and factory canteens, the talk was about personal worries and difficulties; the majority felt 'very much more seriously ... about private than about public affairs'.[102] Two years later, with victory now guaranteed, there was little to suggest that this situation had changed. Touring Britain for the Ministry of Information, the experienced writer Bernard Newman noted that most people were talking about relatively trivial personal problems and not the big issues of the day:

> One day in May, 1944, I was involved in several conversations – one in a roadside cafe for lorry drivers, one with women in a queue for cakes, and a third in a fish-and-chip shop. I noted down the principal topics of conversation: post-war housing, the Bevin boys, strikes, one-man businesses, the second-hand furniture ramp, equal pay for equal work, income tax, the cut in the cheese ration, poor quality of corsets, holidays away from home, overcrowding in trains and buses, wasting petrol, shortage of matches, high wages of boys and girls, and the bad distribution of fish.

He concluded: 'we are indeed parochial in our outlook: "selfish" is probably a better word'.[103]

Notes

1 For a contemporary gloss on these themes see Odhams Press, *Ourselves in Wartime* (London, n.d.), passim.

2 The following is drawn from R.M. Titmuss, *Problems of Social Policy* (London, 1950), pp. 23–44.

3 For the workings of the first evacuation scheme and many of the arguments advanced in this section see J. Macnicol, 'The Effect of the Evacuation of Schoolchildren on Official Attitudes to State interven-

tion', in H.L. Smith (ed), *War and Social Change* (Manchester, 1986), pp. 3–31.

4 G. Field, 'Perspectives on the Working-Class Family in Wartime Britain, 1939–1945', *International Labor and Working-Class History*, 38 (1990), 7–12.

5 O. Lyttleton, *The Memoirs of Lord Chandos* (London, 1962), p. 152.

6 Titmuss, *Problems*, p. 172.

7 *Ibid.*, pp. 355 and 543–9.

8 M. Cole, 'General Effects: Billeting' in R. Padley and M. Cole (eds), *Evacuation Survey. A Report to the Fabian Society* (London, 1940), p. 73. The educationalist H.C. Dent came to a very similar conclusion; see his *Education in Transition* (London, 1944), p. 11.

9 Women's Group on Public Welfare, *Our Towns: A Close Up* (Oxford, 1943), p. xi.

10 See e.g. D. Charques, 'Your Concern and Mine', *The Townswoman*, 11:6 (1944), 73–4.

11 See e.g. F. Le Gros Clark and R.W. Toms, 'Evacuation – Failure or Reform', *Fabian Tract*, 249 (London, 1940), pp. 3–4.

12 W. Boyd (ed), *Evacuation in Scotland. A Record of Events and Experiments* (Bickley, 1944), p. 58.

13 M. Kerr, 'Evacuation', *The Highway*, 34 (1941), 12.

14 Macnicol, 'The Effect of the Evacuation', p. 18.

15 Boyd, *Evacuation in Scotland*, pp. 67–8.

16 J. Simeon Clarke, 'Family Life', in Padley and Cole, *Evacuation Survey*, p. 162. Such problems were clearly widespread: see, among many, C.D. Rackham, 'Some Thoughts on Evacuation', *The Highway*, 32 (1940), 102.

17 Quoted in Titmuss, *Problems*, p. 394.

18 Barnett House Study Group, *London Children in War-time Oxford* (London, 1947), passim.

19 Quoted in S. Isaacs (ed), *The Cambridge Evacuation Survey* (London, 1941), p. 37.

20 Anon., 'The War and the People – No. 1', *Social Work*, 2:1 (1941), 8–9.

21 This paragraph is based on T.H. O'Brien, *Civil Defence* (London, 1955), especially pp. 508–9 and 681.

22 T. Harrisson, *Living Through the Blitz* (Harmondsworth, 1978), pp. 109-10 and *Tribune*, 29 November 1940. For the means by which this version of the Blitz was promoted see A. Calder, *The Myth of the Blitz* (London, 1991), passim.

23 *New Statesman*, 21 September 1940.

24 Anon., 'The War and the People', 14.

25 *Wimbledon Borough News*, 28 March 1941.

26 B. Betts, 'Let "Blitz" Failures Show the Way to Social Betterment', *Local Government Service*, 20:12 (1940), 263. For the extent of local bureaucracy see T. Harrisson, 'Blitzinformation', *Local Government Service*, 21:8 (1941), 177–83.

27 *New Statesman*, 8 March 1941. For an example of the varied activities of shelter committees see B. Sokoloff, *Edith and Stepney. The Life of Edith Ramsay* (London, 1987), pp. 107–10.

28 *Tribune*, 27 September 1940.

29 O'Brien, *Civil Defence*, p. 508.

30 Harrisson, *Living*, p. 311. For a personal account of the frictions of shelter life see B. Kops, *The World Is a Wedding* (London, 1973), p. 68.

31 M. Banton, *The Coloured Quarter* (London, 1955), pp. 76–7.

32 J.C. Heenan, *Not the Whole Truth* (London, 1971), p. 247.

33 Referred to in the *Independent*, 26 January 1991.

34 Tom Harrisson Mass-Observation Archive [hereafter THMOA], TC Forces 1939-56, Box 2, File D, H. Novy, 'RAMC Depot report 5', 5 January 1941, p. 1.

35 Harrisson, *Living*, pp. 281–2.

36 *Ibid.*, pp. 116–24.

37 There were remarkably few cases of panic or hysteria, see e.g. P.E. Vernon, 'Psychological Effects of Air-Raids', *Journal of Abnormal and Social Psychology*, 36:4 (1941), 457–76.

38 T. Harrisson, 'Who'll Win?', *Political Quarterly*, 15:1 (1944), 26.

39 See pp. 63–4.

40 The following is largely drawn from S.P. Mackenzie, *Politics and Military Morale* (Oxford, 1992) and P. Summerfield, 'Education and Politics in the British Armed Forces in the Second World War', *International Review of Social History*, 26 (1981), 133–58.

41 *Us 3. Mass-Observation's Weekly Intelligence Service*, 17 February 1940.

42 See e.g. T. Stevens, 'Army Education', *Fabian Research*, 53 (London, 1940), pp. 4, 20–1.

43 Collected in The Directorate of Army Education, *The British Way and Purpose* (London, 1944).

44 P. Addison, *Churchill on the Home Front* (London, 1992), pp. 354–5.

45 Mackenzie, *Politics*, chapters 5 and 6, passim.

46 W.E. Williams, 'Education in the Army', *Political Quarterly*, 13:3

(1942), 257. See also Political and Economic Planning, 'Education in the Services', *Planning*, 234 (1945), 6, and *Economist*, 4 March 1944.

47 *Times Educational Supplement*, 29 November 1941.

48 *New Society*, 11 July 1974.

49 Mackenzie, *Politics*, p. 184.

50 See e.g. THMOA, File Report 948, 'Report on ABCA', 3–4 November 1941, passim.; A. Correspondent, 'Contact with the Forces', *Socialist Commentary* (1943), 24.

51 Anon., 'Homeward Bound', *Army Education Corps Quarterly Bulletin*, October (1945), 13.

52 W.E. Williams, 'Lost Time?', *Industrial Welfare*, 27:298 (1945), 45.

53 THMOA, File Report 948, p. 7; *Army Education Corps Quarterly Bulletin*, February (1944), 10.

54 Anon., 'Army Education', *The Highway*, 34 (1942), 101.

55 A.J.P. Taylor, *English History 1914–1945* (Harmondsworth, 1985 ed.), p. 668.

56 THMOA, TC Reconstruction 1941-43, Box 2, File K, 'Fourth Report on Reconstruction IV. Basis of Political Trends in the Army', 31 October 1942, pp. 17–18.

57 N. Scarlyn Wilson, *Education in the Forces 1939-46* (London, 1948), p. 90. See also Cmd 6348, *Report of the Committee on Amenities and Welfare Conditions in the Three Women's Services* (London, 1942), pp. 44–6.

58 THMOA, File Report 948, pp. 2–3.

59 T. Mason and P. Thompson, '"Reflections on a Revolution"? The Political Mood in Wartime Britain', in N. Tiratsoo (ed), *The Attlee Years* (London, 1991), pp. 57–8.

60 For the working class see R. Hoggart, *The Uses of Literacy* (Harmondsworth, 1958 ed.), p. 320; for the middle class see G. Gorer, *Modern Types* (London, 1955), pp. 52–5 and S.R. Parsons, 'Communism in the Professions. The Organisation of the British Communist Party among Professional Workers, 1933-1956' (University of Warwick Ph.D., 1990), pp. 487–8.

61 R.C. Grundy, 'Where Do We Stand?', *Conservative Agents' Journal*, (1944), 55-6.

62 For detail on those that advanced this argument, see R. Croucher, *Engineers at War* (London, 1982).

63 Unless stated otherwise this section is drawn from H.A. Clegg, *A History of British Trade Unions since 1889. Volume III 1934–1951* (Oxford, 1994), pp. 239–57; P. Inman, *Labour in the Munitions Indus-*

tries (London, 1957), pp. 393–402; and H.M.D. Parker, *Manpower* (London, 1957), pp. 455–7, 504–5.

64 The years 1939 and 1945 are excluded since they include several months of peace.

65 For an insider's account of industrial relations in coalmining see B.L. Coombes, 'Points of View: 1. The Miner', *Fortnightly*, 151 (1942), 233.

66 Public Records Office [hereafter PRO], LAB 10/446, Regional Industrial Relations Officer [hereafter RIRO] – Wales, Weekly Report, 8 December 1944, p. 1.

67 PRO, LAB 10/445, Weekly Reports from Deputy Chief Industrial Commissioner re Scotland, 28 January 1944, p. 1 and 17 November 1944, p. 1.

68 PRO, LAB 10/534, RIRO – Scotland, Weekly Report, 13 April 1945, p. 1. For similar comments re production bonuses see LAB 10/553, RIRO – London, Weekly Report, 2 March 1945, p. 1.

69 See, for the general background, P. Addison, *The Road to 1945* (London, 1975) and K. Jefferys, *The Churchill Coalition and Wartime Politics, 1940-45* (Manchester, 1991).

70 J. Jacobs, 'December 1942: Beveridge Observed. Mass-Observation and the Beveridge Report' in J. Jacobs (ed), *Beveridge 1942–1992* (Brighton, 1992), p. 20.

71 British Institute of Public Opinion, *The Beveridge Report and the Public* (London, n.d. but 1943), p. 5. Unless otherwise stated, all subsequent figures come from this report.

72 For an example of one woman's incomprehension see V. Hodgson, *Few Eggs and No Oranges* (London, 1976), p. 274.

73 J. Harris, 'Did British Workers Want the Welfare State? G.D.H. Cole's survey of 1942', in J. Winter (ed), *The Working Class in Modern British History* (Cambridge, 1983), p. 214.

74 Jacobs, 'December 1942', p. 21.

75 Mass-Observation, 'Social Security and Parliament', *Political Quarterly*, 14:3 (1943), 250.

76 G.H. Gallup, *The Gallup International Public Opinion Polls. Great Britain 1937–1975, Volume One* (New York, 1976), p. 73.

77 This paragraph is drawn from L. Moss, *Education and the People* (The Social Survey, No. 46, 1945), passim.

78 Gallup, *Opinion Polls*, p. 91.

79 See e.g. Modern Records Centre, University of Warwick, MSS 200/B/3/2/C940 Pt.1, letter from J.G. Gribble to Sir J.F. Watson, 31

August 1942; and Mass-Observation, *An Enquiry into British War Production Part 1. People in Production* (London, 1942), p. 329.

80 See e.g. PRO INF 1/282, Weekly Report no. 158, 14 October 1943.

81 P. Thompson, 'Citizen Soldiers: The Resettlement of Ex-Service Men and Women in Britain, 1939-51' (University of Warwick Ph.D., forthcoming), chapter 2.

82 For further evidence on this issue, see G. Jeffery, 'Points of view: III the shipyard worker', *Fortnightly*, 152 (1942), 44; R.P. Lynton, 'Factory Psychology in the Transition', *Pilot Papers*, 1:1 (1946), 62; and B. Roberts, 'A Mining Town in Wartime: the Fears for the Future', *Llafur*, 6:1 (1992), 83–4.

83 For a fuller elaboration of some of the themes raised in the following paragraphs, see N. Tiratsoo, 'The Reconstruction of Blitzed British Cities 1945–55: a general introduction', in J. Hasegawa (ed), *The Reconstruction of British and Japanese Cities* (Tokyo, 1995).

84 Anon., *Your Inheritance. The Land: an Uncomic Strip* (Cheam, Surrey, n.d.), n.p.

85 Gallup, *Opinion Polls*, pp. 96, 97, 105, 115.

86 Titmuss, *Problems*, pp. 329–30.

87 M. Galton, 'Houses Wanted', *Women in Council Newsletter*, 50 (1944), n.p.; O. Alsager MacIver, 'Family Life in War Time, 1939-1945', *Social Work*, 3:10 (1946), 236; and *Picture Post*, 7 October 1944.

88 *Architects' Journal*, 15 January 1942.

89 THMOA, File Report 1162, 'Propaganda for Town Planning', 18 March 1942. For similar comments on the relative unimportance which the 'vast majority' attached to town planning see W.A. Robson, *The War and the Planning Outlook* (London, 1941), pp. 5–6.

90 Summarised in T. Tsubaki, 'Postwar Reconstruction and the Question of Popular Housing Provision, 1939-1951' (University of Warwick Ph.D.. 1993), Vol. 1, chapter 5.

91 There were, for example, some 60 million changes of address between September 1939 and June 1945. See S. Ferguson and H. Fitzgerald, *Studies in the Social Services* (London, 1954), pp. 3–4.

92 Quoted in E. Slater and M. Woodside, *Patterns of Marriage* (London, 1951), p. 215.

93 For a contemporary overview of the problems involved, see Sir A.S. MacNalty, 'Influence of War on Family Life', in Lord Horder (ed), *Rebuilding Family Life in the Post-War World* (London, n.d.), pp. 128–36.

94 For the problems of living with relations see Slater and Woodside,

Patterns, pp. 216–17.

95 Labour Party, *Report of the Twenty-Second National Conference of Labour Women, 1943* (London, 1943), p. 11.

96 Mass-Observation, *People's Homes* (London, 1943), p. 171.

97 See, among many, Report by the Scottish Housing Advisory Committee, *Planning Our New Homes* (Edinburgh, 1944), pp. xix and xxix.

98 Mass-Observation, *People's Homes*, pp. xxii and 208; B.S. Townroe, 'What Do the Services Think?', *Architectural Design & Construction*, 12:10 (1942), 202.

99 Anon., 'The Englishwoman's Castle', *Town and Country Planning*, 11:43 (1943), 106.

100 PRO CAB 117/209, 'Ministry of Information Survey on Public Reaction to Reconstruction Plans', November 1942.

101 Mass-Observation, 'Social Security', 245 and, more generally, Mass-Observation, *The Journey Home* (London, 1944).

102 G.D.H. Cole, *Fabian Socialism* (London, 1943), p. 14.

103 B. Newman, *British Journey* (London, 1945), p. 29.

3

Party politics in wartime

Following the declaration of war in September 1939, the Labour Party joined the Conservatives and the Liberals in an electoral pact. In future, any seat that became vacant was to be retained by the previous incumbent's party. The agreement covered by-elections and, from 1940, local elections. However, this was not a political truce. Party organisation and activity, in the metropolis and the constituencies, could continue. The collapse of the Chamberlain Government in May 1940 and the subsequent formation of the Churchill Coalition, with its prominent Labour members, did not significantly alter this situation. The main parties eschewed electoral confrontations but were not prevented from campaigning at other times if they could. This chapter deals with the way these unique conditions shaped party politics during the Second World War. It begins by looking at how the principal organisations coped with wartime privations, and then traces the public's reaction to their various efforts. A final section examines the 1945 election and discusses what lay behind the Conservative's unexpected defeat.

During the first years of the war Labour was keen to maintain its organisation at all levels. The annual conference continued to be held, though usually in London rather than on the coast and rarely for a full week. Policy making at the centre was also successfully maintained, despite the loss of two leading members of the Research Department to the Coalition Government in May 1940.[1] From 1941 onwards, the Party's Central Committee on Reconstruction Problems oversaw the formulation of post-war plans in a variety of policy areas, including education, employment and health.[2] Similarly Party propaganda was not neglected. The Press and Publicity Department continued to function notwithstanding paper shortages and a reduction of staff which, by 1940, left only one journalist still working in the Department.[3] In fact, the publication of pamphlets, leaflets and a number of Party journals continued throughout the conflict.

The message from Labour's headquarters at Transport House in London to ordinary Party members was simple: keep at it. In September 1939, *Labour Organiser*, the journal for agents and constituency officials, reminded its readers of 'the great emphasis placed by Headquarters on the continuance of the ordinary work of the Local Parties'.[4] This was only the first statement of what was to become an oft-repeated theme: Labour had signed an electoral, not a political, truce. In the months ahead the constituencies had two tasks. On the one hand, they were to prepare for the inevitable disruption that war would bring. The imposition of conscription, for example, meant that mundane organisational matters like maintaining contact with members and collecting subscriptions would be of vital importance. Thus, constituencies should instigate a variety of precautionary administrative practices, including the election of duplicate officers in case the incumbent was called-up.[5] If possible, local parties should also continue to publish newspapers and promote the sale of pamphlets and leaflets. With the inevitable reduction in public meetings due to the commandeering of halls and the inconvenience of the black-out, printed propaganda would be especially important.[6] On the other hand, local parties must also be alive to the opportunity presented by the conflict, both to serve the nation and to demonstrate Labour's values in action. Constituencies and individual activists were thus urged to co-operate with other organisations involved in the war effort, like the Civil Defence Services, and to represent Labour on appropriate public bodies. Moreover, all parties should establish an Advice Bureau to provide assistance on allowances, pensions and other practical matters of especial importance in wartime. In the words of *Labour Organiser*: 'Make your Party a refuge for all who are in trouble'.[7] To this end, Transport House published a monthly *Bulletin* with summaries and guidance on new legislation.[8]

What impact did this advice actually have? During the first phase of the war, and often beyond, many parties were certainly able to develop a number of strategies for dealing with organisational difficulties. A survey of about 250 constituency and borough parties in the winter of 1939 revealed that the majority were adapting to wartime circumstances with some success.[9] Secretarial posts were filled as soon as they became vacant, in many cases by those not yet subject to conscription, like women and older activists.[10] Local party newspapers continued to be published – including a number of established weeklies like Birmingham's *Town Crier* and the *Leeds Weekly Citizen* – though there was considerable variation across the country. Encouraging signs could be found in, for example, Middlesex, where in early 1940 most parties were issuing bulletins to their members. Moreover, such developments were thought to be 'one of the main contributory factors' to the 'healthy' state of Labour activity in that area. In Brighton, the local Party had even managed to turn its monthly paper into a 'lively weekly' during wartime.[11] Party meetings were also the object of organisational change. In Woolwich (East London), as in many other branches, Labour members now met at constituency rather than ward level.[12] In some areas meetings were held in private homes rather than public halls with considerable success.[13] By 1942, such 'cottage meetings' were regularly advocated by the Party's national organisation as one way of maintaining activity and comradeship.[14]

A number of local parties also involved themselves in the war effort. Internal reports revealed that within a few weeks of the outbreak of war nearly every constituency had set up an Advice Bureau or Vigilance Committee. These enabled local activists to monitor the extent of profiteering and any other abuse of wartime conditions.[15] By 1941 a number of parties were described as 'taking the initiative' in war work in their locality.[16] In Birmingham, for example, the Borough Labour Party, the Co-operative Party and the local Trades Council were particularly active in agitating for better air raid protection (ARP) and in helping to re-house those who had been bombed-out during the Blitz.[17] The possible political benefits of this work was not lost on activists or Transport House. A leading Labour figure in Cambridgeshire believed that his work in ARP was 'making many people revise their previous views about Labour':

> from a great many people I hear such sayings as 'I am Labour after this war' ... 'You Labour people are great, and if you can do this in war why not in Peace', and I believe that through the part our people are playing all over the country Labour is made.[18]

Labour Organiser drew a similar conclusion. The Blitz in East

London and in the coastal towns of East, South-East and North-East England, saw Party activists 'solving problems instead of merely passing resolutions about them'. Labour in these localities was now associated with 'doers' rather than 'talkers' and as a consequence, the Party was 'highly esteemed'.[19]

Yet, as those at Transport House knew only too well, such activity, though obviously welcome, was increasingly a substitute for, rather than supplementary to, more explicitly political work. In fact, as the war progressed it was clear that in many areas constituency organisation amounted to little more than a skeleton of central committees.[20] The effects of conscription, evacuation, the Blitz and black-out, were all too evident.[21] Premises were destroyed, agents and key activists absent, subscriptions remained uncollected and meetings problematic.[22] In such circumstances, it was hardly surprising that Labour's local political presence was often low key. One indication of this decline in public political activity can be found in the number of speaking engagements Party figures made across the country. In the eighteen months prior to June 1939, the constituencies had sent some 13,000 requests for speakers to the Party's Propaganda Department. In 1941 that figure had fallen to just 220.[23] Moreover, it was clear that local activity was poor, not only where Labour was weak, as in Scotland, for example.[24] This was also the case where it had been relatively strong: in much of the North-East, for instance, Labour had, apparently, 'ceased to function'.[25] In County Durham, all seventeen Divisions had (or shared) political agents before the war, but by January 1942 only eight enjoyed this organisational advantage.[26] Party meetings in Bishop Auckland were infrequent and poorly attended.[27] On Tyneside, rank-and-file activity was minimal, while Divisional meetings were described by one local Party official as 'more or less mechanical'.[28]

In an attempt to 're-animate' constituencies, Headquarters regularly reviewed existing arrangements, instigated membership drives and provided financial assistance to various branches for the continued employment of full-time agents.[29] It also established a number of regional 'policy conferences' with the express intention of keeping members aware of developments in Party thinking, and at the same time encouraging discussion.[30] This initiative met with some success. Thus in 1940 Labour's declaration of 'Peace Aims' was debated at thirty-six conferences across the country. The fol-

lowing year, members met in sixty different towns and cities to consider 'Labour and the War' and a further twenty groups examined
'Home Policy'. Activity continued into 1942 when sixty-four
assemblies addressed the topic of 'Democracy and Reconstruction',
and thirty-three examined the Party's Interim report, *The Old World
and the New Society*, which advocated the continuation of wartime
planning into the peace.[31]

Despite these efforts, Labour experienced numerous problems.
Individual membership almost halved between 1939 and 1941 –
from 408,844 to 226,622 – and continued to fall, albeit more
slowly, to a wartime low of 218,783 in 1942.[32] Decline was particularly severe in London where the effects of evacuation and
bombing had been most intensive. By 1942, individual membership
in the capital stood at one-third of its pre-war level, while the
number of full-time constituency agents had fallen from thirty-one
to six.[33] Even the Party's Women's Sections experienced set-backs.
Labour women had been central to the survival of several constituencies during the disruptions of 1940–41.[34] In Portsmouth, for
example, seven of the eight Party officials in the city were women.
Yet, as a report from the Chief Women's Officer made clear, the
extension of conscription to younger women in 1942 meant that
few could continue active membership. Increasingly, the Party
would have to rely on the energy of older activists, and this situation was likely to worsen in the months ahead.[35]

From the vantage point of early 1942, therefore, Labour's position looked bleak. In March of that year the Party's General Secretary, J.S. Middleton, compiled a daunting catalogue of difficulties.[36]
Individual membership was in decline; propaganda considerably
reduced; constituency and local parties less active; and social activities almost completely abandoned. The war, it seemed, had undermined the possibility of effective action. However, in the months
that followed, Labour gradually began to revive. Britain's victory at
El Alamein and the publication of the Beveridge Report produced a
new mood amongst members. Final victory now seemed guaranteed and this made discussions about reconstruction much more
relevant. Activity had a focus, since a peacetime general election
was definitely on the horizon.

The Party's renewed vigour was apparent in a variety of ways.
Discussion of Beveridge was intense and pulled both leadership and
local activists together in common cause.[37] More generally, the

3 An 'Improving' Pastime? Morgan Phillips and Aneurin Bevan at the 1952 Labour Party Conference (see Chapter 6)

years 1943–44 saw an intensification of Labour's reconstruction planning. By the end of 1944, detailed policy documents had been prepared covering social and welfare policy (education, housing, the national health service and social security), economics (full employment, the nationalisation of public utilities and finance) and foreign affairs (including a paper on world peace). The Party's membership was informed of these developments through the already-established network of regional 'policy conferences', some of which attracted large audiences.[38] There were also various initiatives intended to improve organisation. Efforts were made to extend the Party's overall presence by creating more regional councils. By 1944, six such bodies were functioning, twice the number of 1940, with a further four planned.[39] In addition, campaigns were launched to increase both individual and trade union membership.[40] Finally, in 1944, with the general election very much in mind, the Annual Conference endorsed a proposal to provide extra funds for constituency parties so they could employ full-time agents.[41]

At the level of central organisation, then, it is clear that the national Party was increasingly active as the war drew to a close. Was this pattern mirrored in the constituencies? Some local organisations remained largely moribund, and were hardly touched by the centre's new sense of purpose.[42] However, the majority seemed to have responded in a more positive way. *Labour Organiser*'s monthly round up of local Party activity grew ever more optimistic. Constituencies up and down the country were involved in fundraising – 'Aid for Russia' being especially popular; membership was at least being consolidated, and in many cases increased; and social activities, once the lifeblood of many parties, were finally taking place again.[43] Moreover, local parties had sometimes creatively reorganised their administrative structures to counter wartime difficulties. In Coventry, for example, the Party lost all membership records when its headquarters were bombed in November 1940. By 1942 individual membership had fallen to 247, barely three-quarters of the 1939 total. Thereafter, Labour followed the Communist Party's example and organised on a factory as well as constituency basis. By 1944, three Coventry factories had functioning groups with a combined total of 160 members. Not only did this keep the Party ticking over: organising in factories probably assisted in rebuilding some ward organisations towards the end of the war.[44]

In 1944, therefore, the Labour Party was in better health than many would have predicted three years earlier. Individual membership stood at 265,793, 65 per cent of the pre-war total but an increase over the nadir of 1942.[45] In addition, activity rates were generally improving. The proliferation of public meetings was a potent illustration of the Party's renewed spirit. In 1943, Transport House received over 550 requests for Party speakers from the constituencies – greater than in any previous year of the war. In 1944, with the added complication of particularly severe travel restrictions, the demand for speakers was even greater.[46]

Turning to other political parties, it is perhaps appropriate to begin with those on the left. Had they fared any better than Labour during wartime? The fortunes of the Communist Party of Great Britain were determined, in large part, by its relationship with the Soviet Union.[47] After the signing of the Nazi–Soviet Pact in September 1939, British Communists, who had spent much of the

1930s agitating against fascism, were instructed by Moscow to oppose any conflict with Germany. This was on the grounds that the combatants were involved in an 'Imperialist War', just like the 1914–18 conflict. Over the following months, Communist propaganda was largely directed at encouraging anti-war sentiment. With Labour in the Coalition, Communists were well placed to exploit popular dissatisfaction over, for example, inadequate shelters and shortages.[48] During the winter of 1940–41, the Party formed a 'front' organisation, the People's Convention, where some 2,300 delegates (claiming, quite falsely, to represent a further 1.2 million people) called for the immediate implementation of a six point programme including, most notably, a 'People's Peace'. Mass-Observation thought the majority of delegates were not of the extreme left and many, in fact, resented the presence of Communists. With the Blitz at its height, they were simply '"looking for a way out of the present mess"'.[49]

Despite such activity, the Party's about turn in 1939 had alienated many supporters. Membership declined from a pre-war peak of 18,000 in the summer of 1939 to perhaps as few as 12,000 by June 1941. Yet, with the German invasion of Russia in that same month, and an equally abrupt change of Party policy, Communist fortunes improved significantly. In the new conditions, all political activity was directed towards the successful prosecution of the war effort. In the military sphere, Communists pressed for the opening of a Second Front. In the industrial sphere, they fought for increased war production for both British and Russian forces. For once benefiting from an association with the Soviet Union, and in particular the Red Army, the Party saw its membership increase dramatically. In December 1941, there were some 23,000 Communists, but by late 1942 the Party claimed over 64,000 members – an all-time high – and something like this figure was maintained for much of the rest of the war.[50] Communist growth and influence was especially marked in industrial trade unions, notably the engineers, and in centres of war production like London, Scotland, Lancashire and the Midlands.[51] Party policy emphasised factory rather than constituency organisation and there may have been as many as 2,000 functioning groups by the spring of 1943.

However, as the war drew to a conclusion, it became clear that these achievements were insecurely based. The difficult conditions, including the black-out and the increased tempo of work, meant that many members in factory branches remained largely inactive. Thus, meetings tended to be dominated by the same few enthusiasts, engaged in what one sympathetic commentator described as a quasi-religious ritual where the words '"Strike, strike"' had replaced '"yes"' and "Amen, brother"'.[52] More significantly, it was quite apparent that the Party had failed to develop any civic presence outside the factory gates. This situation had become serious enough by early 1945 for the national leadership to order a reorganisation on residential rather than workplace lines. The Communist Party, therefore, ended the war on an uncertain note, largely marginalised and with a branch organisation marked by low levels of activity, high membership turnover and slow recruitment of converts.

The other significant organisation on the left that made an impact during the war was Common Wealth. This was launched in July 1942 through a merger of two informal left groupings: the 1941 Committee, led by the radical writer and broadcaster J.B. Priestley, and Sir Richard Acland's Forward March movement.[53] Its foundation owed much to the prevailing anxiety following the fall of Tobruk. In 1942 Common Wealth was only one indicator of a widespread disaffection with the conduct of the nation's war effort.[54] British military failure, it was argued, was largely due to sectional party interests near the top of government. Indeed, anti-party feeling reached its apogee in the spring and summer of that year, when Independent candidates won by-elections in the Conservative strongholds of Grantham, Rugby, Wallasey and Maldon.[55] Common Wealth gave this mood a focus.

However, by the end of 1942, the organisation found itself facing entirely new conditions. British victories in North Africa had changed public perceptions and diminished anxiety about the country's war leaders. Consequently, Common Wealth was forced to look for new issues on which to campaign. After a disagreement, Priestley left the movement and as a result it became increasingly dominated by the ex-Liberal MP Acland. He wanted to turn the war into a moral crusade in which private property, and with it class interest, would be replaced by common ownership and self-sacrifice.[56] Acland was a wealthy landowner who, practising what he preached, donated his hereditary estates to the National Trust in 1943. Although Common Wealth welcomed all, its appeal was almost entirely directed at the middle classes. In meetings up and down the country, Acland would ask them to exchange their obsession with rank and status and join in the creation of a classless utopia. This was socialism with a high moral Christian tone, a point made all the more evident in the organisation's three guiding principles: the 'common ownership' of industry and land; 'vital democracy' in elections and industrial relations; and 'morality in politics'.

In a number of ways, this approach met with success. At a peak in 1944, Common Wealth had over 300 branches and claimed membership of some 12,000, a fifth of which were in the forces. It tended to be strong where Labour was weak (the wealthy suburbs of London and the Home Counties, the South, South-West and North-West) and weak where Labour was strong (the working-class districts of the major industrial conurbations). Members were overwhelmingly middle-class, with perhaps nearly three-quarters drawn from the professions, including, most notably, teachers, local government officers, low-grade civil servants and scientists. Most were without any previous experience of party politics.

By early 1945, it was apparent that Common Wealth had failed to increase its influence. The organisation was not a signatory to the wartime truce and so had been able to win three by-elections, at Eddisbury, Skipton and Chelmsford. However, rank-and-file members were increasingly aware that they could not compete with the major parties and some sought to affiliate with Labour. Common Wealth had risen in exceptional wartime conditions and did not seem likely to survive the return of normality.

Turning from the left, what had been happening to the Tories? Following the outbreak of war, the Conservative Party, like Labour, was quick to remind activists of the necessity of maintaining organisation. Within days of the electoral truce, the Party Chairman, Sir Douglas Hacking, had sent the officers of every local constituency association a dossier of statements from prominent Labour and Liberal figures on the importance of political activity in wartime. Given the opposition's tactics, he advised, 'it would seem unwise for any but the junior movements of the Conservative Party to disband'.[57] In the months ahead, Conservative Central Office would repeatedly claim the high moral ground. They were only interested in winning the war, leading figures repeated, but since the other parties continued to engage in public agitation it was essential that Conservative organisation be maintained.[58] Local branches were constantly advised to involve themselves in war work. Party officers and executive committees were to keep in personal touch with members and collect information on the state of public opinion in their constituencies. Local branches were to assist in the running of information bureaux, aid evacuees, distribute Party literature and, if possible, recruit new members. Meanwhile the women's branches, ever mindful of a strict gender divide in political activity, were to form working parties for the Red Cross, visit evacuee mothers and hold social events.[59]

Despite Central Office's exhortations to the localities, Conservative activity at the national level was severely hampered within weeks of the outbreak of war.[60] The most obvious sign of this was the virtual suspension of the Party's annual conference. Last held in 1937, the Tories were not to arrange another such event until 1943. Party organisation was similarly effected. A number of key staff at Central Office left to take up work of national importance, including the Chief Organisation Officer, Marjorie Maxse.[61] The majority of full-time Party agents and Area Officers were conscripted, though the National Society of Conservative Agents continued to meet throughout the conflict.[62] The Party's youth organisation (for those aged sixteen to thirty), the Junior Imperial League, was disbanded following the outbreak of war and only reformed (as the Young Conservatives) in late 1944.[63] Finally, policy making also fell into abeyance because the Conservative Research Department was closed for most of the duration.

The next two years were difficult for Tory headquarters, but by late 1941 there was evidence of a modest recovery.[64] A key development was the formation of the Post War Problems Central Committee (PWPCC) under the direction of R.A. Butler. During 1943–44 the PWPCC's findings were made public through a series of pamphlets called *Signposts*. These provided much needed evidence that the Conservative Party was thinking about the post-war world. Such publications were also thought to be important for the development of Party organisation, providing an important focus for activist discussion in 'Looking Ahead' circles which acted as a kind of Tory ABCA.[65]

How was constituency activity effected by these developments? Party reports during the winter of 1939–40 suggested that a majority of local branches had managed to hold meetings. Out of a total of forty-two associations in London, for example, twenty-nine still carried out their duties.[66] Moreover, those constituencies that had closed down were grouped together in an attempt to overcome the loss of Party agents.[67] By April 1940, it was also clear that many associations had involved themselves in various aspects of war work, including the running of local information bureaux and the organisation of working parties producing comforts for the troops.[68] A year later, the Party journal, *The Onlooker*, confidently claimed that it was 'only in a very few constituencies that the associations are inactive, while in many an efficient organisation is being maintained'.[69] Yet, there was general agreement that very little of such activity could be described as overtly political.[70]

In fact, as an Executive Committee report to the Party's Central Council in October 1941 made clear, every month the war continued 'the difficulty of preserving Constituency Associations in their peace-time vigour and efficiency' grew 'greater'.[71] Indeed, by 1942 many local branches had, in one anxious Party member's words, 'gone into cold storage for the duration'.[72] In some regions financial constraints limited the scope for activity. At Cambridge, for example, the Eastern Area office was closed in July 1941, due to lack of funds. Thereafter, the Central Office Agent for the area was instructed to spend the majority of his time in London where all future meetings were to be held.[73]

This was a fairly desperate situation, but in 1943 there were signs that the worst might have passed. The Eastern Area, for instance, reported that annual meetings were being held in 'practically every division', social functions were more frequent, and perhaps most significantly, several associations had set up committees to consider reconstruction questions.[74] Nevertheless, difficulties remained. Some claimed that 'Looking Ahead' circles were the key to the revival but, in fact, most were of limited size and concentrated in a few locations.[75] Furthermore, the *Signpost* pamphlets, supposed to be the basis for group discussion, had to be re-thought since sales did not cover production costs. What was intended as a mass circulation primer in civic affairs had become a highly priced series with a small print run.[76] In addition, promoting debate was by no means easy in a Party where, according to several disgruntled activists, local associations were often run by 'small cliques'. By the summer of 1944 contributors to Party journals were regularly complaining that Executive Committees were the preserve of well known 'county families' or those with titles. Consequently, branches were lifeless, and in many parties the rank-and-file did not consider it worth their while attending Annual General Meetings.[77]

In the winter of 1944–45, therefore, Conservative Party organisation tended to be weak and much of the rank-and-file were either acquiescent or disengaged. The new Party Chairman, Ralph Assheton, acknowledged as much in his address to the East Midlands Area Council in November 1944. Constituency organisations, he told his audience, 'must be restored to their pre-war strength' and, given the shortage of full-time agents, 'rely more upon themselves than they have done hitherto'.[78] At the Conservative conference in March 1945, Churchill, for once paying attention to Party matters, echoed this theme and added that Labour was better prepared for the forthcoming election.[79]

Having surveyed the fortunes of the main political parties during the war it is now time to turn to the general election of 1945. Before considering the campaign, some attention must be given to the state of public opinion on the eve of the election. What would an informed observer in early 1945 make of the various parties' prospects? On the basis of public opinion polls it would be hard not to conclude that Labour would win any forthcoming election. From June 1943 to April 1945, in answer to the question 'If there was a general election tomorrow, how would you vote?', Labour was consistently supported by between 37 and 42 per cent of those interviewed, in contrast with the 23 to 31 per cent who chose the Conservatives.[80] Popular support for Labour was also evident at a number of by-elections held during this period.[81] Fourteen contests were held between February 1943 and May 1945 in which electors had the option of voting for an Independent candidate with socialist beliefs. There was a movement to the left in all but two of the seats, with four contests registering a swing of over 10 per cent. This trend was most apparent at Chelmsford in Essex during April 1945, when the Common Wealth candidate defeated the Conservative with a swing of 28 per cent.

Voting preferences, therefore, revealed considerable support for Labour or other 'substitute' candidates. Moreover, the trend was confirmed by popular attitudes to specific policies. As has already been suggested in Chapter 2, public enthusiasm for post-war social reform, most notably the provision of housing and social security, was clearly evident from late 1942 onwards. Opinion polls on a number of other policy areas also indicated that many accepted some of the more ideological features in Labour's programme. For example, between March 1944 and April 1945, the nationalisation of the coal industry, the railways and the land all received majority approval.[82] A substantial number were also in favour of the continuation of wartime government intervention. In June 1944, 68 per cent of those questioned agreed that post-war reconstruction should be mainly conducted under state control.[83]

Such enthusiasms were, however, always tempered by a certain amount of cynicism. What the public wanted from politicians were firm commitments not empty promises. This point was often made to Bernard Newman on his travels round Britain. Few electors in 1945, Newman believed, would be taken in by the candidate 'who tries to outpromise his opponent'. Moreover, now that several million more manual workers were playing income tax for the first time, there was 'a growing realization that some high-sounding schemes might mean no more than the transfer of money from one pocket to another'. All of this, Newman concluded, meant that 'Most of the new electors, in particular, will demand a constructive and practical programme rather than a negative diatribe'.[84]

Nevertheless, Labour still had to contend with the undoubted popularity of Churchill. On thirty-four separate occasions during the war, the British Institute of Public Opinion (BIPO) asked the public whether they approved of Churchill as Prime Minister. Only once did his popularity fall below 80 per cent, and that was in the summer of 1942 after a number of military set-backs culminating in the fall of Tobruk.[85] Given these figures, it was hardly surprising to find that most commentators concluded that as long as Churchill remained their leader, the Conservatives would be triumphant.[86] Any dissenters from this view – such as Mass-Observation's Tom Harrisson – were considered to be simply misinformed.[87]

By the spring of 1945 the defeat of Germany was imminent.[88] With the approach of peace, both Labour and Conservative leaders began to face up to the reality of having to fight a general election. The main question was one of timing, in particular whether a contest should be held after Germany's surrender or be delayed until Japan had succumbed. The prevailing opinion within the Conservative Party was that an election should be contested soon after the end of the European conflict. This was because the Tories wanted to maximise Churchill's appeal as a war leader. Labour Party activists also preferred a quick poll. Mistrustful of Churchill and the effect of high office on their own leaders, they had long called for the break-up of the Coalition. Attlee, in contrast, favoured an autumn election, hoping that the Prime Minister's wartime reputation might have dimmed somewhat by that time. Churchill was unwilling to accept this slight postponement. Thus, unable to agree a polling date, Labour formally left the Coalition on 23 May 1945 only two weeks after the German surrender. Churchill formed a caretaker administration which, because it contained a handful of Liberals, was described as the National Government. The dissolution of Parliament was set for 15 June and 5 July established as polling day, except in a handful of seats where the coincidence of local holidays caused it to be delayed by a few days. Due to the need to transport votes cast by service personnel stationed across the globe back to their home constituency, ballot boxes were not to be opened until 25 July.

At the start of the campaign, both parties outlined what they saw as the crucial issues facing the electorate.[89] They agreed that Britain was in a very difficult position because of the huge economic and social costs imposed by the war. However, their prescriptions varied considerably. Labour argued that the state would have to be closely involved in solving the nation's problems. Private enterprise had failed during the 1930s and could not be trusted in the future. If Britain was to thrive industrially and become a fairer society, a large dose of state-led reform was imperative. The Conservatives proposed an almost wholly contrasting strategy. They believed that wealth creation was best left to the free market. The main duty of an incoming government was to cut red tape and official bureaucracy. Entrepreneurial spirit, rather than state action, would ensure popular prosperity.

These themes were repeated in much of the election propaganda distributed throughout the country. The situation in the constituency of Plymouth Devonport was fairly typical. Here, Labour's Michael Foot stood against the incumbent Leslie Hoare-Belisha, Minister of National Insurance in Churchill's caretaker Government.[90] Plymouth had been especially badly damaged by German bombing because of its naval dockyards, so both candidates stressed the need for new housing. Foot, for example, wrote:

> Home is the best word in the English language. We shall not have won the peace until every citizen in Devonport and every citizen of England has a good roof over his head, the chance to marry and

bring up his children, safe from the fears of unemployment, sickness and war.

There was, however, little agreement about the way this might be best achieved. Foot called for the nationalisation of major industries so they could be run on behalf of the whole community. Only state planning would ensure the maximum output of houses. On the other hand, Hoare-Belisha argued that private enterprise should be left to handle the job. Rebuilding Plymouth would be costly and could only be achieved if industry thrived. Nationalisation was not an option, Hoare-Belisha told his constituents, as the 'State can no more run British Industry successfully than it can replace the housewife in the home'.

As the election campaign developed, it became obvious that the Conservatives were experiencing some difficulties conveying their message to the electorate.[91] For reasons of expediency, the Party used Churchill as the spearhead of its national appeal. Tory strategists believed that his wartime stature would outweigh popular resentment about the Party's responsibility for endemic unemployment and appeasement in the 1930s. This was a serious miscalculation. Most voters agreed that Churchill deserved credit for helping defeat Germany, but far fewer thought he would be a good peacetime leader. Moreover, Churchill's performance in the campaign was erratic, raising questions about his judgement. His assertion that Labour would have to rely on 'some form of Gestapo' to implement its policies caused widespread offence, particularly when it was recycled by more sanguine Conservatives as the slogan 'Remember Belsen'. Compounding these errors, Churchill appeared oblivious to popular concerns. Most importantly, he underestimated the importance of housing, merely repeating a promise to build 220,000 new homes within two years. This was widely viewed as an inadequate response to the problem.

Labour's campaign, in contrast, generally ran according to plan. Attlee proved an effective figurehead: calm and moderate in the face of Churchill's bluster. Furthermore, Labour successfully portrayed itself as the Party most interested in practical solutions to everyday problems. The ideological aspect of nationalisation was deliberately played down. Industries were to be transferred into the public sector to make them more efficient, not because this would extend working-class power.[92] Labour candidates stressed their empathy

with the hopes and fears of ordinary families as they looked
uneasily into the future. For example, Percy Daines, standing in
East Ham, told local electors that he was 'The People's Advocate'
and went on to describe himself in the following terms:

> You have before you a man of the PEOPLE; a tough Londoner;
> a Trade-unionist; Co-operative Committee-man; ex-Councillor;
> ex-Royal Engineer (this war). A vigorous, forthright Britisher,
> with an International outlook; a Family Man, son in the Royal
> Navy. Advocate at Party Conferences of the Soldiers' Charter.

> *Daines* knows the value of every shilling to a worker's home.

> DAINES IS ONE OF US.[93]

The public's response to these assertions is hard to gauge. Few
showed much interest in abstract ideological issues. Thus, when
voters in Fulham were asked what attracted them to one or other
of the parties only 7 per cent of prospective Conservative supporters mentioned private enterprise whilst a mere 6 per cent of those
intending to vote Labour spoke of nationalisation.[94] What most preoccupied people, as the previous chapter has underlined, was how
to end the acute housing shortage. In July 1945 63 per cent of
voters thought this to be the most important question facing any
incoming government.[95] Yet, it was not altogether clear what this
meant in terms of party preferences. A few indicators suggested
that Labour was gaining ground. Some 42 per cent of those polled
shortly before the election believed that an Attlee administration
would be best able to solve the housing crisis, compared to only 25
per cent with faith in the Conservatives.[96] On the other hand, most
informed commentators continued to believe that Labour had
simply too much ground to make up. The best the Party could hope
for, the pundits agreed, was a reduced Tory majority.[97]

In the light of such expectations, the final result came as a
great shock to both ordinary voters and party leaders. Labour had
won a landslide victory – at least in terms of Parliamentary seats.
The Party had made 203 gains over its 1935 position, finishing
with 393 MPs to the Conservatives' 213, the Liberals' 12, the Communists' 2 and Common Wealth's 1. Not only did the Party clean
up in the big industrial cities, it also did remarkably well in rural
areas, especially Norfolk, and in seats located in comfortable sub-

urban areas, in particular those which ringed London. This appeared to indicate a seismic shift in the political loyalties of a hitherto staunchly Conservative social group: the English middle class. More specifically, Herbert Morrison's victory in East Lewisham, which had returned a Tory throughout the interwar years, was taken to signify the defection of much of the lower middle class to Labour's cause.

Notwithstanding this impression, Labour's share of votes cast was rather more modest than its Parliamentary majority would suggest. At 47.8 per cent, this was Labour's best showing to date. Yet, the Conservatives had still managed to gather 39.8 per cent of the poll, hardly a disastrous performance. This was a solid core of support to take into Opposition. Labour's total was even less striking if viewed as a proportion of those on the electoral register, not all of whom exercised their franchise. In fact, Attlee won the support of just over one-third of those entitled to vote.

How had Labour achieved this unprecedented victory? Contemporary opinion varied. Some argued that there had been a decisive switch in middle-class loyalties. Others suggested that the services' vote explained the result: the army in particular had 'gone Labour'. Conservative analysts felt cheated: their opponents had not respected the political truce, while influential sections of the media had spread what amounted to left-wing propaganda. Are any of these explanations convincing?

Psephological data on the 1945 election was collected by BIPO.[98] This organisation found significant variations in the way different social groups had cast their votes. Men were more likely to have supported Labour than women. This gender gap was particularly pronounced in the working class: some 65 per cent of working-class men but only 52 per cent of their female counterparts had voted for Attlee. Of greater contemporary significance was the way in which political loyalties appeared to be structured by occupation (see Table 2). Thus, at the extremes, whilst just over three-quarters of those employed in industrial occupations supported Labour barely more than one-fifth of small shopkeepers and business people were similarly inclined.

These observations were fairly straightforward, but it was less easy to determine whether *changes* in middle-class party loyalties had proved decisive. It was clear that Labour had improved its vote amongst all sections of the population since 1935. Moreover, many activists on both sides believed that middle-class sympathies had moved significantly in Labour's direction.[99] Nevertheless, the extent of this shift was overestimated. John Bonham collated BIPO's data on this subject and found that middle-class voters varied considerably in their response to Labour. The Party's support was concentrated in the lower echelons of the group. As he concluded, 'The Labour party's best friends in the middle class are the clerks, typists, canvassers, and agents'. About one-third of such people had voted Labour. Elsewhere in the middle class, affiliations were very different. Only about 10 per cent of top business people and 15 per cent of higher professionals were Labour supporters.[100] Overall, therefore, the middle-class vote made less of a difference than some imagined. Labour's victory was principally the result of the support of wage earners. Lower middle-class votes were useful, however, as they gave the Party an edge in closely contested constituencies.

Table 2   *Voting in the 1945 general election, by occupation (per cent)*

Occupational Group	Labour	Conservative	Liberal	Other
Professional	26	60	12	2
Salaried	30	53	16	1
Small proprietor	21	71	8	-
Waged, industrial	77	15	6	2
Waged, agricultural	53	34	11	2
Waged, other	55	35	8	2

Source: H.W. Durant, *Political Opinion. Four General Election Results* (London, 1949), p. 7.

Claims about the services' vote were made by both sides, but, again, interpretations seem to have been subject to exaggeration and misunderstanding.[101] The previous Chapter has shown that radicalism amongst members of the armed forces was hardly pronounced: this position had not changed by the start of the campaign. Many soldiers had required much persuasion to put their names on the electoral register and in the end nearly 40 per cent actually failed to vote.[102] Thus, in simple numerical terms, the forces' vote cannot have made a significant difference to the result. Moreover, it is by no means certain that all service personnel supported Labour. One member of the Royal Artillery stationed in Germany during 1945 noted that only a few of his colleagues were either convinced Conservatives or socialists. The majority was composed of a 'fluid mass' which leant 'more to the left than to the right', but could not be described as either enthusiastic or committed. Most soldiers were:

> not so much interested in ideologies as in how their own lives will be affected especially in relation to their jobs, their wives and their children. So far no one has come forward with a programme which catches their enthusiasm.[103]

Conservatives had a twofold explanation of their Party's defeat. Some accused Labour of maintaining its organisation during the war, thus breaking the spirit of the political truce. The Tories, went the argument, had put the country first and neglected party activity, to their eventual great disadvantage.[104] Assessing the merits of this case is far from easy.[105] As this chapter has demonstrated, the Conservatives did not suspend activity during the war; even so, their organisational capacity was badly disrupted. The Party saw many full-time officials drafted into the war effort away from their constituencies. By 1944 some 313 Conservative agents and organisers were either in the forces or engaged in work of national importance. In comparison, Labour suffered less from the demands of war. It depended on voluntary effort, many activists being trade union members in reserved occupations who were consequently able to maintain local parties despite the disruption.[106] Thus, by the start of the campaign, a number of local Labour parties were considerably better equipped to fight an election than their rivals. In the safe Labour seat of Bishop Auckland Hugh Dalton faced a badly prepared National Liberal candidate who had only recently returned from service in Italy. As Dalton noted of his opponent:

> It is said that he had never made a speech in his life before and he had very few regular meetings during the campaign – never more than one a night. His wife and daughter went around in a car with a loudspeaker, exhorting anyone who might hear to vote for him, and also, apparently, calling out, 'What about Dalton in 1938?' But neither I nor anyone else knows what this meant.[107]

Such an argument, however, should not be pushed too far. Labour was not a wealthy party; in many areas it also suffered from lack of funds and resources. In West Fife the young Willie Hamilton was in the unusual position of standing against Willie Gallacher, the incumbent Communist MP. With no money, no previous political experience and initially no place to stay in the constituency, Hamilton did not benefit from an organisational advantage. Such was the poverty of his campaign that he was forced to walk the streets of one pit village ringing a hand bell to publicise a meeting. Despite this, Labour still came a respectable second in the constituency.[108]

The biggest flaw in the Conservative claim that the key to Labour's victory was its superior organisation lies in the fact that a majority of voters had decided how they were going to vote well before the start of the campaign. Despite the considerable energy expended on party rhetoric, most people were left unmoved by manifestos, meetings and broadcasts.[109] If the campaign had any impact on voting intentions it was to reinforce pre-existing Labour inclinations. However, superior organisation probably ensured that Labour sympathisers were more likely to turn out and vote than potential Conservatives. This would have enabled Labour to win seats which, in other circumstances, might have slipped through its grasp.

A second Conservative argument concerned the media. Party officials claimed that some influential newspapers and magazines, a variety of book publishers and even elements in the employ of the BBC had favoured Labour during the war. As the Party Chairman protested, 'The flow of propaganda never ceased'.[110] It is not unusual for a losing party to blame the media for defeat. Nevertheless, there seems to be some substance to this particular claim. During the war a number of views had been given a platform by the BBC which, due to their left-wing character, would have been excluded prior to the conflict. J.B. Priestley, the radical but popular author, had broadcast on the radio during the summer of 1940 and was credited with helping to give form to a popular mood which laid the ground for the Conservatives' eventual defeat. He was no friend of the Tories and during the 1945 campaign advocated a Labour victory.

This contention also needs qualification. First, the impact of radio on political attitudes can be exaggerated. The wartime public's favourite listening was dominated by variety shows: political talks and discussions came well down the list.[111] Even when they tuned to programmes with some political content, the public did not always draw the intended conclusions. It was for this reason that the future Labour MP Tony Crosland questioned the effect of J.B. Priestley. Writing in 1941 he speculated that:

> Although one can't prove it, I don't myself believe that Priestley's popularity on the B.B.C. had anything to do with his politics ... I believe it is almost entirely his skill as a broadcaster ... I well remember last summer, when I was at Northwich, listening every Sunday night to him with two middle-aged Tories, one of them Secretary of the local Conservative Association. They absolutely lapped it up, blissfully unconscious of any real Left tendency – and will go on voting Tory all their lives.[112]

Second, it is doubtful that the press played the part some Conservatives imagined. Labour was actually supported by fewer mass circulation newspapers than the Conservative Party. The Tories commanded the loyalty of Lord Beaverbrook's *Daily Express* which remained the biggest selling morning paper during the war. It is true that the editorial columns of the increasingly popular *Daily Mirror* vigorously supported the promise of social security contained in the Beveridge Report.[113] However, as high a profile was given to murder stories and Hollywood gossip as domestic political news. Furthermore, it was only on the eve of the poll that the *Mirror* explicitly called on readers to vote Labour. In any case, the evidence suggests that the newspaper reading public of the time took little notice of editorial lines, be they Labour- or Conservative-inclined.[114]

Labour's 1945 victory owed much to the way the Second World War led many voters to regard the Conservatives in a new and critical light. As a few, more perceptive contemporary commentators noted, a large number of people supported Labour for the first time because they actually disliked the Conservatives more than Attlee's Party.[115] Whilst an unprecedented proportion of the middle class had turned their back on Churchill, the most significant movement of opinion had occurred in the manual working class. Labour's supporters were not for the most part enthusiastic about the cause of 'socialism' – as some in the Party considered.[116] They were not even particularly sympathetic to Labour's nationalisation programme –

as various political commentators supposed.[117] However, they did
hope – manual working class and middle class alike – that Labour's
support for welfare reform was genuine. By implementing Beveridge and building houses they trusted that Labour would stand a
good chance of preventing Britain returning to pre-war poverty and
misery. This was the foundation of Labour's eventual electoral triumph. The Party had successfully maintained a public profile
during the war and in 1945 held an organisational advantage over
the Conservatives. Its eventual victory at the general election produced a huge Commons majority but this obscured the more
modest nature of its popular support.

Notes

1 H. Pelling, 'The Impact of the War on the Labour Party', in H.L.
   Smith (ed), *War and Social Change. British Society in the Second World
   War* (Manchester, 1986), pp. 132–3.
2 For the development of Labour's policy making in this period see I.
   Taylor, 'Labour and the Impact of War 1939–45', in N. Tiratsoo (ed),
   The Attlee Years (London, 1991), pp. 7–28.
3 Labour Party, *Report of the Fortieth Annual Conference of the Labour
   Party* (London, 1941), p. 34.
4 Anon., 'The Party at Work in War', *Labour Organiser*, 20:219 (1939),
   167-8.
5 Administrative advice and innovation in response to wartime developments was a constant theme; see, for example, J.T. Baxter, 'Contact. A Job for All Parties' and Anon., 'War-time Collecting Problems.
   Some Hints and Suggestions', both in *Labour Organiser*, 20:222
   (1940), 22–3 and 30.
6 Anon., 'Wanted in War-time. Your Local Labour Paper and What to
   Do with It', *Labour Organiser*, 20:219 (1939), 174–5; Anon., 'Party
   Literature', *Labour Organiser*, 20:220 (1939), 187.
7 Anon., 'The Party at Work in War', 168. See also the comments of
   Margaret Cole regarding the role local parties could play assisting
   evacuees: M. Cole, 'Wartime Billeting', *Fabian Research*, 55 (London,
   1941), p. 24.
8 Labour Party, *Report of the Forty-First Annual Conference of the Labour
   Party* (London, 1942), p. 24.
9 Anon., 'Around the Parties', *Labour Organiser*, 20:220 (1939), 178–9
   and J.T. Baxter, 'Around the Local Parties', *Labour Organiser*, 20:221

(1940), 1–4.

10 See, for example, the report from East Lewisham in Anon., 'Six Months After', *Labour Organiser*, 20:224 (1940), 51.

11 Anon., 'Local Reports on the Condition of the Labour Movement', *Labour Discussion Notes*, 9 (1940), 1–7. See also Anon., 'Around the Local Parties', *Labour Organiser*, 21:231 (1941), 165–6, and, for the role of the party paper in Reading, I. Mikardo, *Back-Bencher* (London, 1988), pp. 58–9.

12 Anon., 'Six Months After', 49–50.

13 Baxter, 'Around the Local Parties', 3.

14 Anon., 'Cottage Meetings – Should Be Revived in War-time', *Labour Organiser*, 22:251 (1942), 9.

15 Anon., 'Around the Parties', 178. For the activities of one Vigilance Committee see, Tom Harrisson Mass-Observation Archive [hereafter THMOA], TC Political Attitudes and Behaviour, 1938-56, Box 9, File I, South Hammersmith Labour Party, 'Special Divisional News Bulletin', 3 (1939), 3.

16 Anon., 'Labour Reports No.2', *Labour Discussion Notes*, 20 (1941), 5.

17 A. Sutcliffe and R. Smith, *Birmingham 1939–1970* (Oxford, 1974), p. 53.

18 Cambridgeshire Record Office, 416/0.23, Cambridgeshire Divisional Labour Party, letter from F. Adams to J. Kearsly, 19 November 1940.

19 J.T. Baxter, '"And Yet It Moves": a Country-wide Review of Labour's Forces', *Labour Organiser*, 21:229 (1940), 129–30.

20 In the south-west London suburbs of Merton and Morden, for example, activity was confined, almost exclusively, to the Party's General Committee. British Library of Political and Economic Science, London School of Economics [hereafter BLPES], Merton and Morden Labour Party, Files 1/2 and 1/3.

21 For a summary of the effects of the war on Party activity see Labour Party Archive [hereafter LPA], Organisational Sub-Committee Minutes, 17 February 1942, Memorandum on 'Individual Membership'.

22 Party premises which suffered direct hits in the Blitz included, for example, Acton and Bermondsey in London, together with Bradford, Bristol, Manchester, Middlesbrough and Yardley (Birmingham) in the provinces. See Anon., 'Hit', *Labour Organiser*, 21:231 (1941), 167. For the difficulties of holding Party meetings, see LPA, Organisational Sub-Committee Minutes, 16 December 1941, 'Memorandum on Platform Propaganda'.

23 For 1942 see LPA, Organisational Sub-Committee Minutes, 16

December 1941, 'Memorandum on Platform Propaganda', p. 3; for 1938–39 see Labour Party, *Report of the Thirty-Eighth Annual Conference of the Labour Party* (London, 1939), p. 69.

24 Following the secession of the Independent Labour Party in the early 1930s, Labour in Scotland was notably weak, see C. Harvie, 'Labour in Scotland during the Second World War', *Historical Journal*, 26:4 (1983), 921–44.

25 Anon., 'Local Reports on the Condition of the Labour Movement', 6. Another Labour city, Sheffield, was similarly inactive: see A. Thorpe, 'The Consolidation of a Labour Stronghold 1926–1951', in C. Binfield, et al. (eds), *The History of the City of Sheffield 1843–1993. Volume 1: Politics* (Sheffield, 1993), pp. 109–10.

26 LPA, National Executive Committee Minutes, 28 January 1942, 'Individual Membership. Resume of Suggestions from District Organisers and Women Organisers', p. 3.

27 Durham Record Office, D/BAL1/2, Bishop Auckland Labour Party minute book, 11 January 1940 – 23 January 1942.

28 Anon., 'Labour Reports No.2', 6; see also *Tribune*, 6 September 1940.

29 LPA, Organisational Sub-Committee Minutes, 17 February 1942, Memorandum on 'Individual Membership'.

30 G.D.H. Cole, *A History of the Labour Party from 1914* (London, 1948), pp. 402-3.

31 Labour Party, *Report of the Thirty-Ninth Annual Conference of the Labour Party* (London, 1940), p. 24; Labour, *Fortieth Conference*, p. 17; and Labour, *Forty-First Conference*, p. 10.

32 Labour Party, *Report of the Forty-Fifth Annual Conference of the Labour Party* (London, 1946), p. 35.

33 For the breakdown of membership by region see LPA, National Executive Committee Minutes, 26 November 1941, Appendix 'Individual Membership', p. 1. The particular problems of London are discussed in B. Donoughue and G.W. Jones, *Herbert Morrison. Portrait of a Politician* (London, 1973), p. 322.

34 Labour Party, *Report of the Twenty-Second National Conference of Labour Women* (London, 1942), p. 5. For a detailed picture of the activities of Women's Sections see the 'Women's Work in the Districts' column in *Labour Woman*, monthly throughout the war.

35 LPA, Organisational Sub-Committee Minutes, 3 March 1943, Memorandum on 'Notes on Organisation of Women in 1942'.

36 LPA, National Executive Committee Minutes, 25 March 1942, Memorandum on the 'Condition of the Party'.

37 For Beveridge's reception amongst the Labour Party policy makers see J. Harris, 'Political Ideas and the Debate on State Welfare, 1940–45', in H.L. Smith (ed), *War and Social Change. British Society in the Second World War* (Manchester, 1986), pp. 250–4.

38 LPA, Policy Committee Minutes, 1944, passim.; Labour Party, *Report of the Forty-Second Annual Conference of the Labour Party* (London, 1943), p. 29.

39 Labour, *Thirty-Ninth Conference*, p. 26; Labour Party, *Report of the Forty-Third Annual Conference of the Labour Party* (London, 1944), p. 14.

40 LPA, National Executive Committee Minutes, 24 November 1943, and Pelling, 'The Impact of the War on the Labour Party', p. 137.

41 Labour, *Forty-Third Conference*, pp. 141–2.

42 See e.g. National Library of Scotland, Dep. 200, Dalkeith Labour Party minute book, 1935–51.

43 See the columns 'Local Party Reports and Balance Sheets' and 'Round the Parties', *Labour Organiser*, 1943–44, passim.

44 N. Tiratsoo, *Reconstruction, Affluence and Labour Politics* (London, 1990), p. 149; T. Mason and P. Thompson, '"Reflections on a Revolution"? The Political Mood in Wartime Britain', in N. Tiratsoo (ed), *The Attlee Years* (London, 1991), p. 60.

45 Labour, *Forty-Fifth Conference*, p. 35.

46 Labour, *Forty-Second Conference*, p. 29; Labour, *Forty-Third Conference*, p. 13.

47 The following is largely drawn from J. Hinton, 'Coventry Communism: A Study of Factory Politics in the Second World War', *History Workshop Journal*, 10 (1980), 90–118.

48 For an insider's account of these activities see D. Hyde, *I Believed* (London, 1951), p. 94.

49 Quoted in A. Calder, *The People's War. Britain 1939–1945* (London, 1971 ed), p. 283.

50 F.H. Hinsley and C.A.G. Simkins, *British Intelligence in the Second World War. Volume 4 Security and Counter-Intelligence* (London, 1990), pp. 82, 84, 283.

51 K. Newton, *The Sociology of British Communism* (London, 1969), pp. 162-3, 177–8.

52 M.L. Settle, *All the Brave Promises* (London, 1984), pp. 135-6. For a more sympathetic picture see R. Samuel, 'The Lost World of British Communism', *New Left Review*, 154 (1985), 48–9.

53 Unless stated otherwise the following is drawn from A.L.R. Calder,

'The Common Wealth Party 1942–45' (University of Sussex D.Phil., 1968), especially Part II, pp. 77–91, 146–64 and 175–89; and D.L. Prynn, 'Common Wealth – a British "Third Party" of the 1940s', *Journal of Contemporary History*, 7:1–2 (1972), passim.

54 For fuller analysis of the mood in 1942, see S. Fielding, 'The Second World War and Popular Radicalism: the Significance of the "Movement away from Party"', *History*, 80:1 (1995), passim.

55 P. Addison, 'By-Elections of the Second World War', in C. Cook and J. Ramsden (eds), *By-Elections in British Politics* (London, 1973), pp. 171–8.

56 For an early statement of Acland's philosophy see his *Unser Kampf* (Harmondsworth, 1940).

57 Conservative Party Archive [hereafter CPA], CCO 500/1/9, letter from D. Hacking to all officers of Constituency Associations, 12 September 1939.

58 CPA, CCO 500/1/9, see e.g. letters from R. Topping to all Agents and Women Organisers, 13 November 1939, and D. Hacking to all Constituency Association Chairmen, 6 February 1940.

59 CPA, CCO 500/1/9, letter from D. Hacking to all Constituency Associations, 26 October 1939, and Memorandum 'Party Activities in War-Time', 14 June 1940.

60 For a general picture of the impact of the war on Central Office see CPA, P. Cohen, 'Disraeli's Child. A History of the Conservative and Unionist Party Organisation', unpublished manuscript, chapter 31.

61 Anon., 'Organisation News', *Onlooker*, 7 (1940), 4.

62 R. Topping, 'A New Year Message from the General Director', *Conservative Agents' Journal*, (1942), 3; Westminster City Library Archives Department, Acc. 485/5, National Society of Conservative Agents, Minute book, 1927–1949.

63 Anon., 'Youth and the Party', *Onlooker*, 7 (1943), 5; and Anon., 'Youth Marches On', *Onlooker*, 9 (1944), 2.

64 The following is based on J. Ramsden, *The Making of Conservative Party Policy. The Conservative Research Department since 1929* (London, 1980), pp. 95–103.

65 Anon., '"Looking Ahead" Circles', *Onlooker*, 5 (1943), 3.

66 Anon., 'London Agents' Meeting', *Conservative Agents' Journal*, (1940), 14.

67 Anon., 'Organisation News', *Onlooker*, 3 (1940), 8.

68 R. Topping, 'Party Organisation and the War', *Conservative Agents' Journal* (1940), 42.

69 Anon., 'Organisation News', *Onlooker*, 4 (1941), 8.

70 See e.g. the picture of Tory activity on war committees and charities in Anon., 'Labour Reports No. 2', 5. .

71 Anon., 'Organisation News', *Onlooker*, 10 (1941), 8.

72 See, among many, 'Looker-On', 'A Story of Apathy', *Onlooker*, 1 (1942), 2.

73 CPA, ARE 7/1/8, The National Union of Conservative and Unionist Associations, Eastern Provincial Area, Minute book, 31 July 1941.

74 *Ibid.*, 24 March 1943. For another area's similar experiences, see e.g. CPA, ARE 3/1/2, The National Association of Conservative and Unionist Associations, North Western Area, Area Council Minutes, 20 March 1943.

75 See 'The Convener', 'Our Looking Ahead Circle', *Onlooker*, 7–9 (1943), passim.

76 Ramsden, *The Making of Conservative Party Policy*, p. 99.

77 Anon., 'Where Do We Stand?', *Conservative Agents' Journal* (1944), 41; H.V. Henthorn, 'Get Rid of the Cliques', *Onlooker*, 9 (1944), 6; and G. Rippon, 'Live Men and Live Methods', *Onlooker*, 11 (1944), 6.

78 Anon., 'Prepare for Political D-Day', *Onlooker*, 12 (1944), 1.

79 CPA, P. Cohen, 'Disraeli's Child', p. 25.

80 G.H. Gallup, *The Gallup International Public Opinion Polls. Great Britain 1937–1975, Volume One* (New York, 1976), pp. 77, 78, 84, 87, 104, 107.

81 The following discussion is based upon Addison, 'By-Elections', pp. 182–3.

82 Gallup, *Opinion Polls*, pp. 89, 103, 108.

83 *Ibid.*, p. 92.

84 B. Newman, *British Journey* (London, 1945), p. 331.

85 Gallup, *Opinion Polls*, p. 61 and, more generally, pp. 34–109.

86 For a number of examples see T. Harrisson, 'Who'll Win?', *Political Quarterly*, 15:1 (1944), 22.

87 *Ibid.*, 32 and THMOA, TC General Elections 1945-55, Box 3, File H, 'Postscript 1946. General Election and After' (n.d.), p. 166.

88 The period immediately prior to the 1945 General Election has been comprehensively discussed in P. Addison, *The Road to 1945* (London, 1975), pp. 252–69; S. Brooke, *Labour's War. The Labour Party during the Second World War* (Oxford, 1992), pp. 303–27; and K.O. Morgan, *Labour in Power 1945–1951* (Oxford, 1985), pp. 34–44.

89 The General Election is well covered in R.B. McCallum and A. Readman, *The British General Election of 1945* (Oxford, 1947). For two

more recent views, see H. Pelling, 'The 1945 General Election Reconsidered', *Historical Journal*, 23:2 (1980), 399–414 and S. Fielding, 'What Did "the People" Want? The Meaning of the 1945 General Election', *Historical Journal*, 35:3 (1992), 623–39.

90 These two documents are to be found in LPA, Michael Foot Papers, MF/M1, Election Material – Devonport 1945–65.

91 For an assessment of the Conservative campaign see G.D.H. Cole, 'Why England Went Socialist', *Virginia Quarterly Review*, 23 (1947), 509; W. Harrington and P. Young, *The 1945 Revolution* (London, 1978), pp. 164–5; and W.T. Morgan, 'The British General Election of 1945', *South Atlantic Quarterly*, 45 (1946), 300, 306–7.

92 Cole, 'England', 512; Labour Party, *Report of the Forty-Fourth Annual Conference of the Labour Party* (London, 1945), p. 90.

93 LPA, 1945 General Election Addresses.

94 Mass-Observation, 'Post-Mortem on Voting at the Election, *Quarterly Review*, 284:567 (1946), 62–3.

95 H. Cantril (ed), *Public Opinion 1936–1946* (Princeton, New Jersey, 1951), p. 677; Mass-Observation, 'Post-Mortem', 62; A.J.P. Taylor, *A Personal History* (London, 1983), pp. 174–5.

96 Cantril, *Public Opinion*, p. 299.

97 *Picture Post*, 21 July 1945.

98 H.W. Durant, *Political Opinion, Four General Election Results* (London, 1949), pp. 6–8.

99 J. Bonham, *The Middle Class Vote* (London, 1954), p. 26; *Conservative Agents' Journal* (1945), 54.

100 Bonham, *Middle Class*, pp. 118–32.

101 For example, see L. Manning, *A Life for Education. An Autobiography* (London, 1970), pp. 163–4; Editorial, *Conservative Agents' Journal* (1945), 53–4.

102 *Picture Post*, 19 August 1944; Mass-Observation, *Puzzled People* (London, 1947), pp. 149–51; McCallum and Readman, *1945*, p. 30.

103 T. Watson, letter to parents, 17 June 1945. In possession of Mr Watson.

104 Lord Butler, *The Art of the Possible* (Harmondsworth, 1973), p. 129.

105 Historians have generally discounted it. See Addison, *1945*, pp. 258–9; Brooke, *Labour's War*, pp. 320–2.

106 Public Records Office, PREM 4/64/2, Note to the Prime Minister from [unknown], 12 June 1944 and letter from G.R. Shepherd to W. Whitely, 4 September 1944.

107 B. Pimlott (ed), *The Political Diary of Hugh Dalton, 1918–40, 1945-60*

(London, 1986), p. 358.

108 W. Hamilton, *Blood on the Walls* (London, 1992), pp. 49–54.

109 THMOA, 'Postscript 1946', pp. 170–1.

110 R. Assheton, 'Lessons of the Election', *Onlooker*, 8 (1945), 3.

111 R.J.E. Silvey, 'Democratic Broadcasting – 1', *The Highway*, 35 (1943), 47 and 'Democratic Broadcasting – 2', *The Highway*, 35 (1943), 86–7.

112 BLPES, Anthony Crosland Papers, 3/26, letter from Crosland to P. Williams, 22 May 1941.

113 See, for example, *Daily Mirror*, 2 and 4 December 1942 and 10 October 1944.

114 See pp. 149–50.

115 Lord Beveridge, *Power and Influence* (London, 1953), pp. 410–11.

116 See pp. 80–4.

117 *Economist* 28 August 1945; *Daily Worker* 27 July 1945.

4

The vision of socialism

Labour's 1945 manifesto contained this significant statement:

> The Labour Party is a Socialist Party, and proud of it. Its ultimate purpose at home is the establishment of the Socialist Commonwealth of Great Britain – free, democratic, efficient, progressive, public-spirited, its material resources organized in the services of the British people.

In the following paragraph, however, came the caution that 'Socialism cannot come overnight, as the product of a weekend revolution. The members of the Labour Party, like the British people, are practical-minded men and women'.[1] The manifesto, in fact, was mainly concerned to describe and justify those 'practical' policies which Labour wanted to implement in government. It indicated that the Party's programme involved the nationalisation of key industries, the creation of a welfare state, the implementation of planning and the commitment to full employment. Such policies promised to push the boundaries of the state further than would have seemed possible before 1939. A number of these proposals found favour with various political opponents, including a few Conservatives. This did not necessarily compromise Labour's claim to be socialist because, whilst such reforms were considered important – indeed vital – they were seen as only a preliminary step towards the Commonwealth. Few in the Party believed that in themselves nationalisation and a welfare state constituted socialism.

Labour's emphasis on the importance of practical reforms did not please everybody within the Party. In 1943 Harold Laski, Labour's most eminent intellectual of the time, exhorted his fellow members to abandon their 'traditional horror of principles'. Labour had, he suggested, evaded doctrine and focused exclusively on piecemeal measures. As a result, it had become a party of social amelioration rather than – despite protestations to the contrary – of socialism. To 'atone for our neglect' Laski called on members to study the works of Karl Marx.[2] In spite of Laski's point of view, Labour's 1945 conference debate on the manifesto revealed differences of detail and emphasis, but none on fundamentals. The definition of socialism and the strategy of gradual reform outlined in the document were accepted with little dispute.[3] Later in the life of the Labour Government, dissent was expressed by the 'Keep Left' MPs and the journal *Tribune* which supported them. Yet, such divisions remained more a question of timing and tone rather than of basics. Thus, during the 1940s, most in the Party were in overall agreement about where Labour was going and how it intended to get there.

That Labour stood for something less than socialism was unthinkable. After all, the Party sought to transcend capitalism through fundamentally restructuring both society and the individual. Moreover, the 1940s appeared to be a uniquely propitious time for the application of Labour's creed: the Second World War was widely credited with bringing about long-desired changes to the material and moral environment. Party members thought it realistic to expect that a Labour Government could move purposefully and, given the constraints of parliamentary democracy, swiftly towards the Socialist Commonwealth. It was not for nothing that the 1945 manifesto was confidently entitled *Let Us Face the Future*.

The purpose of this chapter is to explain why the building of a socialist society appeared a practical prospect to so many Labour members during the war and the first years of the Attlee administration. To recapture the mood of the time, the chapter will indicate how members interpreted the impact of the Second World War and Labour's famous 1945 general election victory. What most undertood by the term socialism or, what might be more accurately described as the 'responsible society', will then be described. The chapter will, finally, outline the means the Party considered appropriate to build socialism. This discussion will provide a context for the subsequent two chapters which look in detail at some of the measures adopted by Labour to encourage the development of socialist values.

By the end of the 1930s most members of the Labour Party were

4 The funny side of life under Labour: 1. 'You're getting hot, sir –
slightly to the left near that outer pea' (see Chapter 7)

comforted by the thought that whilst socialism might not have been imminent it was at least inevitable. All the necessary economic and social preconditions had, they believed, long been in place. Faith in socialism's ineluctability was widespread, despite the collapse of the minority Labour Government in 1931 and the Party's subsequently disappointing electoral performance. Whilst historical development was assumed to have reached a stage propitious for socialism, further progress, however, was hampered by one vital factor. Labour's inability to return to office after Ramsay MacDonald's 'betrayal' demonstrated how much the Party's prospects hinged on this matter. According to Clement Attlee only the popular fear of socialism stood between the Party and its historical destiny. If Labour was to advance its cause, Attlee suggested, the Party had to work hard to 'convert to its faith many millions of workers who still cling to Capitalism'. Nevertheless, he remained confident that such efforts would eventually be rewarded as the immorality of the economic system became ever more apparent.[4]

Few thought that Labour's cause had been made much easier by Britain's declaration of war on Germany in September 1939. Socialism was still a matter of exhorting the uncertain majority to abandon their doubts. Not long after the outbreak of hostilities, Hugh Dalton called on his fellow citizens to make the necessary change of heart and mind. 'It is not far', he declaimed,

> to the Land of Heart's Desire, not more than a day's march if we could see the way, if the clouds would lift, if we had the will to make the journey. From man as he is to man as he might easily be, it is not so far; from this society to another without war and want, not far. Allons-y! Let us go there.[5]

There was little expectation that this appeal would be met with a more positive response than might have been generated before the invasion of Poland. In fact, during the 'Phoney War' most assumed that hostilities would be limited and their domestic impact minor. Thus, in December 1939 Herbert Morrison thought that Neville Chamberlain would continue as Prime Minister for the duration of the struggle.[6] Yet, even before the events of 1940, the war was considered to have accelerated important changes that would ultimately rebound to Labour's advantage. It was predicted that, for example, increased planning and state control of the economy would make the case for policies Labour had long advocated. As

Attlee told the Party's 1940 conference: the 'world that must emerge from this war must be a world attuned to our ideals'.[7] Despite such apparent confidence, Labour seemed more to hope than expect great change: moreover, it was considered that this would occur in the international system rather than at home.[8]

The events which followed from the fall of France in May 1940 changed all this. After the evacuation at Dunkirk Labour figures openly declared that the war had brought one era to an end and begun another. In *The Old World and the New Society* (1942) the National Executive Committee (NEC) announced that the conflict had, 'socially and economically, effected a revolution in the world as vast, in its ultimate implications, as that which marked the replacement of Feudalism by Capitalism'.[9] In the same year, the Fabian Society was told:

> We are at the end of an age. No matter how the war ends, there can be no return to the old ways of living ... There has been no such holocaust of established institutions since the advent of the Dark Ages: nay, even then much less of the human race was shaken by the collapse of the ancient empires than is being shaken today.[10]

The reason for this sense of wholesale upheaval was partly based on the drastic increase in state direction of economy and society induced by the military crisis. These measures were obviously welcomed by the Party. As Morrison told the *Daily Express*, 'Out of all this must come good ... because we can never go back to the old untidy economy. It has got to be planned, and the most valuable lessons of all are being learned now from our controls'.[11] By 1941 it was considered that after the defeat of Germany the state would retain its grip on economic power.[12] Whilst seen in positive terms, these changes were of a secondary order: after all, the war had only accelerated a previously identified economic process. The unique contribution of Dunkirk and the Blitz to Labour's purpose was thought to be the transformation they had effected in the public mood. It was the interpretation of the people's response to these events, described in Chapter 2, which gave Labour hope that socialism had been transformed from a distant promise into a much more immediate prospect.[13]

None drew the political lessons of the conflict as keenly as Herbert Morrison.[14] In April 1941 he stated that:

If only the British people showed the same united and resolute determination to win the peace, as it now showed to win the war, the world might well enter upon one of the greatest periods of progress and achievement in human history.[15]

Towards the end of 1943 he told an audience in Burnley that:

The free and neighbourly human spirit which has always animated our Civil Defence services combined with the advancement of local authority organisation at its best, has been a model from which any society anywhere has something to learn, as have we ourselves, perhaps, in other spheres of national life.

Let us not lose that spirit, and let us recall this as we stand to-day at the beginning of the last road to victory.

Let us remember the meaning of the struggle and the triumph, and let us carry forward into the peace all that we can of the courage, will, and fine public purpose which will have achieved it.[16]

On occasion Morrison suggested that under German bombing 'civilians learned what co-operation, what good neighbourliness, what common danger and common effort really meant. I want to see that blitz psychology used in the days of peace'.[17] *Let Us Face the Future* made the same plea, stating that the country required 'the spirit of Dunkirk and the Blitz sustained over a period of years'.[18] If Labour could somehow maintain the 'Dunkirk spirit' it seemed that the future of socialism was assured.

There appeared reason to believe that the wartime spirit was more than just the expression of a short-term solidarity that would evaporate with the German surrender. By the spring of 1944 Morrison talked of the 'altered moral sense of the community' and argued that 'we have a social conscience'. In fact, he considered that the war showed the workings of a 'genuine social idealism'. According to him, most people had come to disapprove of extreme forms of competition; their faith in private enterprise was lost; acceptance of severe inequalities of wealth weakened; and unemployment no longer accepted as part of the natural order of things. As a result, he suggested, the British people were 'moving into an altogether different form of society, working in an altogether different atmosphere of ideas'.[19] Morrison went further and indicated that 'we have got past the point where our people, after the experiences they have been through, will ever again be content with limited and material aims'. Thus, if forced to make the choice between private enterprise and socialism, the British people would undoubtedly choose the latter.[20]

Some, however, doubted that the wartime spirit could be sustained into the peace. Laski warned that, due to post-war fatigue and inertia, the 'high mood' produced by war might not last. Whilst hostilities had caused the private individual to be absorbed into the public sphere, it was unlikely that after the conflict had ended this process would continue. Due to this fear, Laski had called on Labour to leave the Coalition Government before the war's conclusion so the Party could take advantage of the 'high mood'.[21] A few in the Party even questioned the extent to which hostilities had brought about change. G.D.H. Cole, for one, noted that whilst many people were dissatisfied with the pre-war order, they were 'not animated by any lively hope that life will take on an essentially new quality, or that the relation of man to man in society will be radically other than it has been in the recent past'.[22] As the defeat of Germany became ever closer even Morrison diluted his optimistic assessment of the wartime spirit with a dose or two of caution. In 1943 he told *Daily Mirror* readers not to expect 'the Promised Land to be handed to you on a silver platter after the war or to be given by some miraculous act of Government'. In post-war Britain, he continued,

> Plans and reforms [will] fail if they [do] not have within them the gutsy and live spirit of an alert and intelligent nation, accepting their responsibilities to their neighbours, understanding the need of co-operative effort and shunning individual, selfish profit ... The one fatal thing would be to relax, to go back to superficial pleasantries, to think the battle was to give us the freedom of the West End.[23]

In 1945, with the German surrender an immediate prospect, he asked:

> Is the great moral purpose of standing by the nation going to snap? We have developed a high public and social morality during the war.
>
> If we can maintain that we will get through our troubles and do great things for our country, but if that purpose snaps and if we forget the nation and only think of ourselves individually, then I am afraid we can be in for a very bad time.[24]

Despite such circumspection, by the time of the fall of Berlin most

Labour members remained confident that the war had shifted the public mood substantially towards the Party. Whilst socialism was no longer deemed imminent – as some had thought during the excitement of 1940 – it was still considered much closer to hand than ever before. However, if Labour's position had been improved since the 1930s, a lot of hard political work remained to be done in order to ensure that the wartime spirit continued into the peace.

Notwithstanding the assumed effect of the war on the popular temper, few in the Party could bring themselves to believe that Labour would win the 1945 general election. Most considered that, whilst Labour would improve on its 1935 position, Attlee would fall short of a Commons majority. Due to their gratitude for his wartime leadership, it was expected that many voters would stay true to Churchill. Despite Aneurin Bevan's best rhetoric, enough people would be persuaded to trust the Tories to deliver social and economic improvement.[25] That Labour actually won under such circumstances took the best part of the Party by surprise. Moreover, the election of an unprecedented number of Labour MPs in previously unwinnable rural and suburban constituencies, appeared to suggest that the nation's wartime spirit was much stronger and more Labour-inclined than had ever been thought. Unalloyed optimism was restored: socialism was most definitely in view. As Dalton recalled of this time:

> ... we all knew that, within us, and because of us, and around us, something had suddenly changed.
>   England arise, the long, long night is over;
>   Faint in the East behold the dawn appear.
> Edward Carpenter's Socialist Hymn at last had found fulfilment.
> After the long storm of war, after the short storm of election, we saw the sunrise. As we had sung in the shadows, so now in the light,
>   England is risen and the day is here.[26]

The transition from capitalism to socialism had begun: in a relatively short period of time Britain would become a Socialist Commonwealth.[27] It became inconceivable that the Conservatives could recover from such a defeat: history had finally passed them by. There could be no turning back. Whilst Labour embodied enlightenment and progress the Conservatives were considered to represent ignorance and reaction. Whitelaw's cartoons in the *Daily*

Herald made this point on a regular basis. From the platform and in print, the Conservatives, those 'astrologers of a dead tradition', were assailed for proposing to return to the 1930s.[28] As the *Daily Herald* suggested, Labour's opponents 'want to bring evolution to a standstill'. Laski even suggested that the Tories were the 'enemies of reason'.[29] Such was the swelling of optimistic sentiment that it was considered possible that Labour would, at worst, be in power for a very long time; at best there would never again be another Conservative Government.[30] The *Herald* summed up this mood, suggesting that:

> A whole world has died ... It was a world in which private interests were allowed to lord it over the community, a world in which Britain's position was steadily undermined by tolerance of industrial inefficiency and moral decline.
>
> The war was won by the British people's resolve to break with these bad traditions. They have made it clear to all the world that they are ready to transform our country into a Socialist Commonwealth.[31]

As a correspondent wrote to *Tribune*: 'today the 26th day of July, 1945 sees Britain reborn'.[32]

Victory was explained by reference to numerous factors, not all of them wholly consistent, but each the culmination of a progressive and irreversible process. For example, Hannen Swaffer felt that 1945 marked 'a spiritual resurgence of the British people ... the result of the determination of countless thousands to apply the principles of their religion to everyday politics'.[33] Others considered that it was the result of advances in standards of education.[34] The dominant interpretation of victory was, inevitably, connected to the impact of war. This was seen to have caused those from different social groups to realise their common self-interest in the face of the small minority who controlled capitalism. Consequently, Labour was described as having won the support of 'men and women of goodwill among all classes'.[35] The main division within the electorate was between the vast majority of 'productive workers' who now voted Labour and the tiny minority of 'non-productive workers'.[36] The war had finally enabled Labour to become the 'People's Party', uniting behind its banner members of that nine-tenths of the population forced to work for a living. It had become the party of 'the producers, the consumers, the useful people'.[37] Thus, Labour

MPs were presented to the public as 'your own men and women, who stand with you in the workshops and factories, the offices, the fields, and men and women of attainment in professional spheres'. In contrast, Conservatives were characterised as 'the big landowners, the captains of industry, the financial magnates, the powerful merchants, the cartel controllers, the bankers, the landlords and the rentiers'.[38] Those voters who turned to the Tories did so only because of an accident of birth or a 'warped psychology'.[39] As *Tribune* stated, factory managers had been persuaded that Labour was the only party able to achieve industrial efficiency: in fact, the 'whole country and every industry and profession' sustained Labour in power.[40] Indeed, when the first post-war County Council elections were held in the spring of 1946, the claim that 'Labour *is* the Nation' had become something of a cliche.[41]

Labour thought the war had immeasurably improved socialism's prospects and saw 1945 as a vindication of this point of view. What most in the Party understood by socialism now needs to be established as this determined how members viewed the possibilities inherent in Labour's assumption of office. Surprisingly, perhaps, given its profound impact elsewhere, the Second World War did not change Labour's vision of the Socialist Commonwealth. The Party's new-found popularity had not been the result of Labour adapting its message to suit the electorate's wishes. Rather, the reverse was thought to have occurred: the people had moved towards Labour. Thus, the experience of war was taken to have simply vindicated Labour's central beliefs. As Laski stated in 1943: 'We need proclaim no new truths, we need only re-energise ancient values'.[42] This was most obviously evident in policy: *Let Us Face the Future* and the 1937 *Immediate Programme* were very similar documents.[43] Indeed, according to a 1946 Research Department memorandum, the programme on which Attlee won power embodied 'the thinking of two decades which ... offered practically no opportunity of carrying out Labour's programme'.[44] More substantively, the fundamental meaning of socialism in the 1940s would have been familiar to members of the turn-of-the-century Independent Labour Party (ILP). The pioneer Robert Blatchford would have felt very much at home with most of the sentiments expressed during the decade. Thus, for Labour members, 1945 marked an end as much as a beginning: marching forward into the future, they looked back for guidance. It was a moment during which newly-elected MPs asked:

'What would Keir Hardie think of this?' and 'What would William Morris say?'.[45]

Consequently, when discussing socialism, contemporaries contented themselves with familiar definitions; they did not consider it necessary to develop ones of their own. A 1948 Party pamphlet even approvingly quoted from Labour's 1928 manifesto, despite its connection with the still much-despised former leader Ramsay MacDonald. According to this twenty-year old formulation, socialism stood for:

> the deliberate establishment, by experimental methods, without violence or disturbance, with the fullest utilization of scientific knowledge and administrative skill, of a social order in which the resources of the community shall be organized and administered with a single eye to securing for all its members the largest possible measure of economic welfare and personal freedom.[46]

Labour's sense of continuity was complemented by the belief that, as was claimed in 1948, 'The Socialism of the Labour Party is as British as beer, and bread and cheese'.[47] Indeed, the Party's alleged empiricism and reluctance to theorise was ascribed to its very British character.[48] A correspondent to *Tribune* considered that Labour embodied Socialism in a form 'suitable for our English way of life, our tradition and existing economic structure'.[49] On hearing Churchill describe socialism as an alien creed, Wright Robinson, a leading member of the Labour Party in Manchester, angrily refuted the claim. He wrote that Labour adhered to 'a brand of nonconformist Socialism [which is] strictly home made by Robert Owen, the Fabians, the I.L.P. and revolters against a too hidebound and complacent Christianity'.[50]

Thus, Labour believed itself to be the consummation of an indigenous progressive political tradition. With this in mind, Herbert Morrison told a BBC radio audience in 1947 that: 'If we look back in history, ever since Magna Carta, or earlier, there has been in the minds of Englishmen an unspoken promise that some day there would be a real "Merrie England"'. Labour's socialism was an attempt to realise that vision.[51] Similarly, both the Fabian John Parker and Arthur Greenwood saw Labour as the legatee of a political heritage established by Wat Tyler and the Peasants' Revolt. Parker deemed that Labour's antecedents included Puritans, Whigs, Nonconformists, Chartists and the old Liberal Party. To his mind,

Labour's socialism embodied 'the latest attempt of the forces of the Left to extend the rights of common people against the forces of privilege'. It was 'the inheritor of the achievements of those who fought for liberty in the past'.[52] Michael Foot also emphasised Labour's affinity with eighteenth and nineteenth century radicals such as Tom Paine, William Cobbett and Francis Place.[53] Even Laski was happy to talk of the 'great tradition' of Liberalism and describe it as Labour's 'parent'.[54] Few would have disagreed with Emmanuel Shinwell when he claimed that, 'the birth of the Labour Party marked one of the great stages in the political evolution of this country'.[55] Subsumed within Labour's own history, therefore, was the attempt to democratise political life. Whilst the creation of the Party marked an important stage in that process, the election of a majority Labour government indicated the imminence of its apotheosis. Hence, *Tribune* stated that by voting Labour in 1945 the British people 'have grown to full democratic stature. They have risen to the opportunity and promise of political democracy'.[56]

As a result of this view, the national constitutional framework within which Labour had developed was thought to require little change. During the early stages of the war, Greenwood considered that, 'Parliament as it exists to-day ... is the outward and visible sign to the whole world of the freedom of the British people'. This was because it allowed 'ordered, lawful, democratic progress ... subject to the will and the approval, through constitutional channels, of the ordinary man and woman'.[57] Parliament, therefore, was more than sufficient for the implementation of socialism. In this, as in other areas, the war had merely vindicated an already entrenched Labour position. As the *Daily Herald* asserted, 'The flexibility and poise of the British Parliamentary institution has been a beacon to democrats everywhere throughout the war'.[58] Just as Labour was the summit of British democracy, so Parliament, honed by historical development had become a genuinely democratic institution. Labour and Parliamentary democracy were closely tied together.[59] As *Tribune* stated in 1948:

> Here in our own land ... we have the chance to put political democracy to its greatest test. Fascism and Stalinism pour scorn on the very name. We, in our democratic Socialist movement, have never subscribed to those sneers. Political democracy was won for us in fierce battles against property. In the American War of Indepen-

dence, in the French Revolution, in the struggles of the Chartists and all the other great battles, this instrument was fashioned for us. All those, our great forebears, believed they were sharpening a weapon which would be our strongest aid in the challenge to property and inequality and the other evils of society. To discard it now in favour of the blunt axe of totalitarianism would be the rankest treachery and folly.[60]

Even on the night of Labour's 1951 general election defeat, the young MP Tony Benn could refer to the 'miracle of British democratic decision making'.[61]

Labour's socialism was not just concerned to consummate democracy in the political sphere: it also envisaged a similar change within economic life. The influence of Marx's materialist theory of history was most evident here. Not all Party members were, as Laski had claimed, ignorant of the former's work. It seems likely that Morrison, who considered Marx 'worth studying', was not alone in learning his economics from the pre-1914 Marxist Social Democratic Federation.[62] Like other members of the Second International, Labour believed that socialism was only possible once capitalism had reached a certain stage of development. It was widely considered that this point had been reached some time before 1939. Indeed, the Second World War was seen to be a result of the inherent instability of capitalism.[63] Furthermore, if socialism was not applied after the war, it was believed that this situation would return, bringing fascism and another world conflict within a generation. Capitalism, it was thought, now needed fascist methods to work: even in Britain, some considered that the economic status quo could not survive within a democratic framework. By the end of 1944 a number of Labour members had already identified a 'Fascist drift' within the Coalition Government.[64]

An important part of the case for socialism was, therefore, closely tied to an interpretation of economic development. The argument that capitalism promoted enterprise and efficiency was rejected. This was due to the emergence of monopolies – in the form of trusts or combines – whose sole object was to restrict production and limit the market because this suited the interests of those who controlled them.[65] Consequently, groups wishing to improve efficiency and increase production were frustrated by limitations deliberately imposed by the capitalist system of ownership.[66] This led to low productivity which harmed the interests of the many because it caused unemployment, poverty and ill-health. Such suffering was considered to be wholly unnecessary. In 1940 the future Labour Chancellor Hugh Dalton admiringly quoted the Liberal economist J.M. Keynes' opinion that 'the problem of want and poverty and the economic struggle between the classes and the nations, is nothing but a frightful muddle, a transitory and an unnecessary muddle'.[67]

This analysis led Labour to consider that capitalism had become irrational. In contrast, what the Party proposed was, according to Morrison, 'not much more than applied commonsense'.[68] Labour looked to state-directed planning and public control to ultimately modify capitalism out of existence. The initial target of state control would consequently be those monopolies which enjoyed the most power to influence economic activity. Government control would ensure that the whole community benefited from its labour rather than just a few individuals. The result would be economic growth on an unprecedented scale. The possibilities of technological advance in Labour's 'ordered society' were predicted to be considerable; indeed they were, in the *Daily Herald*'s view, 'illimitable'.[69]

It was confidently expected that, by tackling the power of the trusts, increased state control would prove to be beneficial. There was another reason to expect that socialism would increase productivity: individuals would be enabled to apply their initiative untrammelled by capitalism's constraints.[70] Labour would properly utilise the skills of managers, technicians and white-collar workers as well as the industrial working class. These were the 'useful people'. Hence, in 1944 the *Daily Herald* distinguished between the backward-looking 'Blimps of the directors' parlours and the Stock Exchange bars' and the more progressive 'practical men who do the job of management'.[71] Prior to the 1945 general election, Morrison also talked of the need to free British industry from the burden of the 'privileged, uncreative, ... amiable, useless, part-time, old school-tie, aristocratic or M.P. nominee director' who treated their posts as sinecures. As a result, efficient, salaried management – in whose hands technical skill was concentrated – would be free to pursue a more productive working partnership with the rest of the labour force.[72] As one of Labour's propagandists announced, 'Socialism is, in fact, the culmination of the managerial revolution'.[73]

Those who had a material interest in the continuation of capi-

talism were, therefore, thought to be few in number. According to
Shinwell this group included those 'who have never done any
useful work in their lives – but who are quite prepared to live on
the results of the labours of others'. He went on:

> The time is passed when we can afford to maintain a 'leisured class'.
> It is economic democracy that we are after, and that means the elim-
> ination of dividend-collecting drones. The multiple company director,
> the flashy manipulator of the stock markets, the army of commis-
> sion-chasers and brokerage collectors – all the tribe of hangers-on
> who can produce nothing themselves ... can, in the future, be so dis-
> couraged that they will have no successors.[74]

Thus, as it embodied a commitment to maximise production, socialism was considered to be in the interests of all but a small minority of people. This meant that Labour's potential constituency even
included industrial employers who found their investment plans
thwarted by financiers.[75] It also implied that Labour was much
more than a trade union party. During this period there was criticism of those who persisted in viewing Labour in such terms. Union
influence was increasingly seen to be debilitating by those wanting
Labour to become a genuinely mass party.[76] Even some trade union
leaders considered that Labour needed to open out its ranks to other
social groups. John Benstead, general secretary of the National
Union of Railwaymen, told union delegates that it was time for the
Party to accept 'every worker, whether he uses a shovel or a pen,
whether he works at law or at the bench'.[77] Since 1918 Labour had
appealed, with little effect, to 'workers by hand or brain'. Due to the
perceived effect of the war on popular attitudes, it seemed possible
to expect that this call would meet with a more positive response
than ever before.

The Party stressed that socialism would accomplish much more
than the creation of 'public economic order' in the place of 'private
economic muddle'. In Morrison's view, by ensuring mankind's mastery over the material world, socialism would free humanity from
the scramble for mere existence and allow the development of 'a
more educated and cultured, as well as happier and freer type of
human being'.[78] Materialism was emphasised in the Party's immediate programme because it was considered that this would maximise support amongst those not fully committed to socialism.
However, material advance was never completely detached from

the declared need to develop the individual and apply ethical standards to society. Indeed, it was suggested towards the end of the war that because fascism, like socialism, entailed economic planning, Labour had to distinguish its own programme by stressing that 'under Socialism material well-being is merely the means to an end, the end being a full and complete life for all'.[79]

Emphasis on the development of the individual and the importance of freedom showed a strong affinity with the English Liberal tradition, in particular the form that had evolved under the influence of John Stuart Mill and the turn-of-the-century New Liberals.[80] Labour's connection with the Liberal Party had, after all, been close during its earlier history and many ILP activists had been educated within the radical Liberal tradition. The collapse of the Liberal Party after 1918 had also brought a number of important recruits into Labour's ranks. Similarly, the Second World War initiated another Liberal migration, from the venerable Lord Simon to the youthful Harold Wilson. Others, such as the former Liberal MP and founder of Common Wealth, Richard Acland, found a place within the Party soon after 1945. This later influx only reinforced a pre-existing tendency. Thus, even Laski could declare that the 'preservation of individuality, its extension, indeed, its ability to affirm its own essence' was one of Labour's most important objectives.[81] As Clement Attlee put it in 1943:

> We, of the Labour Movement, are the inheritors not of a body of economic doctrines only but of a great urge of the human spirit. The demand of the human soul is not just for security from fear, not just freedom from want, though both are necessary, but for room to grow to its full stature. We demand freedom. We are Socialists because we demand the same freedom for all that we demand for ourselves ... We seek to build a society where the great qualities of the common man may find full expression.[82]

The full development of the individual was not the only goal Labour set itself. The economic order to be inaugurated by the Party implied responsibilities, a responsible society in fact. Morrison often talked of the importance of 'public service' and even described the spirit of modern socialism as being a 'sober sense of social responsibility'. This is what Attlee meant when he referred to 'an active spirit of service to the community'.[83] Without the development of this sense of social responsibility in each and every individual few considered socialism possible. Indeed, the need for the British people to become 'in spirit Socialist' was decisive. This was because what 'matters is the spirit in which we act, more than the precise form our action takes' as these forms were 'matters of expediency rather than principle'.[84] In practical, every day terms, this 'spirit' was within the grasp of most, even under capitalism. A speaker concluded a talk to one Manchester Labour Women's Section meeting in 1947 by stressing 'the need for us all to re-affirm our faith in Socialism – to practise it in our homes – also to practise truth and friendship'.[85] Socialism's object, the only basis upon which it could ultimately succeed, remained what it had been for the ILP in the 1890s: 'Fellowship'.

As Attlee stood on the threshold of 10 Downing Street the route to socialism seemed, to most Labour members at least, clearly signposted. By causing significant change in the public mood, the Second World War had helped create circumstances in which Labour could finally apply a creed promulgated since the late nineteenth century. The Party realised that Labour in power had to achieve substantial material reform in conjunction with an ethical transformation of the population. Together, these would form the basis of the responsible society – in other words socialism. The sheer magnitude of this a task meant that nobody expected that socialism could be built before Attlee was obliged to seek re-election. Some suggested that socialism would be achieved by 1960 at the very earliest; others talked in terms of it taking at least a generation.[86] The remainder of this chapter surveys in general terms how the Party thought it could build socialism. In the following two chapters, this matter is described in greater detail.

As already mentioned, the Party understood that socialism relied on two preconditions. The first was the implementation of economic reforms, many of which had been outlined in *Let Us Face the Future*. It was expected that these would transform the material environment by bringing important sections of the economy under public control and guaranteeing minimum standards of living for all. The achievement of material change appeared the easiest of socialism's two requirements. Much of Labour's work had, in fact, been anticipated by the Coalition Government which had been forced to increase state control of the economy due to the wartime emergency. Once installed in power, Labour regularised and extended these measures: it nationalised key industries, created a

National Health Service and implemented planning. The Government could do this, safe in the knowledge that the Party's Commons majority made it possible.

On their own, it was considered, these reforms would not lead to socialism: they required individual moral change to make them work. Thus, the second precondition, that the public had to become socialist in both thought and deed, was as vital as the first. No matter how many Acts of Parliament were passed, without a refashioning of individual values the Socialist Commonwealth would not emerge. Morrison was especially concerned to emphasise this point. In 1948 he told Labour's conference that, if the Government's reforms were not to become 'just another bit of bureaucratic routine' the people themselves had to want to make them work.[87] Such a goal could not be achieved as simply as the Royal Assent.

By voting Labour in unprecedented numbers and with such apparent fervour the post-war public was thought ready to set out on the road to socialism. The 'Dunkirk spirit', however, was not sufficient: if the Commonwealth was to be reached this spirit had to be developed and improved upon. Many in the Party recognised that even a large proportion of Labour voters were not fully socialist. The Party had, it was realised, made an explicitly broad appeal to 'all men and women of progressive outlook'.[88] It was appreciated that a substantial number had supported the Party mainly for material reasons. Trade unionists, for example, had been exhorted to advance their self-interest by voting Labour.[89] It was up to the Party to show such voters that, as Barbara Castle put it, socialism was 'something bigger than just ending queues and raising pensions and wages'.[90]

Thus, the most compelling and difficult question which faced Labour after 1945 was: how to make socialists? For reasons outlined above, this task was to be accomplished within the existing political framework. The Party's faith in Britain's constitution had been confirmed by wartime experience. This was further reinforced by the ease with which after 1945 the Labour Government implemented its manifesto pledges. As Richard Acland pointed out in 1947, there was pride in 'the unprecedented British Revolution of the mid-twentieth century. No corpses, no guillotines, no secret police'.[91] Gradual reform through representative democracy appeared to work: Labour's strategy of 'planning with freedom' seemed fully vindicated.

There was a perceived need, however, to encourage active participation within the political system. As Shinwell had stated towards the end of the war: 'I am anxious for the preservation of parliamentary institutions. I want them to be taken seriously'.[92] This was even more important as the Attlee adminstration increased the size and scope of central government. A state which dominated people's lives would undermine an important element of the responsible society: public-spirited citizens. During the war G.D.H. Cole had suggested that 'real neighbourhood organisation' needed to become the basis of 'popular authority' to offset the centralising and bureaucratic trend within government.[93] Those of a more conventional turn of mind, such as James Griffiths, were also concerned to create 'a real civic consciousness' by encouraging involvement in the existing system of local government.[94] At the very least, therefore, Labour needed citizens with an 'active and informed interest' in political affairs if socialism was to be achieved.[95]

The Labour Party itself was considered to have a decisive role to play in encouraging popular participation in public life. By joining the Party voters would at once be integrated into the political process and also help advance socialism. Close after the 1945 election, the Party issued *Labour's Call to Labour's Voters*. This announced that, 'Every elector who voted Labour has a moral as well as a political responsibility to assist the Government to do the job that was entrusted to it'. It continued:

> Your responsibility did not end with your voting Labour. You cannot afford to say to the Government 'Now go on and do your Job' and yourself take little or no further interest in the matter. The strength and power of the Government can be eroded more quickly by its supporters becoming indifferent or complacent than by anything else. Continued active personal support is needed from every supporter and that support can best be harnessed and made effective through membership of the Labour Party.

The pamphlet concluded that 'The goal should be Every Labour Voter a Labour Party Member'. Other Party publications stressed the need for such recruits to be active rather than passive members.[96]

If they were to be enthused with the desire for participation, the Party had to show new recruits that it was a model of the respon-

sible society.[97] A *Tribune* correspondent considered it essential that
Party stalwarts made novice members aware that they were 'out to
give rather than get, to serve rather than to satisfy only personal
ambition'.[98] In the words of one delegate to the 1944 Party conference, 'membership involves an obligation to act, to learn, to
think'.[99] Yet, the Party was not considered wholly adequate to meet
this challenge. Even many established members were thought to
require some form of instruction in socialist principles. To this end,
Transport House encouraged the formation of Labour discussion
groups in constituency and ward parties, the model for this initiative being the Army Bureau of Current Affairs. To facilitate the
development of informed debates on contemporary topics the
Research Department produced a series of pamphlets to focus discussion. The journal *Labour Forum* was established with the same
aim in mind. The expectation was that, in the words of Director of
Party Research Michael Young, participants in discussion groups
would:

> give democratic leadership to the people on the Councils, in the fac-
> tories, in the fields, in every activity of the national life, so that there
> is a wholehearted collaboration between people and Government –
> between 'us' and 'them'.[100]

The education of members was also considered important
because of their prospective role in informing the electorate about
the progress of the Labour Government. Of indifferent voters, members were exhorted to 'Pelt him with facts'. Only an informed
public, it was said, would be a bulwark against the 'power of reaction' during the transition to socialism.[101] Hence, in 1946 the NEC
decided that the public needed to be taught, 'a higher conception
of social ideas and values' and be reminded of 'the personal obligations of duty and service which are necessary for the realisation
of a social civilisation'. At the same time it also discussed establishing a national network of bookshops in order to distribute
Labour and progressive literature in the hope they would form 'centres of literary culture and knowledge'.[102]

Many Labour activists already considered that 'educating' the
public was the prime responsibility of Party members. Like their
predecessors, Labour's rank-and-file were expected to regard themselves as missionaries bearing the socialist gospel. No annual conference was complete without at least one delegate calling for the

[*Illingworth cartoon, reproduced by permission of the "Daily Mail."*

The customer is always left.

" *We know that the organised workers of the country are our friends . . . As for the rest, they don't matter a tinker's cuss.*"—Mr. Shinwell at Margate on May 7th, 1947.

5   The funny side of life under Labour: 2. 'The customer is always left'
(see Chapter 7)

'old evangelical spirit', for the Party 'to go back to the street corner where we came from, to go back to the doorstep, to the factory gate, and to express what is truly within us'.[103] Morrison told the 1948 conference:

> We must have an active, living democracy in our country and we must whip up our citizens to their responsibilities just as we canvass them in elections or just as the air-raid wardens did in the war.[104]

Not only this, but Party members were also expected to 'shoulder personal responsibility' to increase productivity during the Government's export drive. Their personal example was deemed to be of great importance in generating enthusiasm amongst the wider workforce.[105]

The most enthusiastic of Party activists could not make socialism more likely if the appropriate material environment was absent. Thus, Acts of Parliament still had an important part to play in Labour's strategy. Part of the Attlee Government's legislative programme was passed in the hope that it would create the appropriate conditions for individual change. In particular Labour hoped to stimulate the desire for 'community' and 'improving' leisure activities as these were thought crucial to the formation of responsibile citizens. The next two chapters look more closely at how Labour tried to put these two abstract ideas into practice. Even such initiatives, however, relied on the willingness of people themselves to embrace reform. The Labour Party could not force people to become socialists. In 1945 most members thought, however, that the war had caused the British public to see the Socialist Commonwealth in a new and more positive light. The experience described in the following chapters indicates that this was a rather optimistic assessment.

Notes

1 Labour Party, *Let Us Face the Future* (London, 1945), p. 6. Parts of this chapter have appeared in S. Fielding, 'Labourism in the 1940s', *Twentieth Century British History*, 3:2 (1992), pp. 138–53.

2 H.J. Laski, 'Marx and Today', *Fabian Research*, 73 (London, 1943), pp. 3–5, 7–9, 16–17, 24–5 .

3 Labour Party, *Report of the Forty-Fourth Annual Conference of the Labour Party* (London, 1945), pp. 89–104.

4 C.R. Attlee, *The Labour Party in Perspective* (London, 1937), pp. 277–9, 281–4.

5 H. Dalton, *Hitler's War. Before and After* (Harmondsworth, 1940), p. 179.

6 P. Addison, *The Road to 1945* (London, 1975), p. 61.

7 Labour Party, *Report of the Thirty-Ninth Annual Conference of the Labour Party* (London, 1940), p. 125.

8 See, for example, A. Greenwood, *Why We Fight. Labour's Case* (London, 1940) and Dalton, *Hitler's War*.

9 Labour Party, *The Old World and the New Society. A Report on the Problems of War and Peace Reconstruction* (London, 1942) p. 17.

10 Fabian Society, 'A Word on the Future to British Socialists', *Fabian Tracts*, 256 (London, 1942), p. 3.

11 *Daily Express*, 21 August 1940.

12 F. Williams, *Ten Angels Swearing ... Or Tomorrow's Politics* (London, 1941), p. 184; G.D.H. Cole, 'The War on the Home Front', *Fabian Tracts*, 247 (London, 1940), pp. 5–6.

13 Labour Party Archive [hereafter LPA], National Executive Minutes, February 1944, 'Mr. Attlee's Call – "I Want the Party to be Ready!"'

(pamphlet); S. Cripps, *Democracy Alive* (London, 1946), pp. 13, 22–3, 37, 62–3; M. Young, *Labour's Plan for Plenty* (London, 1947), p. 9.

14 B. Donoghue and G.W. Jones, *Herbert Morrison. Portrait of a Politician* (London, 1973), pp. 324–7.

15 *Daily Herald*, 7 April 1941.

16 *Daily Mail*, 15 November 1943.

17 *Daily Mirror*, 18 January 1943.

18 Labour, *Face the Future*, p. 3.

19 LPA, Herbert Morrison News Cuttings, Press Releases 4 March and 29 April 1944.

20 LPA, Herbert Morrison News Cuttings, Press Release 29 April 1944; *News Chronicle*, 1 October 1943.

21 Laski, 'Marx', pp. 31–2; *Tribune*, 7 May 1943.

22 G.D.H. Cole, 'Plan for Living', in G.D.H. Cole *et al.*, *Plan for Living* (London, 1943), pp. 1–3.

23 *Daily Mirror*, 18 January 1943.

24 *Daily Telegraph*, 24 April 1945.

25 H. Dalton, *The Fateful Years. Memoirs, 1931–1945* (London, 1957) pp. 465–6; E. Shinwell, *I've Lived Through It All* (London, 1973), p. 180; A. Bevan, *Why Not Trust the Tories?* (London, 1944).

26 Dalton, *Fateful Years*, pp. 482–3.

27 Harvester Press, *The Archive of the British Labour Party. Series II. Pamphlets and Leaflets. Part III. 1940–52* [hereafter *LPPL*] (Brighton, 1981), 1945/34; Anon., 'Labour Women M.P.s Look Ahead', *Labour Woman*, 33:8 (1945), 175.

28 Labour Party, *Report of the Forty-Eigth Annual Conference of the Labour Party* (London, 1949), p. 118; *Daily Herald*, 9 April 1945; *Tribune*, 8 June 1945 and 2 November 1951.

29 *Daily Herald*, 21 April 1945; Labour Party, *Report of the Forty-Third Annual Conference of the Labour Party* (London, 1944), p. 110.

30 P. Duff, *Left, Left, Left. A Personal Account of Six Protest Campaigns, 1945–65* (London, 1971), p. 9; L. Manning, *A Life For Education. An Autobiography* (London, 1970), pp. 164–6.

31 *Daily Herald*, 3 November 1945.

32 *Tribune*, 3 August 1945.

33 *Daily Herald*, 14 October 1946.

34 P.G. Richards, 'The Labour Victory: Election Figures', *Political Quarterly*, 16:4 (1945), 356.

35 F. Williams, *Fifty Years March* (London, 1951), pp. 358–9.

36 Editorial, *Labour Woman*, 38:3 (1950), 50–1.

37 H. Morrison, *The Peaceful Revolution* (London, 1949), p. 47.
38 Harvester, *LPPL*, 1945/32.
39 *Daily Herald*, 1 September 1945.
40 *Tribune*, 3 and 10 August 1945.
41 *Daily Herald*, 9 March 1946.
42 *Tribune*, 7 May 1945.
43 I. Taylor, 'Labour and the Impact of War, 1939–45' in N. Tiratsoo (ed), *The Attlee Years* (London, 1991), pp. 21–6.
44 LPA, RD32/October 1946, Anon., 'Research Programme', [n.d.].
45 *Daily Herald*, 30 July 1945.
46 LPA, RD114/June 1948, Anon., 'Welcome to the Labour Party', [n.d.], p. 7.
47 *Ibid.*, p. 5.
48 Lord Lindsay, 'The Philosophy of the British Labour Governments', in F.S.C. Northrop (ed), *Ideological Difference and World Order* (London, 1949), p. 250.
49 *Tribune*, 27 August 1943.
50 Manchester Central Reference Library, Local Studies Unit [hereafter MCRLLSU], M284/Boxes 8–11, Wright Robinson Papers, Diary, 1 June 1945.
51 *Listener*, 4 July 1947.
52 J. Parker, *Labour Marches On* (Harmondsworth, 1947), pp. 13–15; Greenwood, *Why We Fight*, p. 204.
53 *Daily Herald*, 15 February 1946.
54 Labour, *Forty-Fourth Conference*, p. 143.
55 E. Shinwell, *When the Men Come Home* (London, 1944), p. 66.
56 *Tribune*, 24 August 1945.
57 Greenwood, *Why We Fight*, pp. 108–9.
58 *Daily Herald*, 7 October 1944.
59 *Daily Herald*, 8 February 1946.
60 *Tribune*, 14 May 1948.
61 Tony Benn, *Years of Hope. Diaries, Papers and Letters 1940–1962* (London, 1994), p. 157.
62 Donoghue and Jones, *Herbert Morrison*, p. 33; Morrison, *Peaceful Revolution*, p. 56.
63 LPA, RDR 279/January 1945, Anon., 'Draft of a Short-Term Programme', [n.d.].
64 Fabian Society, 'Word', p. 23; Labour, *Forty-Third Conference* (London, 1944), p. 114; Laski, 'Marx', p. 19; *Tribune*, 7 May 1943.
65 Fabian Society, 'Word', pp. 9–10.

66 Cole, 'Plan', pp. 14–15.

67 Dalton, *Hitler's War*, p. 181.

68 Morrison, *Peaceful Revolution*, p. 21.

69 Morrison, *Peaceful Revolution*, p. 9; *Daily Herald*, 31 July 1945.

70 Labour, *Forty-Fourth Conference*, p. 91.

71 *Daily Herald*, 31 July 1944.

72 *Daily Herald*, 30 April 1945.

73 'Licinius', *Vote Labour? Why?* (London, 1945), pp. 23–4.

74 Shinwell, *Come Home*, pp. 8–14, 45.

75 Labour Party, *Full Employment and Financial Policy* (London, 1944), pp. 2–3.

76 *Tribune*, 26 March 1945.

77 Anon., 'Whom Do We Want in the Party?', *Labour Organiser*, 23:262 (1943), 3–4; *Daily Herald*, 5 July 1944.

78 H. Morrison, 'Man: The Master or the Slave of Material Things?', *Barnett House Papers*, 18 (London, 1935).

79 *Tribune*, 28 January 1944.

80 M. Freeden, *The New Liberalism. An Ideology of Social Reform* (Oxford, 1978), pp. 24–32, 254–6.

81 Laski, 'Marx', pp. 28–9.

82 Labour Party, *Report of the Forty-Second Annual Conference of the Labour Party* (London, 1943), p. 122.

83 Morrison, *Peaceful Revolution*, pp. 23, 43; *Daily Herald*, 26 February 1945.

84 Fabian Society, 'Word', pp. 16–19.

85 MCRLLSU, M450/1, Openshaw Ward Women's Section Minute Book, 11 September 1947.

86 Young, *Plan*, p. 11; Fabian Society, 'Word', p. 15.

87 Morrison, *Peaceful Revolution*, pp. 45–6; H. Wratten, 'Are We Making Socialists?', *Labour Organiser*, 27:315 (1948), 6–7; *New Statesman*, 27 November 1948.

88 Labour, *Face the Future*, p. 12.

89 Harvester, *LPPL*, 1944/25.

90 Anon., 'M.P.s Look Ahead', *Labour Woman*, 33:8 (1945), 166.

91 *Tribune*, 5 December 1947.

92 Shinwell, *Come Home*, p. 31; Young, *Plan*, p. 8.

93 Cole, 'Plan', pp. 23–32.

94 *Tribune*, 5 December 1947 and 14 January 1949.

95 *Daily Herald*, 28 April and 13 August 1945.

96 Harvester, *LPPL*, 1944/27, 1945/22, 1946/70.

97 M.A. Hamilton, *The Labour Party To-Day* (London, n.d. but 1939), p. 94; Young, *Plan*, p. 9; Harvester, *LPPL*, 1944/5.

98 *Tribune*, 20 July 1945.

99 Labour, *Forty-Third Conference*, p. 111; Harvester, *LPPL*, 1945/1.

100 *Tribune*, 11 January 1946; P. Gordon-Walker, 'Party Education: The Next Step', *Labour Forum*, 1:1 (1946), 3–5; Harvester, *LPPL*, 1946/17 and 24.

101 Harvester, *LPPL*, 1945/6 and 29.

102 LPA, National Executive Minutes, 18 September 1946, 'A Note on Education in the Labour Party'; Labour Party, *Report of the Forty-Fifth Annual Conference of the Labour Party* (London, 1946), p. 116.

103 Labour Party, *Report of the Forty-Seventh Annual Labour Party Conference* (London, 1948), p. 130; Labour, *Forty-Eigth Conference*, pp. 115–17.

104 Labour, *Forty-Seventh Conference*, p. 132.

105 LPA, National Executive Committee Minutes, 'The Labour Party and the Production White Paper', 24 February 1947.

5

Creating the 'Responsible Society', part one: building community

In thinking about how they were going to change British society, Labour leaders recognised that the current situation was far from acceptable. The electorate had demonstrated its political maturity by voting in a Labour administration but many everyday social attitudes remained very much less satisfactory than this advance might suggest. The ordinary citizen appeared often alienated from decision-making, able to exert very little control over home, leisure or work life. In addition, the dominant popular culture seemed frivolous, a celebration of the lowest common denominator rather than a channel for improvement and developing horizons. Britain might now have a socialist Government but it was certainly not a socialist society. Labour's task was to correct this imbalance.

The following chapter looks at various methods employed in pursuit of this objective. The particular focus is on the question of community. Labour believed that, as things stood, people were often driven apart, to live separate and perhaps damagingly introverted lives. In the future, they must be drawn together and thus reminded of their common humanity and deeper purpose. This meant a range of policies designed to shift the balance between private and public, selfish and selfless. In each case, the central aim was to create the kind of infrastructure that would encourage participation and overcome helplessness. To illustrate what was at stake here, and what was achieved, attention will be given to developments in three key areas – housing, civic affairs and the workplace. A final section examines the broader context, in order to assess how far Labour's ideals concerning community were consistent with the general pattern of developments in post-war Britain.

In 1945, Labour recognised that housing was the most important domestic problem it had to solve. Many homes had been destroyed or damaged during the war. Furthermore, those who had been forced to share accommodation were now anxiously waiting to begin life on their own. The priority was for a building pro- gramme designed to produce units as fast as possible. However, Bevan, the Minister responsible, emphasised that quantity must not be allowed to dominate at the expense of quality. The new houses must be soundly built and of adequate size. Moreover, care would need to be taken about their positioning and relationship to ameni- ties. Indeed, grouping homes in the right way might well be crucial to the success of shaping communities.

The insistence on this latter point derived from Labour's belief that interwar urban development had gone drastically wrong. Housing had been built by private speculators and was therefore largely unplanned. As a consequence, many urban areas were functionally inefficient, choked, for example, by traffic congestion.[1] In addition, there had been widespread damage to the social fabric. The neglected inner-city areas were obviously unsatisfactory since, as Cripps explained, slums produced 'only too often slum minds and slum habits'.[2] But newer, outlying estates were in many ways little better. The houses might be well built, but there was usually a chronic shortage of facilities, producing a sense of isolation. Women were particularly likely to suffer in these circumstances. As one Labour local councillor noticed, the estate-dwelling housewife might well be 'confined to the four walls of her home ... [with] little time or energy for a life of wider interests'.[3] Finally, there was the problem of segregation. The tendency had been to build groups of houses for particular social classes. The result was what Bevan called 'castrated communities', a pattern he felt to be deeply dam- aging:

> You have colonies of low-income people, living in houses provided by the local authorities and you have the higher income groups living in their own colonies. This ... is a wholly evil thing, from a civilised point of view ... It is a monstrous infliction upon the essen- tial psychological and biological one-ness of the community.[4]

Given such criticisms, Labour decided that in future much more attention should be given to the housing pattern. The first indica- tion of this new priority had come at the 1944 Conference, when the party accepted that a technique recommended by the prominent architect Sir Charles Reilly should be used as a model in all future development.[5] Reilly had been appointed Planning Consultant to Birkenhead City Council earlier in the year, and had produced a plan for an estate lay-out which continued to divide the local political establishment.[6] What Labour liked about the architect's ideas was their emphasis on community: Reilly wanted houses to be 'placed in friendly relation to one another'.[7] His conception was to build homes in relatively small numbers around village greens. Four or five of these groupings would be arranged like the petals of a flower around a central area, equipped with appropriate facilities for education, recreation and shopping. Such 'neighbourhood-units' could then be aggregated into larger conurbations.[8] The objective was to allow real communality to flourish amongst all sections of the population. As Reilly noted of his basic tier, the village green:

> With all the ways of meeting one's fellows such an estate would provide ... a great many of the advantages of a residential university would accrue. It should make for a more intelligent community whose members do not rely on a single newspaper for their information[9]

This was a forceful theme, and once in office, Labour continued to be guided by its general thrust. Bevan was an especially strong proponent of the neighbourhood-unit idea, yoking it to his particular concern about class segregation. In a typical speech, reported in the *Architects' Journal* during 1948, he reached back into history to illustrate the ideal:

> We cannot have aggregations of ostentatious living in one place and in another colonies of obvious, self-evident workers. We have to have communities where all the various income groups of the population are mixed; indeed, we have to try and recapture the glory of some of the past English villages, where the small cottages of the labourers were cheek by jowl with the butcher's shop, and where the doctor could reside benignly with his patients in the same street.[10]

Despite this rhetoric, actually creating neighbourhood units in the years after 1945 proved to be a very much more difficult proposition than many had imagined. Most architects were broadly sympathetic to Labour's views. The neighbourhood unit had been recommended in the 1944 *Housing Manual*, an official guide to

good practice, and it continued to be widely accepted by the profession throughout the later 1940s.[11] In addition, many local
authorities, now charged with a key role in house building, adopted
the idea as a central planning tool. A Midlands' mayor of 1946 was
by no means alone in hoping that a division of his city's suburbs
into 'definite zones, each with its own identity, and ... centre' would
promote 'a social sense'.[12] Nevertheless, when practical decisions
had to be made, other influences often came to dominate. The Government's investment controls, particularly after 1947, meant that
few councils could contemplate even basic infrastructure provision.
Relatively small sums for features like health centres were judged
too extravagant. Meanwhile, the sheer scale of demand for accommodation also exerted strong pressures. As one observer noted,
local authority housing departments 'found themselves over-
whelmed by the enormous queues of homeless people ... and it soon
became evident that the long-term aims of good community would
have to be subordinated to ... more immediate needs'.[13]

In these circumstances, the ideal and the reality of new building
began to become very different things. Critics recognised that
Labour wanted to pursue a new direction, and was quite sincere
about its objectives, but they were also scathing about what had
actually been achieved. A review of the situation in 1950 came to
the following conclusions:

> *Most* of the bigger new estates have been *planned* on neighbourhood
> lines ... In general however, only the houses (and a few shops) are
> actually being built, so that in many places conditions similar to
> those of the 1930s are unfortunately beginning to appear. Trans-
> port, shops, schools, churches and medical services are all inade-
> quate, whilst facilities for entertainment and recreation are almost
> non-existent.[14]

A numerical survey, completed shortly afterwards (see Table 3)
made this point even more forcefully.

These figures were certainly disturbing, but Labour and the other
proponents of the neighbourhood unit also had to accept another
unpalatable fact. For it was gradually becoming clear that even
where building had been relatively enlightened in the post-war
years, there was no necessary growth of community feeling. A
National Council of Social Service handbook of 1950 concluded
that new one-class housing estates were often completely lacking

in common purpose: 'it must be admitted that sometimes the difficulties have been so great that the community spirit has withered and the only solution has been to import help and leadership from outside'.[15] More significantly, an investigation by Birmingham University sociologists into one of Coventry's new neighbourhoods came to very similar conclusions. Tenants, it was found, were continuing to rate each other on a rough to respectable continuum, and mix accordingly. The prevailing ethos could be illustrated by the pattern of neighbouring. Living in proximity encouraged mutual help but 'hazards' like gossip and the perceived threat to privacy pulled in an opposite direction. The result was a general uneasiness and considerable discrimination in actual contacts:

> The restraining of neighbourliness is illustrated by responses to questions dealing with borrowing and lending. There is pressure on neighbours to borrow from each other but this is restrained by the judgement that borrowing and lending is undesirable. Indeed very few of the women accept borrowing or lending as a normal incident of social relationships and the general standard for the group is disapproval.[16]

Table 3 *Planned and actual provision of various facilities on 100 post-war housing estates, 1952*

Facility	No. planned	No. built	No. built as % of no. planned
Day nursery	13	–	–
Nursery school	46	1	2
Infant welfare clinic	24	6	25
Infant play space	22	2	9
Open playground	52	14	27
Health centre	33	–	–
Community centre	50	4	8
Branch library	46	11	24

Source: C. Madge 'Survey of Community Facilities and Services in the United Kingdom', *U.N. Housing and Town and Country Planning Bulletin*, 5 (1952), 31–41.

A final problem concerned the middle class. Bevan, as has been noted, was in favour of inter-class mixing, and in 1949 actually passed legislation allowing councils to build for all income groups.[17] Nevertheless, there were few signs that middle-class people wanted working-class neighbours. In several cases, residents in better-off districts campaigned against council houses being built in their midst.[18] A leading opponent of the Stevenage New Town plan displayed typical attitudes. He lived down a secluded lane, behind high hedges, and feared for his privacy and his individuality should neighbourhood units be built:

> Why [the Minister's] idea ... is they'd have all the houses built around a park, and two mothers would take turns minding the children, two in the laundry, and so on, every day ... We don't want people looking in our windows while we eat. I bought this extra acre of land just to keep anyone from building on it.[19]

By the end of Labour's period in office, therefore, few of those involved in planning were as optimistic about the neighbourhood unit idea as they had been in 1945. Some continued to believe that when full facilities were finally provided, living communities would quickly emerge. On the other hand, majority opinion had more or less concluded that the whole conception was flawed. It might certainly be worth providing people with a range of services close at hand. But to believe that a change in the physical environment could so easily alter long-held social attitudes was simply naive.[20]

In addition to neighbourhood schemes, Labour also tried to create a sense of local community by boosting civic culture. The commitment here was sometimes ambiguous. The Government's belief in national welfare provision tended to downgrade local authority involvement and led to allegations of over-centralisation. However, the impact of legislation was not all in one direction, and the Local Government Act of 1948 actually widened municipal power.[21] More significantly, the pursuit of local democracy (and thus local community) remained important to many in the Party. Labour journals emphasised that 'Democracy, to be virile, must be local democracy'.[22] In towns and cities, this enthusiasm was even more forcefully presented. Coventry's George Hodgkinson, leading a Labour administration, argued that involving people in their city's affairs was vital and demanded innovative thinking:

the citizen must be in day to day contact with the activities of the
local authority through the medium of the Press and the voluntary
associations ... Here is the embryo of the new democratic technique
which will make the citizen conscious of the vital part, the living part
he has to play as a citizen in a real democracy.[23]

Given such attitudes, the 1940s did sometimes witness the flowering of civic culture, with Labour authorities presiding over an
extended range of services and a freshly created sense of local identity.[24] Nevertheless, progress was rarely straightforward in such
places and could easily be thwarted. To illustrate the range of problems Labour faced, the following paragraphs concentrate on two
examples, the provision of municipal eating facilities, known widely
as British Restaurants, and the attempt to involve ordinary people
in city planning.

British Restaurants (BRs) were first established in 1941 as part
of the Government's wartime emergency feeding programme.[25]
They aimed to provide cheap meals in locations convenient for factory workers. By October 1943 there were 2,140 BRs in operation
providing 615,000 meals per day, an impressive figure though
actually only about 2–3 per cent of all the meals served daily in
catering establishments.[26]

BRs were administered under the 1939 Emergency Powers Act,
and so at the end of the war there was speculation as to what
would happen once this legislation lapsed. Some argued that a fresh
Bill should be introduced to allow city councils to take over the
facilities. Local Labour politicians believed that commercial caterers
were unreliable and uninterested in the poorer sections of the community. If they were handed BRs they would need to be closely controlled, and so it seemed wiser to have the undertakings run by the
municipality.[27] Feminist opinion reached similar conclusions. Communal restaurants owned by public authorities would be an 'economic aid' to the poor and at the same time free many housewives
from the burden of endless cooking.[28] The wider public apparently
agreed with these views: in January 1945, 60 per cent told Gallup
that they would like to see BRs continued after the war, with only
17 per cent against.[29]

The catering trade, not surprisingly, was vehemently opposed to
any municipalisation of the BRs. It argued that the restaurants had
been set up in an emergency, and promised as only temporary. The

catering industry was quite capable of meeting future demand, especially when ex-servicemen returned to re-open their cafes. The optimum solution was to shut BRs; if they must be kept open under local authority control, they should at least be fully self-supporting and not subsidised from the rates.[30] To publicise their case, the Caterers Association of Great Britain lobbied hard in Whitehall. Meanwhile a 'sinister whispering campaign against British Restaurants' was 'spreading through the country', allegedly orchestrated by 'vested interests'.[31]

The Labour Government's response to these arguments was announced in 1946. Ministers were worried about the possible cost of municipalising BRs – a number had already shut because of falling revenue – but in the end decided that this was the best course of action.[32] The resulting Civic Restaurants Act of 1947 allowed local authorities to run refreshment services (and thus take over BRs) provided that they did not show a deficit for three years in succession.[33] This seemed to satisfy the twin objectives of improving social welfare while maintaining budgetary constraints.

During the next few years, some local authorities made a great success of their new powers. A description of the Chesterfield Civic Restaurant, opened in 1950, noted that it was a modern building with big windows, situated in the town centre. Breakfasts, lunches, teas and suppers were all provided, and there was room for over 350 people at any one time.[34] However, many councils found catering much more difficult. Some struggled to finance their operations, as costs increased faster than inflation, and this was particularly evident where a 'fair wages' policy had been adopted.[35] For others, the greatest problems revolved around the restaurant buildings themselves. Many BRs had been established in temporary locations (such as schools, shops, hotels, churches and warehouses), either under agreement or through requisition. After the peace, original users were often increasingly eager to regain possession of their sites, sometimes threatening legal action if they were opposed.[36]

To make matters worse, popular feelings about public communal feeding were gradually becoming less positive. Firstly, the demand for cheap meals, especially at mid-day, appeared to be contracting. Many workers were reverting to the habit of returning home at lunch, a trend encouraged by some wives on the grounds that their cooking was cheaper and more satisfying.[37] At the same time, competition in the restaurant trade as a whole was gradually intensifying. More factories and schools were opening canteens, while independent caterers had begun offering a better range of fare.[38] The changing situation was highlighted when the first of Littlewoods' thirty-three planned cafeterias opened at the company's Oxford Street store in 1947.[39]

Meanwhile, there was growing unease about the idea of municipal catering in general. The Beaverbrook press campaigned against the continuation of civic provision, arguing that it was 'an example of a war-time emergency device being perpetuated for the sole purpose of destroying free enterprise at the expense of the ratepayer'.[40] Local chambers of commerce made much the same point, lobbying councillors on the grounds that their responsibility was 'to govern, not to trade'.[41] The electorate was not necessarily persuaded by such rhetoric, but nevertheless appeared to be becoming more 'rate conscious' and less willing to support any non-essential council expenditure. Everywhere, the pressure for municipal provision seemed to be declining.[42]

In these circumstances, there was an understandable tendency for local administrations to economise over catering whenever possible. In the early 1950s, a Fabian enquiry found 'many instances' where authorities had adopted 'a take-it-or-leave-it attitude to their customers and not really set out to compete in excellence of service or cooking'.[43] Elsewhere, the preferred solution was to leave the trade altogether. In early 1945 there had been 1,843 BRs; four years later, only 654 civic cafes and canteens were still operating.[44] Vested interests, in conjunction with public indifference and parsimony, had begun to win the day.

Labour's attempt to involve the public in city planning revolved around several initiatives. The 1947 Town and Country Planning Act devolved responsibility for planning on to certain kinds of local authority (usually county borough or county councils).[45] These bodies were instructed to prepare development plans for their areas by 1951 and then review them quinquennially. Such a process was expected to encompass consultation with every relevant interest. This was not a legal obligation, since the Minister responsible wanted to maintain maximum flexibility in what would be very diverse circumstances, but it continued to be heavily emphasised in official instructions.[46] As a further safeguard for the citizen's position, the Act also introduced a new right of appeal. In future, objectors to a planning authority's recommendations could have their cases heard in public before a Ministry inspector.

These legislative measures were accompanied by a propaganda campaign providing information and emphasising the merits of popular participation.[47] Local authorities were encouraged to launch social surveys in their districts, if possible using volunteers from appropriate clubs and societies. Several responded, while others held meetings or displays on plans and planning. Accompanying literature and public statement stressed that ordinary people could and should exert a real influence. At an exhibition held in East Ham library during 1951, the Mayor expressed fairly typical sentiments:

> [He] said that a mystical people believed to be all powerful and referred to as 'they' occupied far too large a place in our thinking ... 'It isn't "they", it is "we"', he said. 'Not just your town, but my town, ours; together we hold its privileges and together we share its obligations.' 'The exhibition is provided to provoke a healthy interest seeking to incite not merely comment, but inviting constructive criticism.'[48]

All told, this was a much more open system than had ever existed before, but it was not matched by any great flowering of public interest in town planning. Objectors were keen to use the appeals machinery and by 1950 the Ministry was adjudicating on over 2,000 cases per year (upholding about one half).[49] However, for most people (as has been suggested) the priority was housing, with planning considered a very low priority. Jean Mann, Labour MP for Coatbridge in Scotland, reported that all her constituents wanted was a house with a bathroom: 'Housing is an acute election issue. "Town Planning" is regarded as a fanatic's dream. No one connects the extreme densities ... of Glasgow with the high disease and death rate'.[50] A local councillor in London reported similar attitudes:

> Why don't they build some dwellings on that bomb-site? The town planning says it's to be open space. What's the use of open space? Isn't there the doorstep and the street? What we want is homes.[51]

As a leading academic planner commented, 'Houses anywhere, at once, were preferred to houses in the right place five years ahead'.[52]

In this situation, direct questioning of the public on wider planning issues tended only to emphasise the general state of uninter-
est and confusion. A social survey of Middlesbrough at the end of
the war had found only restricted consensus on suggested improvements and great apathy amongst the less well-off ('Interest in
replanning is, as might be expected, highest in the group whose
wage rate is over £5 per week').[53] Enquiries in Willesden, a suburb
of London, during 1947, produced similar impressions:

> In addition to the restricting effect of the informant's preoccupation
> with housing, even those who were able to turn their thoughts to
> other matters at this point were frequently unable to offer any sug-
> gestion for local improvements. Of these, according to the inter-
> viewer's reports, some definitely were not interested or said no
> improvement was needed, whilst the replies of others might have
> been more fruitful had they had more time to think about them.[54]

A reformed planning system, it appeared, was no necessary guar-
antor of increased public interest or participation.

Labour's strategy to promote community in the workplace
hinged on the establishment of Joint Production Committees (JPCs)
– forums composed of equal numbers of managers and workers
which were charged with resolving problems arising in the running
of industrial units. Such bodies had been established in the war to
involve workers in the national effort, but though judged generally
successful, few had survived into the peace. Labour's campaign to
re-introduce JPCs began in 1947 and can usefully be examined as
it affected first private industry and then the nationalised sector.

Labour was attracted to the idea of JPCs in private industry for a
number of reasons. Ministers knew Britain was involved in a 'battle
for production' but recognised that this would not be won unless,
as in the war, workers and employers could be persuaded to moderate their sectional interests. At the same time, the JPC idea fitted
in with wider Labour ideals about how people should be treated, at
work as much as in society. Ernest Bevin was a particular proponent of this view:

> Men will follow when they know they are getting a fair deal, and at
> this time in our development this means that they must be treated
> as equal partners and must be given the facts.[55]

Further to the left, finally, the JPC seemed a possible first stage in establishing a more thorough-going industrial democracy.

Reactions to Labour's view amongst employers and trade union-ists were unsurprisingly mixed.[56] The Trades Union Congress (TUC) was an enthusiastic advocate of JPCs and pressed for discussion about their early creation. Nevertheless, there could be no question of departing from voluntary principles: as a staunch defender of free collective bargaining, the TUC felt that the two sides of industry should be left alone to develop any new programme. Amongst employers, attitudes were far less enthusiastic. Business leaders remained very wary about resurrecting what they saw as an emer-gency measure necessary in wartime, which might well now chal-lenge the manager's long-held right to manage. In addition, there were less publicised worries that JPCs might easily be infiltrated by Communists.

As a consequence of these various pressures, the final agreement to push for joint consultation, signed in 1947, was rather less far-reaching than some had envisaged. The TUC and the employers' associations concurred that appropriate machinery should be intro-duced to facilitate 'the regular exchange of views between employ-ers and workers on production questions'. But they also wanted it 'clearly understood' that: 'a) the machinery would be purely vol-untary and advisory in character; b) it would not deal with terms and conditions of employment; [and] c) it would be up to each industry to decide the appropriate form of machinery'.

Over the next three years, JPCs grew in number at a fairly steady rate. An enquiry by the British Employers Confederation (BEC) in 1950 found that thirty-five out of forty-seven trade associations contacted had arranged for JPCs to be created in their industries. The 'big majority of the large firms', it was reported, had JPCs.[57] In engineering, 63 per cent of employees were in factories with joint consultation machinery.[58] Nevertheless, it was also apparent that the general situation was somewhat less satisfactory than these figures suggested. Companies in engineering employing less than 150 people, a large slice of the total, were more likely not to have JPCs than their larger competitors, and this pattern was repeated in several other industries.[59] Moreover, there was growing evidence that when JPCs had been established, they were not performing as once expected. In 1951, the journal *Future* asked managers what they felt about JPCs: 'In your experience is joint consultation useful as evidence of desiring good relations, not even that but completely useless, or really valuable?'. It found that only 6 per cent of those questioned were very positive; 22 per cent agreed JPCs could be described as worthless, while 57 per cent believed that they had symbolic importance but little else.[60] H.A. Turner, writing with rather different sympathies in *Socialist Commentary* during the same year, reached broadly similar conclusions. Joint consultation as a whole, he alleged, had produced 'remarkably little impact on industrial working life'. The JPC campaign, in particular, seemed to be very disappointing. Relatively few firms were involved – it was 'notable that the same two or three' had been 'continually cited as examples to be emulated'. Secondly, there was 'a general tendency' for discussions in functioning units to focus on welfare alone, to become bogged down in 'tea and toilets' as a popular dismissive epithet had it.[61]

Given such views, there were those who readily asserted that the JPC campaign had been a failure. The whole episode, it was argued, illustrated the Government's lack of will in enforcing radical ideas and its readiness to compromise with vested interests. However, looking at the evidence closely suggests that the real situation over JPCs was much more complex than such criticism allowed. It is evident, firstly, that not all judged operative JPCs harshly. The Engineering and Allied Employers National Federation reported that many member firms looked at joint consultation favourably, since it stimulated team spirit, 'with consequent improvement of production, reduction in absenteeism and so on'.[62] In addition, the 'tea and toilets' point could easily be overdone. As a careful study of joint consultation in nine Yorkshire firms argued, welfare matters dominated because it was 'the smaller and particular, as opposed to the general matters which touch the ordinary worker most'.[63]

Having said this, however, there is no doubt that some JPCs were relatively ineffective, and so there are legitimate questions about why problems occurred. Here, contemporary opinion was rather divided. Employers argued that the workers were not interested in joint consultation. 'The general difficulty most frequently mentioned', according to the BEC, was 'lack of interest on the part of the work people'.[64] Trades unions countered that employers were fundamentally opposed to the whole idea of joint consultation. Allan Flanders, an academic expert on industrial relations, felt that neither side could claim much credit: 'It cannot be said that the employers' associations or the trade unions have put much drive into the campaign ... The main impetus has come from the government'.[65]

Disentangling such claims is not easy, but some conclusions do seem reasonable. Firstly, it is clear that the Government was firmly behind the JPC campaign. However, attitudes elsewhere were more ambivalent. Most employers remained suspicious of joint consultation and were not unduly upset when it failed. Trades unions expressed nominal agreement with the idea, but found it harder to provide much positive support. They jealously guarded any alteration in collective bargaining and (like the employers) were often afraid of Communist or rank and file incursion.[66] The engineering union was most in favour of JPCs, yet had provided relatively little practical assistance:

> the Executive have urged the importance of these committees only in general terms, and have not set the District Committees or shop stewards targets and specific tasks. Nor have the members been encouraged by any thorough examination of or useful suggestions about the role these committees can and should ... play[67]

Such lassitude was frankly recognised in some quarters. Sir George Chester, replying for the General Council at a TUC debate, was in no doubt that the JPC initiative had not received adequate union backing: 'I regret to have to say that there are many unions now represented in the Congress that have done very little about it except to pay lip service to it and ... expect the Government to act'.[68]

This leaves the ordinary worker. Here, attitudes are very much less easy to gauge. Employers clearly had an interest in exaggerating worker apathy and so many of their complaints can be safely discounted. However, other more reliable accounts pointing in the same direction seem convincing. An American academic from Princeton University interviewed shop stewards in 1951 about JPCs and found them scathing about popular attitudes. The stewards, she reported, 'were more critical than management of the workers' "narrow self interest"'.[69] A National Institute of Industrial Psychology study at about the same time, based on information from nearly 700 firms and over 4,500 interviews, reported similar findings, and ended up concluding:

> It was clear to us that the large number of the rank and file of the workers knew little about joint consultation, and tended to be apa-

thetic about it unless it happened to be dealing with something of immediate concern to themselves.[70]

The Government's problems with JPCs in private industry may, therefore, have been as much caused by worker indifference as the machinations of vested interests.

Turning to the nationalised sector, it might be expected that such problems would be very much less in evidence. The Government was obviously in a much more powerful position with the state run industries and did not have to worry about recalcitrant employers. The relevant unions had often argued for socialisation over many years, and there was obvious goodwill towards Labour as the party which seemed to be turning wishes into reality. To see whether any of this made much difference, it will be sensible to focus on one industry in depth, choosing coal because of its high profile in the 1940s, importance to the economy, and central place in Labour's mythology.

The Nationalisation Act of 1946 imposed legal obligations on the National Coal Board (NCB) to engage in both collective bargaining and consultation. The Board was required to consult on matters of 'safety, health and welfare', as well as secure 'the benefit of the practical knowledge and experience' of its employees with respect to the 'organization and conduct of the operations in which they are employed'.[71] Accordingly, in the years after 1947, the NCB moved rapidly to set up a joint consultation system of several tiers, but based firmly on Pit Production Committees (PPCs). The importance given to the miners' views was symbolised by the promise that one or two from their union would always be appointed to the highest level of the organisation.[72]

The NCB had great hopes of this departure, but within a relatively short period of time faced severe criticism about its inadequacies. At the TUC, left-wingers petitioned for a complete change in the way the industry was organised: the NCB reflected 'not the Social democratic revolution of Mr. Attlee, but ... the managerial revolution of Mr. Burnham'.[73] Within the Labour Party, too, criticism was rife. A motion at the 1948 Conference called for greater workers' participation in all nationalised industries. The current situation was certainly unacceptable. As a Hallam District Labour Party delegate explained, those in the state sector were rapidly becoming alienated: 'They do not feel that they run the industry.

The industry is still run by "them"'.[74] Predictably, this theme was rapidly taken up by the Conservatives. Brendan Bracken told the House of Commons in 1949 that 'many miners are deeply disillusioned, not to say bitterly cynical' while one of his allies declared that the Government was 'building a bureaucratic machine far removed from those who toil in the bowels of the earth'.[75]

More worrying for the NCB was research which suggested that miners did indeed share some of these feelings. A Mass-Observation investigator found considerable unhappiness at the new arrangements: 'the biggest grumble that occurs amongst miners is the fact that the present Coal Board bosses are the old bosses in new colours'.[76] Ferdynand Zweig's interviews with pit workers yielded similar impressions. Miners felt swallowed up by an enormous new bureaucracy over which they had no control. A Derbyshire informant told Zweig: 'Before, we knew where we stood ... When we had a grievance the manager could settle it in five minutes ... Now we cannot settle anything with the manager. When we come to the manager, he always shifts everything on to the back of the N.C.B. ... But we don't know the N.C.B.'.[77]

Given the strength of such feeling there were many who were ready to agree with the *Economist* that nationalisation had 'brought the worst of both worlds': 'as likely as not ... the old enemy remains in immediate authority, but behind him there looms a huge and sluggish hierarchy in whose mazes (as the worker sees them) either grievance or constructive contribution are likely to get permanently lost'.[78]

These were serious charges and they once again convinced some that the Government was at fault. Labour had not thought closely enough about the worker's place in a nationalised concern and did not really care about participation. However, as with JPCs in private industry, the real situation was rather more complex than it at first sight appeared.

Firstly, not all miners were as disillusioned with nationalisation as some press reports implied. Will Lawther, President of the National Union of Mineworkers (NUM), denounced those who lived 'as far away from the pits as possible' yet were always vocal on how the industry should be run. On consultation, Lawther believed, 'every possible step had been taken'.[79] Rank and file miners might grumble about the new arrangements but few wanted a return to private enterprise. An investigation at a Yorkshire pit in 1948

reported that every miner thought nationalisation 'the only remedy
for the industry': 'Nobody interviewed condemned it, and few
blamed present troubles on nationalisation. The majority realised
that it would take time before the benefits would be felt'.[80]

More specifically, the consultation machinery itself could not
simply be written off as a failure. The Fabian enquiry of 1949,
Miners and the Board, found that only three of the eighty-eight
workers and officials interviewed thought consultation was adequate, yet this was by no means a representative sample.[81] A more
detached evaluation by the Ministry of Fuel and Power in the same
year concluded that the consultative machinery had on balance
'proved itself'. There were problems, certainly, but progress was
being made, too: 'It is obviously difficult to assess its influence in
concrete terms, but all parties agree that it has made a big contribution to freer and healthier relationships within the Industry, and
that it has proved its practical worth on many occasions of material moment'.[82] Perhaps surprisingly, this was a view that the NUM
also partly endorsed. Asked by the TUC to look at the whole question, the union reported that the provision for consultation was
essentially adequate. Problems were still occurring with the way
the new machinery was used, leading to 'a good deal of dissatisfaction', but this was by no means evident in every area. Indeed, at
some pits, the relationship between management and men could be
described as 'good and ... improving at all levels'.[83]

Having said this, it is also by no means apparent that when
difficulties over consultation were, occurring, they could simply be
blamed on the negligence of the Government. The NCB (and the
Ministry behind it) bore some responsibility, no doubt, but so did
the NUM and the miners themselves, as a brief survey of attitudes
will amply demonstrate.

On Vesting Day, the NCB inherited a cohort of mine managers
who had been brought up with a 'captain on the bridge' tradition.
Most were engineers, whose long experience in the industry was
commensurate with their considerable statutory responsibilities for
safety. Such men rarely had any training in personnel management
techniques, and so they sometimes found it difficult to accept
miners as equals on the new PPCs.[84] However, the NCB was not
oblivious to this problem, and did what it could (given the constraints of time and resources) to re-educate. An anonymous high-
ranking civil servant, writing in 1950, felt that the Board had acted

very responsibly: 'For the last four years successive Ministers ... have had weekly meetings with [the] N.C.B. ... And the N.C.B. have satisfied us that over the whole period they have been striving to secure a new outlook on problems of labour relationship'.[85] Moreover, it was also observed that the NCB was not simply concentrating on managers but also trying to build up confidence and involvement amongst miners. Cheap magazines and newspapers, together with films, were used to spread information,[86] and show that popular rumours – for example, that the NCB was a bloated white-collar bureaucracy – were simply untrue.[87] At the same time, real efforts were being made to encourage workers into management grades. An Acton Society Trust enquiry of 1951 concluded that the Coal Board was the only public corporation to have a fully co-ordinated scheme for training and promotion.[88]

The NUM's attitude to consultation was rather more ambiguous. The union had been granted considerable concessions over the way PPCs were elected,[89] but many of its activists were uneasy about any role in decision-making. One widespread view was that the union should concentrate on representing its members; management should manage.[90] As a consequence, there was a reluctance to welcome detailed financial statistics about the industry's working, with one prominent miners' leader in the north declaring: 'it's wrong for unions to expect all the information there is to get, since a union ought not to wish for any more information than it's willing to take responsibility for'.[91] On top of this, wider attitudes in the NUM were hardly helpful. For internal political reasons, many leading figures continued to play an 'anti-bosses card' regardless of context, and even, for example, opposed the appointment of personnel managers at pits.[92] Challenged about its constant assertion that the NCB was being run by retired generals and Whitehall placemen, the NUM finally agreed to hold an enquiry, but took two years to tell its members that there was 'no reasonable cause for dissatisfaction'.[93]

Amongst rank and file miners, attitudes were sometimes equally unhelpful. Long experience of battling against very hostile private owners had inculcated a bitterness amongst some which a few years of nationalisation could not eradicate. The sociologist Mark Benny, who remained sympathetic to the miners' cause, used a portrait of a Durham lodge official ('Jim Edmondson') to illustrate the persistence of long-held attitudes after Vesting Day:

There is a tendency among men of good will to assume that Edmondson, when he comes to [the PPC] ... to advise the engineers on technical matters, will cease to be the same Jim Edmondson who
bargains with the manager about ... payments ... In fact, habit is
extremely strong. Jim expects to dictate or resist demands; he is used
to the tendentious rather than the relevant fact; above all, he wants
to decide rather than to deliberate ... he would like to be able, on a
majority vote, to issue instructions to the management.[94]

However, even where hostility was less in evidence, interest in consultation did not necessarily thrive. Many miners had an extremely
instrumental attitude to their industry – 'in the main they applied
everything to themselves', as one outsider observed[95] – and they
supported nationalisation because it was bringing better wages and
security of employment, not a new set of socialist relationships. 'A
minority', according to Mass-Observation, realised that nationalisation was 'erecting potential assets', but this feeling '[did] not appear
to be widespread'.[96] Accordingly, devoting time to consultation,
after the rigours of work, seemed an unattractive proposition.
Moreover, there was little point in registering for training or promotion schemes. Most miners had a deeply ambivalent attitude to
pit work at the best of times, and few wanted their sons to become
colliers.[97] Running the industry was best left to others, an attitude
shared widely enough to leave some NCB scholarship schemes
occasionally undersubscribed.[98]

In these circumstances, unbiased accounts of the coal industry's
consultation process often underlined the difficulties that faced the
NCB. One investigation, based on 200 interviews at the beginning
of the 1950s, found that the Board was disseminating an impressive amount of data. Problems were occurring, however, because
the miner fitted this information 'into the pattern of his existing
prejudices'.[99] Rectifying such a situation would not be easy during
the short term.

Taken together, in conclusion, Labour's attempts to promote
community achieved rather less than many in the Party were
hoping for. Individual policies had been handicapped by a lack of
resources or effectively opposed by vested interests, but a significant
feature in each case was public apathy or even hostility. Labour's
aims, it seemed, were simply not widely enough shared. Too few
wanted to participate in the prescribed way.

What made this more worrying for those on the left was the wider context, for a good deal of evidence appeared to indicate that however Labour might pursue community in the late 1940s, it would be unlikely to gain much success. Little could be expected of the more affluent – they remained wedded to individualistic ambitions – but there was real disappointment at attitudes in the working class. Ritchie Calder, visiting Stepney in 1946 for the *New Statesman*, believed that a year after the flying bombs, 'few vestiges of the shelter community spirit' remained: 'The shelters themselves are closed, but no new community life has replaced them'. J.B. Priestley, in a broadcast nearly two years later, made a similar point. There seemed to be 'far less kind and neighbourly co-operation' in post-war Britain. 'People', he judged, were 'harder, more selfish, more intent upon looking after Number One'.[100] The fact was that the forces bringing people together were now probably weaker than those pulling them apart. Common habits and lifestyles, of course, persisted, but there was little sign of any corresponding merging of identities. Most ordinary people continued to be preoccupied with their own lives, together with those of family, kin and friends. By contrast, contact with others outside these spheres could be circumscribed or tenuous, perhaps not even really desired. The ideal of community, therefore, was often only weakly developed in reality, as a short summary of attitudes and aspirations will demonstrate.

For most working-class people, the prime objective at this time was to gain or protect independence. The war might have brought relative affluence and full employment, but even with the new welfare state, fear of a descent into poverty remained widespread.[101] As a result, it made sense to hedge, whenever possible, against unforeseen circumstances. One way of doing this was to concentrate on maintaining independence and keep interfering authorities as much at arm's length as possible. Attitudes towards the key question of housing clearly illuminated the prevailing mentality.

Many people who moved into council houses during this period were happy with their new accommodation, if only because it delivered them from sharing or a life in the slums.[102] Nevertheless, rising earnings and memories of the 1930s building boom meant that the desire for home-ownership was growing. A Hulton Research survey of 13,000 people in 1950, structured according to age and social class, described the typical preferences as follows:

Most people like living in houses rather than flats, and they like having a house to themselves. They like their own private domain which can be locked against the outside world and ... they are a nation of garden lovers. They want to grow flowers and vegetables and sit on Sunday afternoons, and they want it to be private.[103]

Enquiries in exclusively working-class areas reached similar conclusions. A social survey of Easington, a mining area of Durham, found that 22 per cent of respondents owned their houses and the aspiration to do so was common. The residents on a new council housing estate in Tulse Hill (London) were similarly inclined. Most liked their current environment but 'many' were reported as preferring a private house 'if they could find one'.[104]

This latter point was inevitably important given the tight building controls of the period, and actual working-class home-ownership probably remained comparatively unusual.[105] Nevertheless, even if the supply of new private houses was 'puny' there was no doubt that demand remained 'bloated'.[106] Prices in cities like Birmingham and Manchester were roughly double their pre-war level, with ordinary 'artisans' dwellings' very much at a premium.[107] Meanwhile, building societies were enjoying boom conditions.[108] In these circumstances, the Ideal Home Exhibition, relaunched in 1947, quickly established itself as a national event. By 1950, it was covering 10 acres, featuring 75 avenues, streets and lanes together with 476 stands, and drawing crowds of 50,000 per day.[109]

If many working-class people placed great emphasis on independence and privacy, they were frequently less sure about what they shared in common with their peers. Zweig believed that there was an instinctive feeling of class, reporting that '[the] average worker has only to look at a man to see whether he is one of them or not'.[110] Orwell was more ambivalent, writing in 1947 that the obvious class differences still surviving in England would astonish a foreigner, but adding that they were 'far less marked, and far less real' than thirty years before.[111] However, both writers seem to have been misled into viewing class as a matter of relatively clear-cut divisions, ignoring the fact that it usually co-existed with other salient classificatory systems.

Certainly, many poorer families did not define themselves as working-class. In Gallup polls of 1948 and 1949, between 47 and 52 per cent of the samples said that they were middle-class, very different to the proportions that might have been obtained using conventional socio-economic criteria.[112] In fact, as is quite evident from contemporary accounts, ordinary people clearly recognised that the social ladder consisted of 'innumerable rungs'.[113] Personal status could be based on several different sets of criteria. There were, firstly, judgements to do with occupation. Blue-collar workers despised clerks, since they had 'cushy' jobs and did not have to sweat. Clerks reciprocated, distancing themselves from the 'dirty trades', and emphasising their middle-class affinities. Craftsmen looked down on labourers. Older men judged their younger counterparts as 'soft'; 'the trouble with the youngsters coming up nowadays', a Clydeside riveter told the BBC in 1950, 'was that they took no pride in their work – a decent day's work'd kill 'em'. Finally, there was an obvious gulf between the sexes. The journalist J.L. Hodson found North-East men contemptuous of the 'Dolls-eye industries' being created in their region and was told by a social worker of the 'great domestic unhappiness' that could occur when women had jobs and men did not.[114]

Alongside these gradations were a complex set of definitions based on place, whether region, city, district or street. Many working-class localities remained highly introverted. One Somerset villager, thinking of moving thirty yards down the road, complained that '"The trouble is, I'll miss my friends"'.[115] Glass and Frankel, investigating Bethnal Green immediately after the war, noted a similar pattern of sentiments:

> The distinction between ... different areas of the Borough are sufficiently important to Bethnal Greeners to make them hesitate or even refuse to move from one part to another. Many stories are told of families who would rather camp in the kitchens of their uninhabitable blitzed houses or sleep in public shelters than accept accommodation in another area of the Borough.[116]

Moreover, there was a general dislike of 'foreigners'. Local men working with the Welsh in the Yorkshire Coalfield described them as 'all piss and wind'.[117] When the NCB asked NUM lodges to accept Italian miners in late 1951, 70 per cent of those approached declined to co-operate, despite the unprecedented safeguards offered. Explaining the position, a civil servant emphasised the vivid prejudices at play: 'at the back of miners' minds ... [there was] a feeling of some contempt for the Italians based on their historical association with ice-cream and organ grinding, and also more lately their rather poor performance in North Africa'.[118]

A final series of distinctions, perhaps most important of all, revolved around perceived respectability. Many were obsessed with not being thought 'rough'. Squatters at a camp in London added 'chromium letter boxes' and 'gaily painted windows and curtains' to their huts so as to underline their 'normalcy'.[119] Slightly better-off housewives would not patronise public washhouses because of a 'certain stigma attached to their use'.[120] The consequence was that, in many areas, the population thought of itself as divided into a hierarchy of micro-distinctions. An ex-inhabitant of a large council estate described one such situation: 'Although it is almost entirely "working-class", every subtle gradation within that class is represented. The flats are arranged in blocks or "closes". Every close has its own character and standard. Tenants in "superior" blocks chafe against the poor status of the estate and are restless to leave'.[121] In these situations, relations with neighbours were often fraught or unwelcome. Gorer reported that the 'typical relationship of the English to their neighbours' could probably best be described as 'distant cordiality' but there were clearly many relationships that did not reach this standard. A survey of London women found a general wariness about being overfriendly: '"Keeping ourselves to ourselves" still prevails, and is felt to be righteous ... "I don't bother with neighbours or anyone outside the family", "I don't drink and I don't smoke; I'm happy to stay at home". The note of self-appro-bation is unmistakable'.[122] Quantitative investigations of neigh-bouring pointed in a similar direction.[123]

In such circumstances, organisations that stressed community (of whatever kind) frequently found it difficult to generate any real or lasting enthusiasm. People would join institutions and perhaps remain members, but they rarely seemed to want any real say in decisions about power or policy. A brief survey of the trade unions, Co-operative societies and voluntary associations will illustrate the dimensions of the problem.

In the six years after 1945, trade union membership rose from 7.6 million to 9.2 million.[124] Moreover, it is clear that many felt the unions were important, both prestigious and essential to safe-guarding working-class interests. Zweig concluded that 'the unions mean a great deal to the men, even to those who do not bother about attending their meetings or who criticise their policy or leadership'. Thus, being called a 'blackleg' or 'scab' was something no man could survive; often, the only possible option open to a strikebreaker was to leave the area.[125]

However, to the trade union activist, the position was rather less satisfactory. Workers in some large sectors – agriculture, clothing, food, drink and tobacco – remained poorly organised.[126] There were also area black spots. A careful study of Dudley found that only 12 per cent of workers were in trade unions. Similarly, though Amalgamated Engineering Union membership in the Coventry District was 27,000 in 1951, local officials believed that this figure could be doubled if all who were eligible joined.[127] Finally, there was the problem of membership apathy or indifference. A Political and Economic Planning (PEP) enquiry in 1946 found that only 20 per cent of trade unionists were 'meeting minded', with a similar proportion normally voting during internal elections.[128] Mass-Observation, reporting two years later, came to similar conclusions: 'Many Trade Unionists appear to have no sense of identification with the organisation to which they belong; some cannot even remember the name of their own union'.[129] The consequence was that many grassroots officials felt isolated. A contributor to the *Chemical Worker* in 1949 repeated a common lament: 'I do not propose to belittle the fame of our Royal Air Force. But the Trade Union Movement can also state: "Never in the History of Human Adversity was so much owed, by so many to so few"'.[130] Similar trends were evident in relation to the Co-op. In formal terms, many of the societies were certainly booming, both in terms of profits and members. However, the real situation was felt to be a good deal less favourable. Many members had joined for the obvious pecuniary benefits, and were too 'divi-minded' for the more ideologically committed.[131] In fact, the journalist Laurence Thompson interviewed one leading Co-op manager who believed that his main task was to keep the dividend up 'at any cost': it was 'the only thing which attracted members, they cared about nothing else'.[132] Certainly, there was little evidence that those shopping at the Co-op wanted to run the organisation. Mass-Observation estimated that the Co-op had nine million members in 1947, but added that 'to the great majority of its users the Co-op is just a shop, and ... a very large number of Co-operators are barely aware of its origins or declared ideals'.[133] A Fabian enquiry of 1948 came to similar conclusions:

[Neb drawing by permission of the "Daily Mail"
" Just for a change from an ordinary anæsthetic
I'll read a Cabinet Minister's crisis speech."

6   The funny side of life under Labour: 3. 'Just for a change from an
ordinary anaesthetic I'll read a Cabinet Minister's crisis speech' (see
Chapter 7)

it would probably upset the pioneers ... to discover how comparatively few in all the millions of Co-operative members are directly
responsible for its activities. Again, it must be frankly admitted that
we do not really know what proportion of the members vote or serve
voluntarily, though it is estimated that not more than one or two in
every hundred attend general meetings. The rest are not actively
interested, and it seems that they do not care about their Society's
future or feel in any way responsible for it.[134]

Detailed local studies confirmed the accuracy of this general picture.[135]

Finally, this pattern could also be observed in the voluntary sector. Most societies were run by small groups and there was always need for many more volunteers, as the National Council of Social Service frequently repeated.[136] However, attracting 'new blood' was never easy. Two campaigning periodicals – the *Citizen* ('The Journal of Civic Affairs and Social Service') and the *Good Neighbour* ('A Woman's Magazine of Public Welfare') – flowered briefly in the late 1940s but were in the end unable to cope with restricted circulations.[137] Here, as elsewhere, the damage was partly self-inflicted. All voluntary organisations might cherish their independent status, but few were prepared to act in unison. Indeed, one authority suggested that the 'most frequently voiced criticism of voluntary organisations' was probably 'their failure to co-operate amongst themselves, whether in raising money or planning their work'.[138] Nevertheless, the shortage of volunteers also reflected the fact that what ordinary people wanted from the different organisations was their benefits, not their ideals. Beveridge largely accepted this point during his exhaustive enquiries on 'voluntary action' in 1947–48, reaching the 'inescapable' conclusion, for example, that what the bulk of eight million friendly society members desired was 'a means of insurance by contract' rather than 'good fellowship'.[139]

The fate of the community association movement in the late 1940s was typical of the wider position. Community associations (CAs) received a boost during the war, being promoted by the Ministry of Education, and by 1945 activists were confident enough to launch an umbrella body, the National Federation of Community Associations (NFCA).[140] However, over the next six years progress was more uneven than predicted. The number of CAs increased significantly and some proved very successful.[141] On the other hand, many continued to be fairly peripheral, unable to attract any vibrant support. A detailed examination of four CAs in the South of England found that they were involving only 'a small percentage' of their target populations. Moreover, attenders were drawn from very specific age and gender groups.[142]

Some of the difficulties experienced by CAs reflected broader economic problems. Little government assistance was available to help construct new buildings, for example, and grants were completely cut after 1947. Nevertheless, the attitudes of many activists did not help. Most were very proud of their local CA but far less interested in parallel organisations. The feeling of belonging to a movement was generally lacking. As a consequence, the NFCA floundered and an attempt in 1948–49 to introduce a national inter-associational membership card (on the lines of that used in working men's clubs) failed through lack of support.[143] To make matters worse, ordinary members were, again, frequently passive. Those using CAs appreciated their facilities but did not necessarily want to become involved in administrative duties. The twenty-first anniversary brochure of the Watling Community Association, published in 1949, admitted that it had always been in 'the hands of a comparatively small group' and added: 'This is sometimes attributed to cliquishness, but [is] ... more truthfully due to lack of effort on the party [sic] of the many, and their willingness to have things done for them'.[144] Occasionally, the situation had deteriorated further, with individuals manipulating apathetic memberships for their own ends. Here, CAs were acting in an opposite way to that intended, accentuating divisions amongst local people rather than healing them.[145]

A number of conclusions emerge, therefore, from this chapter. As has been shown, Labour believed in community and tried to promote it wherever possible. The various initiatives achieved some gains, but were eventually disappointing. Difficulties were caused by a number of factors, but it is clear that many people were not really in sympathy with what Labour was trying to achieve. Britain might have come together to a certain extent during the war, but in the later 1940s had reverted to being a very divided society. Class and gender differences were pronounced, as were those based on occupation, place of residence and notions of respectability. In these circumstances, the impulse to community remained weak. Labour was struggling against the grain. The next chapter examines whether the Party was any more successful with its policies over leisure.

Notes

1 L. Silkin, 'Housing and Planning', *Labour Woman*, 33:2 (1945), 38–9.
2 *The Times*, 30 July 1945.
3 G. Bray, 'Planning Our Housing Estates', *Labour Woman*, 33:6 (1945), 123.
4 *Hansard*, 414, 17 October 1945, col. 1222.
5 Labour Party, *Report of the Forty-Third Annual Conference of the Labour Party* (London, 1944), pp. 123–6.
6 L. Wolfe, *The Reilly Plan* (London, 1945), pp. 9–12.
7 *Tribune*, 16 February 1945.

8 Wolfe, *Reilly Plan*, pp. 9–12.

9 *Tribune*, 16 February 1945.

10 *Architects' Journal*, 24 June 1948.

11 See, e.g., J. Dahir, *The Neighbourhood Unit Plan* (New York, 1947), pp. 77–83, and P. Collison, 'Town Planning and the Neighbourhood Unit Concept', *Public Administration*, 32 (1954), 463–9.

12 *Coventry Standard*, 31 August 1946.

13 L.E. White, *Community or Chaos* (London, 1950), pp. 26–7.

14 *Ibid.*, p. 27.

15 The National Council of Social Service, *Our Neighbourhood* (London, 1950), p. 25.

16 W. Burns, 'The Coventry Sociological Survey: Results and Interpretation', *Town Planning Review*, 25:2 (1954), 132.

17 Anon., 'The Housing Act 1949', *British Housing and Planning Review*, 5 (1949–1950), 50.

18 See, e.g., *Coventry Standard*, 11 September 1948.

19 H. Orlans, *Stevenage. A Sociological Study of a New Town* (London, 1952), p. 162.

20 Collison, 'Town Planning', 465 and P.H. Mann, 'The Socially Balanced Neighbourhood Unit', *Town Planning Review*, 29:2 (1958), 91–8.

21 W.A. Robson, 'Labour and Local Government', *Political Quarterly*, 24:1 (1953), 39–55 and P. Crane 'Enterprise in Local Government', *Fabian Research*, 156 (London, 1953).

22 Editorial, *Fact*, 7:4 (1949), 50.

23 *Coventry Evening Telegraph*, 12 June 1945.

24 See, e.g., *New Statesman*, 26 February 1949 and *Tribune*, 23 September 1949.

25 R.J. Hammond, *Food. Volume Two. Studies in Control and Administration* (London, 1956) pp. 381–94.

26 *Local Government Chronicle*, 16 July 1949; Public Records Office [hereafter PRO], MAF 99/1734, Ministry of Food Wartime Meals Division, Memo. 'British Restaurants ...', December 1944, p. 1.

27 N. Tiptaft, *I Saw A City* (London, 1945), pp. 39–42.

28 Standing Joint Committee of Working Women's Organisations, *Working Women Discuss – Population, Equal Pay, Domestic Work* (London, 1946), p. 10 and B. Drake, 'Communal Feeding in Wartime', *Fabian Research*, 64, (London, 1942), 27.

29 *News Chronicle*, 5 January 1945.

30 PRO, MAF 99/1737, 'Note for Mr Hood ...', [n.d.], p. 1.

31 *Daily Herald*, 5 January 1945.

32 The debate on what to do about BRs can be followed in Ministry of Food files, e.g. PRO, MAF 99/1736, 1737, 1738, and 1760.

33 *Local Government Chronicle*, 16 July 1949.

34 *Municipal Review*, 21:248 (1950), 6.

35 National Council of Social Service, *British Restaurants* (London, 1946), p. 61.

36 *Ibid.*, p. 45; Newham Local Studies Library, West Ham C.B. Council Committee Reports, Education Committee, 14 June 1949.

37 T. Barna, 'Rebuilding London: A Survey of Stepney, 1946', *Review of Economic Studies*, 13:2 (1945–6), 96–8; National Council of Social Service, *British Restaurants*, p. 19.

38 *Local Government Chronicle*, 10 October 1951 and W. McCullough, 'The Trend in Canteen Patronage', *Industrial Welfare*, 32:4 (1950), 126.

39 *Caterer and Hotel Keeper*, 11 June 1947.

40 *Daily Express*, 21 November 1946.

41 *Caterer and Hotel Keeper*, 14 May 1947.

42 See J. Copeland, 'Municipal Enterprise Has a Future', *Citizen*, 2:3 (1948), 68 and *Daily Express*, 2 February 1948 (for a poll showing that a large majority were against any extension of municipal trading).

43 Crane, 'Enterprise in Local Government', p. 24.

44 *Hansard*, 467, 28 July 1949, col. *171*.

45 See Cmd 8204, Ministry of Local Government and Planning, *Town and Country Planning 1943–1951*, (1951), passim.

46 *Ibid.*, p. 26 and *British Housing and Planning Review*, 6:1 (1950), 28.

47 For one example, see *Architects' Journal*, 21 August 1947.

48 *Barking and East Ham Express*, 7 September 1951.

49 Cmd 8204, *Town and Country Planning*, p. 179 and C.M. Haar, 'Appeals under the Town and Country Planning Act, 1947', *Public Administration*, 27 (1949), 37–40.

50 J. Mann, 'Warehousing the People', *Town and Country Planning*, 21:112 (1953), 362–3.

51 E. Pepler, 'London Housing and Planning', *Town and Country Planning*, 29:84 (1951), 157.

52 H. Myles Wright, 'The First Ten Years', *Town Planning Review*, 26:2 (1955), 75.

53 D. Chapman, *A Social Survey of Middlesbrough* (The Social Survey No. 50, 1946), p. 11.

54 B. Hutchinson, *Willesden and the New Towns* (The Social Survey No. 88, 1947), p. 85.
55 Quoted in N. Tiratsoo and J. Tomlinson, *Industrial Efficiency and State Intervention: Labour 1939–51* (London, 1993), p. 47.
56 The following two paragraphs are based on *ibid.*, especially pp. 94–5.
57 Modern Records Centre, University of Warwick [hereafter MRC], MSS 200 B/3/2/C961 Pt. A4, Ref. N.C. 11504, BEC 'Joint Production Committees. Summary of Replies ...', 22 July 1950, pp. 1–3.
58 MRC, MSS 200 B/3/2/C961 Pt. 3, BEC 'Questionnaire on Joint Consultation Machinery. Reply of the Engineering and Allied Employers National Federation', 20 April 1950, p. 1.
59 *Ibid.*, and MRC, MSS 200 B/3/2/C961. Pt. A4, Letter, Secretary, Shipbuilding Employers Association, to K.J. Burton, BEC, 9 June 1950, p. 1.
60 Anon., 'Management Looks at Labour', *Future*, 6:3 (1951), 56.
61 H.A. Turner, 'Is Joint Consultation Enough?', *Socialist Commentary*, 15:6 (1951), 128–31.
62 MRC, MSS 200 B/3/2/C961 Pt. 3, BEC 'Questionnaire', p. 1.
63 A. Tatlow, 'Joint Consultation in Nine Firms', *Yorkshire Bulletin*, 3:1 (1951), 42.
64 MRC, MSS 200 B/3/2/C961 Pt. A4, Ref. N.C. 11504, BEC 'Joint Production Committees', p. 4.
65 A. Flanders, 'Great Britain', in W. Galenson (ed), *Comparative Labour Movements* (New York, 1952), p. 85.
66 Tiratsoo and Tomlinson, *Industrial Efficiency*, pp. 95–7.
67 Anon., 'Enry Straker Teams Up', *Future*, 3:1 (1948), 39.
68 TUC, *Report of the Eightieth Annual Congress of the TUC, 1948* (London, 1948), p. 405.
69 H. Baker, 'Joint Consultation in England – An American Comments', *Journal of the Institute of Personnel Management*, 33:314 (1951), 65.
70 National Institute of Industrial Psychology, *Joint Consultation in British Industry* (London, 1952), p. 211.
71 G.B. Baldwin, *Beyond Nationalization. The Labour Problems of British Coal* (Camb. Mass., 1955), p. 100.
72 The joint consultation machinery in the coal industry is well described in a number of Acton Society Trust pamphlets; see especially Acton Society Trust, *The Framework of Joint Consultation* (London, 1952).
73 TUC, *Report of the Eighty-Second Annual Congress of the TUC, 1950* (London, 1950), p. 513.

74 Labour Party, *Report of the Forty-Seventh Annual Conference of the Labour Party* (London, 1948), p. 169.

75 *Hansard*, 465, 1948–49, 19 May 1949, cols 625 and 672.
Tom Harrisson Mass-Observation Archive, the University of Sussex [hereafter THMOA], TC Coal Mining 1938–48, Box 2, File 2D, Draft Letter L.R. England to T. Booth Waddor.

77 F. Zweig, *Men In The Pits* (London, 1948), pp. 159–60.

78 *Economist*, 19 June 1948.

79 Labour, *Forty-Seventh Conference*, p. 169.

80 THMOA, TC Coal Mining 1939–48, Box 2, File 2G, Report by J.G., 'National Coal Board Survey. Rossington', June 1948, p. 2.

81 M. Cole, 'Miners and the Board', *Fabian Research*, 134, (London, 1949) and *Hansard*, 465, 1948–49, 19 May 1949, cols 665–6.

82 PRO, POWE 37/77, O.P. (49) 4, 25 January 1949, Productivity (Official) Committee, Memo. by Ministry of Fuel and Power, 'Action to Improve Productivity in the Coal Industry', 25 January 1949, p. 8.

83 TUC, *Report of the Eighty-First Annual Congress of the TUC, 1949*, (London, 1949), p. 218.

84 PRO, POWE 37/81, Letter H. Gaitskell to H. Morrison, 12 March 1948 and POWE 37/81, Unsigned Memo., 'Short-Term Managerial Methods of Increasing Production', 30 November 1950, p. 1.

85 PRO, POWE 37/81, 'Short-Term Managerial Methods', p. 1.

86 PRO, COAL 30/46, Memo. by Secretary of NCB General Purposes Committee, 'Publicity Within the Coal Industry', 15 September 1954; National Coal Board, *Films on Coal* (London, 1961).

87 PRO, POWE 37/7, Memo. by Statistics Branch, 'Allegations about Hordes of Officials', 27 January 1951, pp. 1–2.

88 Acton Society Trust, *Training and Promotion in Nationalised Industry* (London, 1951), p. 62.

89 Acton Society Trust, *Framework*, p. 8.

90 See Lawther's statement to the 1948 Labour Conference: Labour, *Forty-Seventh Conference*, p. 170.

91 Baldwin, *Beyond Nationalization*, p. 106.

92 PRO, POWE 37/81, Letter H. Gaitskell to H. Morrison, 12 March 1948.

93 *Daily Dispatch*, 3 August 1951 and *Daily Mail*, 7 July 1953.

94 M. Benny, 'Under New Management', in A.G. Weidenfeld (ed), *Other People's Lives* (London, 1948), p. 35.

95 THMOA, TC Coal Mining 1938–48, Box 2, File 2G, Report by J.G.,

'National Coal Board Survey. Rossington', June 1948, p. 2.

96 THMOA, File Report No. 3007, 'Attitudes to the Nationalisation of Coal', June 1948, p. 40.

97 E.R. Manley, *Meet The Miner* (Lofthouse, 1947), p. 70.

98 Acton Society Trust, *Training and Promotion in Nationalised Industry* (London, 1951), p. 31.

99 Acton Society Trust, *The Worker's Point of View* (London, 1952), pp. 5, 6 and 12.

100 *New Statesman*, 26 January 1948; and *Listener*, 23 October 1947.

101 There was, for example, no strong belief that full employment would persist. See, in relation to the miners, Benny, 'New Management', p. 36, and more generally, F. Zweig, *The British Worker* (Harmondsworth, 1952), pp. 60–1 and 227.

102 See, e.g., *Coventry Standard*, 2 March 1946.

103 Hulton Research, *Patterns of British Life* (London, 1950), pp. 8 and 24.

104 H. Rankin, 'New Town for Old', *Current Affairs*, 75 (1949), 15; and *News Chronicle*, 20 July 1949.

105 Political and Economic Planning [hereafter PEP], 'Home Ownership', *Planning*, 18 (1952), 187–8.

106 *House-Builder*, 7:2 (1948), 92.

107 F. Streeton Steed, 'House Price Trends', *News-Letter*, 10:2 (1947), 50–3.

108 See, e.g., O.R. Hobson, *A Hundred Years of the Halifax* (London, 1953), p. 126.

109 *Public Opinion*, 24 March 1950.

110 Zweig, *Worker*, p. 202.

111 G. Orwell, *The English People* (London, 1947), p. 30.

112 G.H. Gallup, *The Gallup International Public Opinion Polls. Great Britain 1937–1975, Volume One* (New York, 1976), pp. 172, 203, 213.

113 Zweig, *Worker*, p. 21.

114 *Ibid.*, p. 206; *Forward*, 9 August 1947; *Listener*, 28 December 1950; and J.L. Hodson, *The Way Things Are* (London, 1947), pp. 277 and 285.

115 W.J. Turner, *Exmoor Village* (London, 1947), p. 24.

116 R. Glass and M. Frenkel, *A Profile of Bethnal Green* (London, 1946), p. 10.

117 THMOA, File Report No. 3007, p. 31.

118 See material in PRO, POWE 37/234; and POWE 37/233, Note by 'C. de P.', 2 October 1951.

119 *Public Opinion*, 23 June 1950.

120 J.C. Wilson, *An Inquiry Into Communal Laundry Facilities* (London, 1949), p. 11.

121 J. Mills, 'The Tenement Housewife', *The Good Neighbour*, 2:6 (1950), 135.

122 G. Gorer, *Exploring English Character* (London, 1955), p. 52.

123 *Ibid.*, p. 55; The University of Liverpool, *Neighbourhood and Community* (Liverpool, 1954), p. 58; and Gallup, *Opinion Polls*, p. 177.

124 H.A. Clegg, *A History of British Trade Unions Since 1889. Volume III 1934–1951* (Oxford, 1994), p. 430.

125 Zweig, *Worker*, pp. 176 and 178.

126 *Labour*, 11:9 (1949), 282.

127 Liverpool University Department of Social Science, *Social Aspects of a Town Development Plan* (Liverpool, 1951), p. 83; *Coventry Standard*, 10 August 1951.

128 PEP, 'Inside the Unions', *Planning*, 249 (1946), 8 and 13.

129 THMOA, File Report No. 2999, 'Trade Unions', May/June 1948, p. 3.

130 L. Jones, 'Still "The Few"', *The Chemical Worker*, 30:5 (1949), 16.

131 *Co-op News*, 11 January 1947.

132 L. Thompson, *Portrait of England* (London, 1952), p. 69.

133 THMOA, File Report No. 2460, 'A Report on People and the Co-op', February 1947, p. 17.

134 N. Barou, 'Whither Co-operation?', in N. Barou (ed), *The Co-operative Movement in Labour Britain* (London, 1948), pp. 9–10.

135 T. Cauter and J.S. Downham, *The Communication of Ideas* (London, 1954), pp. 104–5.

136 National Council of Social Service, *For the Common Good* (London, 1949), p. 23.

137 Editorial comments in *Citizen*, 2:6 (1948), 163–4; and *Good Neighbour*, 2:6 (1950), 121–2.

138 National Council of Social Service, *Common Good*, p. 24.

139 Lord Beveridge, *Voluntary Action* (London, 1948), p. 293.

140 R. Clarke (ed), *Enterprising Neighbours* (London, 1990), p. 50.

141 S.G. Jones, 'Community Centres and Associations in Manchester', *Social Welfare*, 8:3 (1948), 58–70.

142 H.W. Mellor, 'The Function of the Community Association', *The Sociological Review*, 9 (1951), 1–32.

143 Clarke, *Neighbours*, p. 54.

144 E. Sewell Harris and P.N. Molloy, *The Watling Community Association. The First Twenty-One Years* (Edgware, Middx., 1949), p. 61.

145 University of Liverpool, *Neighbourhood and Community*, p. 33.

6

Creating the 'Responsible Society', part two: reforming popular leisure

When Labour took office in 1945 most of the Party's prominent thinkers, as well as much of its active membership, were dissatisfied with how the majority of Britons spent their leisure time. They believed that most of those who had voted for Attlee – even many ordinary Labour members – were deficient in this respect. It was felt that 'escapist' activities, such as watching Hollywood films and reading detective novels, inhibited qualities associated with the 'responsible citizen' and so impeded the building of socialism. Nevertheless, more appropriate means of enjoying recreation, which encouraged characteristics conducive to sustaining a vibrant civic culture, were considered to be within reach. The wartime activities of the Army Bureau of Current Affairs (ABCA) and the Council for the Encouragement of Music and Art (CEMA) seemed to provide a model. The former had apparently given previously uninterested people a desire to discuss contemporary social and political issues. The latter was credited with imbuing mass audiences with an enthusiasm for classical drama, music and ballet.[1] Moreover, such critics of popular leisure also expected that as Labour's welfare reforms liberated the population from economic adversity so they would become more receptive to the appeal of the higher arts.[2]

Acting on this analysis, the Attlee Governments tried to reform popular leisure through legislation. Despite this, the majority continued to view their pastimes as, quite literally, diversions rather than opportunities for improvement. As the sociologist Ferdinand Zweig concluded during his 1947 study of the subject, for most, recreation was 'the kingdom of perfect freedom' which compensated for a dull and arduous working life.[3] The persistence of this attitude frustrated the ambitions of Labour's leisure critics, whose hostility for the people's pleasures became increasingly apparent. This chapter looks at the desire of such influential Labour members to promote change in popular entertainments and the nature of the public's response. Before embarking on a detailed analysis of this question, however, it is necessary to explain why Labour's leading lights thought such an apparently trivial subject important.

It would be wrong to imagine that everyone in the Labour Party was preoccupied with changing the content of popular leisure. The majority of ordinary members most certainly were not: like the rest of the country they happily consumed commercially provided entertainments. However, activists, the sort who wrote letters to the weekly left-wing journals *Tribune* and the *New Statesman*, as well as MPs, prominent intellectuals and Labour ministers all at one time or another confronted the issue. As will be seen later in the chapter, these individuals shared their 'improving' agenda with more conservative elements, in particular those found in the higher echelons of the British Broadcasting Corporation. More importantly, they also gave voice to opinions embraced by others on the political left, from Liberals to Communists, many of which had been current in the late nineteenth century. Such figures had thought their political objectives imperilled by values promoted by the people's favoured pursuits and looked to education and 'enlightenment' to improve individuals as a precondition to their becoming socialists. This entailed the abandonment of popular institutions such as the public house.[4] This perspective had not much changed by the middle decades of the twentieth century. Politically progressive critics of popular leisure believed that it prevented the development of fully rounded members of society, of socialism – or of any other more limited form of political advance.[5] Thus, one wartime body in which Labour members took a leading role considered that 'funfairs, football pools, chain cinemas, holiday camps, beauty parlours, cheap confectionery and "comics"' only encouraged people's baser instincts.[6] To promote finer feelings, recreations currently enjoyed by the privileged few needed to be put in the place of such pastimes. In the eyes of Labour's leisure critics, one of the evils of capitalism was that it had denied workers all that was best in culture, leaving them with inferior pleasures, the by-products of deprivation. Just as socialism would build on the achievements of capitalism in the realm of the economy, so it would do so culturally. As a correspondent to *Tribune* put it after Labour's 1945 victory: 'the time has now arrived when culture should cease to be the hall-mark of the leisured class and should be available to all'.[7]

Despite such interest in the reform of popular leisure, Labour's 1945 manifesto included only a cautious and brief reference to the topic. Labour-inclined progressives concerned with the question of culture, such as J.B. Priestley, thought the leadership saw art as no more than the icing on the cake. Other more severe critics doubted that the Party had any form of policy on the matter.[8] It is certainly true that Labour ministers considered cultural policy less immediately pressing than improving the country's balance of trade, building new homes or creating the institutional framework of the welfare state. Yet, if other more material problems crowded the scene and pushed the question of leisure into the background, it hardly disapppeared from view.

In early 1945 the MP Philip Noel-Baker made a case for Labour to advocate 'cultural development' in its manifesto.[9] He considered this 'a natural corollary of the principles of the party'. Although Noel-Baker's attempt to place culture high on Labour's agenda failed, few would have disagreed with his general sentiments. As two Research Department memos from 1946 and 1947 stipulated, a 'Socialist policy for leisure [is] essential – Socialism [is] an attitude to life as a whole, not merely that part of it spent in work'. Indeed, 'the aim of socialists has always been wider than a mere change in the ownership of the means of production'. The purpose of a leisure policy – like socialism in general – was to help 'the citizens of Britain to live full and varied lives' and facilitate 'a great extension in the horizons of mind and spirit for the men and women of Britain'. In an economic environment where the majority could not gain fulfilment at work, due to its repetitive nature, leisure activities were seen to be of decisive importance in the formation of social and political attitudes.

These memoranda recognised that there was a 'leisure problem' in Britain. Indeed, the 'failure of the majority of Britain's citizens to enjoy a full life through their leisure pursuits' constituted 'a major social problem'. The narrow range of popular pastimes, their predominantly 'passive' nature and domestic or individualistic orientation were strongly criticised. The popularity of the cinema and gambling, for example, indicated that people pursued little else but superificial thrills and temporary excitement. The reasons for this were thought to be twofold. First, the fact that there were few adequate facilities meant that most people could not spend their time productively. Second, the environmental and economic context promoted trivial pursuits:

> The sordid disorder of ill-planned towns must inevitably drive their inhabitants to the warmth and comfort of cinemas and pubs; and all forms of escapist entertainment or recreation are encouraged by the drabness, insecurity and hopelessness of daily life.

Labour hoped to tackle both these causes. However, it was not considered that building more community centres and improving the lived environment would by itself make the 'problem of leisure' disappear. Yet, citizens could not be forcibly directed to take up alternative pastimes. As the *Tribune* columnist Jennie Lee wrote: 'people should feel free in their spare time to do as they please. We don't want any regimented Strength through Joy or Joy through Strength movements in this country'.[10] The people, however, needed 'guidance'. Thus, there was support for Labour-controlled public authorities to encourage the pursuit of approved leisure activities and implement policies which discriminated in their favour. The hope was that such measures would eventually 'improve' public taste. As a correspondent to *Tribune* commented, 'The love of beauty *can* be inculcated in the mass of the people'. Another declared that 'our [cultural] programme must be based, I am sure, on a *consciously educative* intent'.[11]

As the Research Department memoranda made clear, there was no doubt which recreations were to be promoted. It was confidently believed that some pursuits were 'intrinsically more valuable' and gave 'greater and more permanent satisfaction and enjoyment than others'. The taxonomy was this: 'active' pursuits were preferred to 'passive' ones; 'creative' favoured over 'non-creative'; and those involving communal participation placed higher than primarily individualistic pastimes. There were calls for the creation of a national theatre as well as municipal theatres, concerts halls and art galleries. Focus was also concentrated upon the provision of facilities such as museums, open spaces, sports grounds, bookshops and libraries.

In line with these aspirations, the Labour Government promoted approved leisure activities as best it could, in the face of severe financial restraints and a deeply embedded opposition to state intervention in this field.[12] The Government's attitude was best summed up in Chancellor Stafford Cripps' 1948 comment to a Treasury official that he 'would very much like to have it accepted as part of general Government policy that the enjoyment of leisure should claim a bigger proportion of the total expenditure on the Budget'. In other words, the desire was there, even if conditions were not exactly propitious.

The war had temporarily increased Government responsibility for the provision of leisure to the people and had mobilised support for a state-funded body charged with providing 'the best for the most'. This led to the creation of CEMA which brought 'high' culture to the populace wherever they were, be it in factory canteens or air raid shelters.[13] The organisation won much praise as a result and the Coalition Government agreed to establish the Arts Council to take up CEMA's mantle in peacetime. The Council's first chair, the Liberal peer Lord Keynes, explained in July 1945, that he aimed to make 'the theatre and the concert hall and the art gallery ... a living element in everyone's upbringing'.[14] This ambition was fully endorsed by incoming Labour ministers who had no complaint with such an autonomous body directing state funds to approved cultural endeavours. Consequently, the Government's relatively generous grant to the Council was maintained even during the retrenchment caused by Korean War rearmament in 1950–51. By the end of the 1940s, however, the Council had ceased taking the arts to the people. Instead, it concentrated on supporting institutions of national importance based in London such as Covent Garden, Sadlers Wells and the Old Vic. This was not simply due to the undoubted metropolitan preferences of Lord Keynes: there had been a decline in the popular desire for such entertainments after 1945.[15]

Apart from extending state patronage of the arts, Labour in power tried to promote and co-ordinate the cultural activities of local authorities. The Town and Country Planning Act (1947) required councils to submit their recreation plans for Government approval before July 1951. By this time, however, Labour was only months away from losing office, so the measure accomplished little of note. The most significant piece of legislation passed by the Attlee Government was the Local Government Act (1948) which, amongst other things, permitted authorities to provide entertainment for their citizens. This part of the Act had been pushed through the Commons by Aneurin Bevan in the face of Conservative opposition. Bevan hoped that the Act would encourage coun-

cils to patronise artists who could then use their talents for the
benefit of the community.[16]

A survey undertaken during the year which followed Labour's
1951 general election defeat showed that most local authorities
had failed to take full advantage of the powers granted them in
1948. This was in part due to financial restraints and lack of building materials. Even a Labour council as keen as Coventry's was to
make good the interwar neglect of cultural provision found that its
room for manoeuvre was severely restricted. Thus, community centres, youth clubs and libraries had to wait until blitzed houses,
schools and shops were rebuilt. The Council's desire to put need
before profit in the field of leisure also came up against the vested
interests of brewers and cinema chains. Moreover, when the matter
was put to a referendum, the public showed that it disapproved of
municipally-provided entertainment. Local authorities in other
parts of the country which held concert recitals, and other similarly
'improving' events, found they usually lost money.[17]

The failure of civic entertainment was partly obscured by the
success of the Festival of Britain which lasted from May to September 1951. This was described by Herbert Morrison, who had charge
of the event, as 'the people giving themselves a pat on the back'.
The Festival organisers wanted it to be a time of 'fun, fantasy and
colour' and to a great extent they achieved their aim.[18] Activities
were organised across the country including exhibitions, pageants,
competitions and games. In London, the crowds enjoyed dancing in
the open air at the Pleasure Gardens and wondered over the
exhibits at the South Bank. It was a popular success. J.B. Priestley,
an advocate of 'hard work and high jinks', approved of the scheme
and even wrote a novel, *Festival in Farbridge* (1951), on the
theme.[19] Yet, the Festival lost £1 million and, like the Government's
other ventures, did not alter the way most people usually spent
their leisure time.

Ordinary people's post-war spending on recreations remained
stubbornly set in interwar grooves. The only real difference after
1945 was that, for the working class in particular, working hours
declined, unemployment fell and real incomes increased (see Tables
4 and 5). This meant that there was more time and money to
devote to the pursuit of pleasure than in the 1930s. Cinemas, dance
halls and dog tracks all did very well during the Attlee years. Working-class spending was dictated by the widespread fear that mass

Table 4 *UK labour force: decline of unemployment and working hours, 1939–51*

	% unemployed	Average hours worked per week
1939	11.6	–
1940	9.7	–
1941	6.6	–
1942	2.4	–
1943	0.8	50
1944	0.7	48.6
1945	1.2	47.4
1946	2.5	46.2
1947	3.1	45.2
1948	1.8	45.3
1949	1.6	45.4
1950	1.5	46.1
1951	1.2	46.3

Source: R. Bacon, G.S. Bain and J. Pimlott, 'The Labour Force', in A.H. Halsey (ed), *Trends in British Society Since 1900* (London, 1972), pp. 119–20.

unemployment would inevitably return. Workers looked upon improvements in their standard of living as temporary and considered that they should enjoy their pleasures whilst in possession of a decent and regular income.[20] Due to this sentiment – along with the increased taxation of beer and cigarettes – spending on leisure increased as a proportion of income. The statistics in this field are impressionistic at best, but they do reveal an upward trend. Thus, one survey conducted in Leeds during 1942 discovered that on average 12 per cent of a family's net income went on 'luxuries'. By 1948 it was estimated that about 20 per cent of an average family's income was spent on the 'comforts and luxuries of life'.[21]

Rising living standards were not evenly spread throughout the working class. For example, the skilled benefited to a much greater extent than the unskilled.[22] More striking still, wives did less well than their working husbands. This was because the household 'allowance' given by husband to wife was usually a fixed sum that varied little over the period of a marriage. The 1930s was a decade of deflation: as prices fell, wives of men in work saw the value of their allowance increase in real terms. In contrast, post-war economic conditions induced a degree of inflation which, due to the inelasticity of the allowance, meant it fell in value.[23] This was confirmed by a 1949 Mass-Observation study which suggested that one-third of men benefiting from a pay increase passed nothing of it on to their wives. Thus, it can be no surprise that whilst 16 per cent of women claimed they had no money to spend on themselves only 2 per cent of men said this.[24]

Table 5 *Improvement in standards of living, 1939–51*

	A: weekly wage earnings index	B: cost of living index	C: differential (i.e. A minus B)
1939	–	101	–
1940	141	114.5	26.5
1941	154	124.7	29.3
1942	174	132.3	41.5
1943	191	138.0	53.0
1944	198	140.6	57.4
1945	196	145.7	50.3
1946	207	150.8	56.2
1947	221	159.0	62.0
1948	239	169.8	69.2
1949	249	174.9	74.1
1950	262	180.5	81.5
1951	289	197.1	91.9

Note: 1930 = 100.
Source: Bacon, Bain and Pimlott, 'Labour Force', in Halsey, *Trends in British Society*, pp. 121–2.

What Zweig described as the 'hunger for leisure' was not satisfied in the same way across the population. Age and gender were the main influences here. Thus, the pub remained the preserve of older men: women and younger adults were less in evidence. Similarly, a 1947 study showed that one-quarter of males between fifteen and twenty-nine years went out more than five evenings a week. In contrast, the same proportion of women between forty and fifty-nine years never went out at all. Domestic responsibilities kept women of whatever age at home in the evening to a greater extent than their menfolk.[25] Although the war had brought about certain changes – women were more frequently seen in pubs than in the 1930s – this should not be exaggerated. Female energies were mainly expended in the execution of apparently never ending household chores. As Zweig wrote, 'regular daily leisure for working-class women' was 'still a comparatively new experience'.[26] In fact, one survey revealed that one-third of working-class housewives claimed that they had no leisure time at all, something confirmed by their tendency to fatigue. Those women who 'enjoyed' some time to themselves indicated that much of it was taken up with sewing, mending and knitting.[27] In post-war Britain, it seems that only men and unmarried women were able to fully satisfy their 'hunger' for leisure.[28]

During the 1940s, watching feature films in a cinema was the most common way of spending leisure outside the home. The decade saw cinema attendance reach the peak of its popularity (see Table 6). Between 1938 and 1946 admissions increased by over 60 per cent and notwithstanding a subsequent decline audiences in 1950 still exceeded those in 1940 by over 30 per cent.[29] As a number of surveys indicated, most people went to the cinema at least once every few weeks or so; a hard core went regularly once or even twice a week. Research undertaken during 1949 indicated that two-fifths of adults went at least once a week, one-sixth at least once a month, just over one-quarter attended 'occasionally' whilst only about one-sixth never went at all. Cinema audiences were broadly representative of the population as a whole. They were, however, disproportionately young, rather more working-class than might have been expected but, in contrast, almost equally divided between males and females.[30]

People went to the cinema for a number of reasons. The main factor was that feature films provided cheap, accessible entertainment of a high quality. During this period there were about 4,600 cinemas scattered across the nation, meaning that even the small-

Table 6   *Cinema admissions, 1934–52*

Year	Admissions (millions)
1934	903
1938	987
1940	1027
1942	1494
1944	1575
1946	1635
1948	1514
1950	1396
1952	1312

Source: H.E. Browning and A.A. Sorrell, 'Cinemas and Cinema-Going in Great Britain', *Journal of the Royal Statistical Society*, 117:2 (1954), 134.

est town had at least one. Most cinemas also changed their programmes twice a week thereby maximising choice. Feature films were suffused with glamour, all the more so because of the dominance of Hollywood's fantastic presentation of an idealised society free of class divisions, poverty and shortages. Films such as these provided the masses with a form of 'escape' from everyday reality. Some establishments were almost literally 'dream palaces'. The Rex in pre-Blitz Coventry was one such example: there 'soft music mixed with the twitter of live birds, flitting behind glass along the length of two walls, with a painted back-scene of sea and sand, and a painted signpost marked "Le Touquet"'.[31] Yet, going to the cinema also involved activities other than simply watching a film. Some young women attended in order to take note of the latest fashions current among the stars.[32] Certain male adolescents went in gangs with the object of fighting their rivals. As one weary cinema manager declared, 'Sunday afternoons are a nightmare. They are not much interested in what film is on, though a good gangster film will hold their attention'.[33] A number of overburdened married women went to find temporary relief from arduous domestic duties. A study of working-class wives from Brighton concluded that their 'reason for enjoying the cinema was usually that it took their minds off their home affairs ... a few women said what they most enjoyed was the chance of sitting down'.[34] On the other hand, some married men claimed they accompanied their wives to the cinema only because this legitimised spending most of their other evenings in the pub.[35]

The majority of films shown in Britain were produced in Hollywood and usually dealt with topics in stark contrast to the audience's existence. An analysis of the main subject of the 572 feature films exhibited between October 1948 and September 1950 on the three main circuits showed that 69.5 per cent had been made in Hollywood whereas only 29 per cent were produced in Britain. Crime dramas (27 per cent) and love stories (20 per cent) were the two dominant themes of such films; in contrast, 'social issue' films accounted for only 1 per cent of releases.[36] The main features which found greatest favour with audiences were, according to one early 1950s survey, musicals and musical comedies (27 per cent); domestic or family subjects (16 per cent); historical films (11 per cent) and dramas and adventures (both with 10 per cent). The 1946 Bernstein Survey revealed a similar range of preferences in relation to short features. Cartoons were favoured by 50 per cent of those asked, whilst 'social developments', in which questions of reconstruction would have been to the fore, were liked by only 18 per cent.[37]

The popularity of Hollywood's 'escapist' films had been challenged during the Second World War. In the midst of the conflict British films had improved in quality and popularity. A number of these echoed the 1930s documentary film movement's concern for social 'realism' and progressive political causes. Thus, certain film makers tried to portray the lives of ordinary people in a sympathetic and non-patronising manner whilst indicating their support for post-war welfare reform. Yet, the impact of such films was limited and Hollywood productions remained the most favoured fare.[38] In any case, not all British films were radical: Noel Coward's extremely popular *In Which We Serve* (1942) and *This Happy Breed* (1944) promoted an overtly Conservative message.[39] One reason for the limited impact of films which aspired to realism may have been because, as one critic put it, they were often morality tales which preached against the pursuit of luxury and comfort.[40]

Whatever the limited stylistic changes promoted by the war, after its end, the move back towards 'escapism' was widely noted. By

1947 the cineaste's journal *Sight and Sound* was concerned that British post-war films no longer depicted 'real life'.[41] A small number of production companies continued to aspire to make films that reflected the concerns of ordinary working people. However, there was little desire on the part of audiences to watch films which dealt with 'real' topics. This was illustrated in the case of *Chance of a Lifetime* (1950) which advanced the vaguely Labourist message that workers and management should co-operate on the basis of mutual respect and the common good. The film became a *cause celebre* after the three major circuits refused to distribute it, claiming that it was an uncommercial proposition. Some on the left suspected that they actually disapproved of its political content. After Rank had been prevailed upon to release it, the truth of the matter came to light: the film simply lacked popular appeal. Significantly, even the modest number who watched the film failed to register its message. A Mass-Observation survey of one audience's response revealed that only just over one-third had deliberately chosen to watch the film. In contrast, nearly half had gone to the cinema either out of habit or because they had nothing better to do. As a consequence, just under two-thirds were completely oblivious to the film's political message. Whilst audiences watched films for many reasons, the desire to receive a lecture on industrial relations was not high among them.[42] As the *Daily Mirror*'s film critic pointed out, those millions who went to the cinema wanted romance not realism; they desired good entertainment not 'good cinema'.[43]

Listening to the radio was the predominant home-based leisure activity. Whereas cinema was subject to exclusively commercial considerations, radio output was controlled by a state-appointed monopoly – the British Broadcasting Corporation (BBC). However, commercial stations broadcasting in English from continental Europe were widely accessible. Sir William Haley, Director-General of the Corporation, upheld the original ethic, propounded by its founder Lord Reith, that providing entertainment was not the BBC's prime duty. In his eyes, the purpose of radio was to improve public taste not pander to its lowest desires. As the BBC's wartime Northern Regional Director put it, the Corporation's policy was to 'never fall below certain canons of taste and standards of quality'.[44] Even so, some compromise was considered necessary. After 1946 the Corporation's output was divided between three services: the Light Programme catered to popular tastes, the Home Service was intended to serve more middle-brow inclinations, whilst the Third Programme broadcast plays, operas and classical music. Haley's ultimate ambition was to encourage listeners to move from the Light to the Home and eventually to the Third so that the former two services would disappear.[45] Others within the Corporation, such as Maurice Gorham, the first Controller of the Light Programme, took entertainment as their main duty. Gorham even used the BBC's Listener Research Unit to check he was attracting audiences. Yet, he was in a small minority and constantly battled against those within the Corporation who found his output vulgar. As a consequence, Gorham eventually resigned.[46]

By 1951, 83 per cent of families owned a radio set. However, as one survey stated, radio figured 'largely as an interference' to other home-centred activities like reading, homework, and conversation.[47] As an observer of adolescents commented, the 'ubiquitous wireless [was] so much a part of the wallpaper in most homes that the boys and the girls seldom talked about it'.[48] During week-days, working-class women constituted the single biggest segment of the radio audience. The wife of a Midlands Corporation cleaner had the radio turned on all day as she said it helped to 'keep her going'.[49] The largest radio audiences were registered on Sundays when millions of sets were turned on throughout the day. In 1947 the proportion of this Sunday audience listening to the Light Programme was 67 per cent; to the Home Service 33 per cent; and to the Third Programme 3 per cent. By 1951 this had changed even further to the advantage of the Light, which enjoyed 78 per cent of the audience, whilst the Home secured only 21 per cent and the Third had fallen even further to 1 per cent.[50]

Generally speaking, working-class listeners preferred the Light Programme whilst members of the middle class favoured the Home Service. The tiny Third Programme's audience was almost exclusively composed of middle-class and skilled working-class listeners. Such was the unpopularity of the Third that over two-thirds of those surveyed in 1949 claimed to have never listened to it. Foreign commercial stations, in particular Radio Luxembourg, enjoyed an almost exclusively working-class audience which tuned in to listen to its unrelenting diet of dance band music.[51] Luxembourg's popularity was the result of the BBC's deliberate neglect, a number of successful comedy shows notwithstanding, of popular tastes. The type of programme most favoured by working-class audiences was variety. Lord Simon of Wythenshawe, who as a Labour peer chaired the BBC Governors between 1947 and 1952, conceded that 'Variety is the most criticised department of the BBC. Many people say that it is far from being as lively and entertaining as variety in the USA'. He considered that the cause of this problem was that whilst drama and the classics were granted money sufficient to ensure their quality, variety was the 'Cinderella of the BBC'.[52] This neglect led the *Daily Mirror* to complain about the number of 'priggish talks and discussions' on the radio.[53]

When asked by Gallup in 1946 whether they supported the introduction of commercial broadcasting a majority of working-class respondents said they did. In contrast, those from 'higher' and 'middle' social classes firmly disapproved. As a stern contemporary critic of the BBC monopoly put it, this difference was due to 'the programme policy of the Corporation [which] gave the lower social classes what they ought to have [and gave] the educated classes what they wanted'.[54]

Reading books or newspapers was another popular domestic leisure pursuit, one often conducted within earshot of the radio. In 1945 Gallup revealed that 53 per cent of the population was reading a book at the time of the survey. There was a noticeable difference in the popularity of reading between social groups. Of those on lower incomes, 47 per cent said they were reading compared to 63 per cent of those in the higher income group.[55] A more detailed picture emerged from Mass-Observation's 1947 study of Tottenham in north London. This indicated that reading was the most favoured activity of one-third of middle-class respondents, one-fifth of skilled workers but only one-tenth of the unskilled working class.[56]

Some observers thought the war had transformed reading patterns. The *New Statesman* was not alone in considering that Forces-based adult education, in particular ABCA, had brought about a 'new public' which wanted 'serious books and thoughtful publications'.[57] There is some evidence for this. However, it is also clear that popular fiction retained its overwhelming interwar dominance.[58] Whilst public libraries increased the number of wartime issues, the share of non-fiction works taken out remained static. For example, whilst Luton Central Library doubled the number of books issued during the war, the ratio of fiction to non-fiction remained the same: for every one non-fiction book borrowed, four works of fiction were issued.[59] Mass-Observation's Tottenham study confirmed this pattern. Seventy-seven per cent of respondents who said they read stated that this was mainly confined to fiction; only 15 per cent read non-fiction. Furthermore, the type of fiction favoured by the majority was hardly 'improving'. The three most popular categories were detective and mystery stories (31 per cent), love stories (17 per cent) and adventure and westerns (16 per cent). Whilst men and women read the first category to the same extent, males were disproportionately interested in westerns and females in love.[60] As with cinema, books were mainly used as a form of escape. As one working-class housewife stated: 'I never read non-fiction. I like love-books and murders and happy endings. What seldom happens in real life. It's nice to get away from things'.[61]

Whilst those who read books on a regular basis were in a (substantial) minority, the vast majority were voracious daily newspaper readers and access to a Sunday paper was all but universal. The rise of the *Daily Mirror* was one of the most noteworthy cultural and political events of the Second World War. Iconoclastic and radical, it seemed to echo the temper of the times and in 1945 endorsed the Labour Party. By the end of the decade it had supplanted the pro-Conservative *Daily Express* and become Britain's biggest selling daily paper. Those responsible for the paper's production made it sensationalist and entertaining in order to appeal to young working-class men and women.[62] This meant that the *Mirror* was less concerned with hard news and more preoccupied with pictures of semi-nude 'young ladies', cartoons, crime stories and gossip about glamorous screen stars.[63] News items accounted for just under one-quarter of the paper's editorial space. This set of priorities and the accessible way information was presented met with great favour. Readers most liked the paper's strip cartoons and spent as much time and attention on the cartoon page as on those containing reports of foreign and domestic events. Only 3 per cent of readers consulted the paper's editorial. By no means all newspapers which aimed to attract working-class readers shared the *Mirror*'s priorities. Labour's own paper, the *Daily Herald*, devoted rather more space to news (30 per cent) and considerably more to politics and foreign affairs. The results of such contrasting emphases were obvious: by 1950 the *Mirror* was read by 25.3 per cent of adults and the *Herald* was consulted by only 11 per cent. However, even the *Mirror*'s popularity paled into insignificance when compared to that of the Sunday *News of the World*. This paper's stress on sexual scandals led 48.3 per cent of all adults to read it.[64]

Since the Holiday with Pay Act (1938) an increasing number of employers were obliged to give their workers paid time off work. By 1945 about 80 per cent of the labour force was covered by the Act. Thus, a growing number of people were able to enjoy a regular holiday – defined as a period away from home over seven days in duration. Yet, holidays were not cheap and still required workers to save money over a number of months. This meant that during the late 1940s only half the population went away for at least seven days. Consequently, holidays remained a rarity for unskilled workers: three-quarters of families whose main bread winner earnt under £3 stayed at home throughout the summer. The most they could hope for was the occasional day in the country or by the sea.[65]

Most people's attitude to holidays reflected those to leisure in general: they were seen to be an escape from everyday concerns. One middle-aged working-class housewife spoke for many when she defined her ideal holiday:

> To get away from everything, not to have to do anything for myself, to be able to get right away from duties and shopping. I like to go somewhere quiet. I like to be served hand and foot and not have to think or worry about a thing.

The desire for rest and relaxation was widespread, especially amongst the working class and working-class women in particular. Activity holidays were largely the preserve of the normally sedentary middle class.[66]

Holiday camps, most famously those owned by the showman entrepreneur Billy Butlin, increased in popularity during the postwar years. So far as the masses were concerned the holiday camp typified the ideal holiday and gave rise to the popular film *Holiday Camp* (1947). Significantly, a Mass-Observation survey discovered that the camps' appeal was largely restricted to the working class. Only 10 per cent of middle-class respondents looked on them in a positive light, compared to 50 per cent of skilled and 46 per cent of unskilled workers. Butlins promised that guests would escape from their workaday world: 'Ride or relax, as you please, but ENJOY yourself. That's the Butlins idea'. In advertising, the lounge bar at Skegness was described as among the most luxurious in the country, while Filey's alleged 'quiet elegance' was emphasised. Value for

7 The funny side of life under Labour: 4. '"Wotcher, folks! 'Appy New Year!"' (see Chapter 7)

money was also underlined. By 1947 Butlins catered for half a million visitors. Yet, only a minority of workers were affluent enough to stay at a camp: in 1947 this lucky band amounted to a mere 8 per cent of the population. Most of the rest dreamed of the day they could afford such a vacation.[67]

One Mass-Observer spent a week at Butlin's Filey camp towards the end of the 1947 summer season.[68] There she experienced a degree of regimentation. For example, campers were given no choice of food at meal times; strangers had to share chalets; each morning Radio Butlins exhorted guests to wake up and go for breakfast; and community singing preceded every evening's entertainment. Campers were also divided into two houses and encouraged to compete against one another in a variety of games in order to win the camp cup by the last Friday. As the reporter noted, such a controlled holiday allowed working people – and especially women – freedoms they had hitherto lacked. Children were looked after by Butlins' staff and there was no housework, cooking or washing up to perform. She also observed that many had come to feel 'a special kind of mateyness and comradeship with all their fellow campers'. This sentiment was the foundation of the hundred or so Butlin's social clubs established in towns and cities across the country which met during the winter months to sustain the 'Butlin spirit'.

The appeal of 'escapist' pastimes was in stark contrast to that of further education. The failure of the adult education movement confounded the hopes of Labour's NEC and educationalists that the war had increased demand for enlightenment.[69] ABCA's apparent success in stimulating the interest of ordinary soldiers in social and political affairs was thought to have fundamentally changed popular attitudes. Thus, it was with some optimism that W.E. Williams, ABCA's wartime Director, established the Bureau of Current Affairs (BCA) in 1946. Williams intended to create a peacetime ABCA by supporting discussion groups he expected would spring up at workplaces and in voluntary bodies such as trade unions.[70] These efforts were supplemented by the Education Act (1944) which stipulated that local education authorities had to take the needs of adults seriously. As a result, groups active in the field received welcome amounts of government funding, the Workers' Education Association (WEA) in particular. Thus, the years after 1945 saw a general expansion in the organisational basis for adult education. The WEA increased its teaching staff threefold, a number of universities established extra-mural courses and the Women's Institute also enhanced its range of didactic activities.[71] The WEA reflected the sense of expectation by announcing that it stood 'on the threshold of greater opportunities for the expansion of its work than ever before'.[72]

Despite this, most people – workers in particular – did not respond to the call. A study of adolescent boys undertaken during the late 1940s discerned that over the three years of the survey only 29 per cent attended an evening class. A mere 13 per cent sustained their interest throughout the whole period. Of those who attended regularly the skilled were disproportionately represented whilst 94 per cent of the unskilled did not attend a single class at all. Those youths who stayed the distance were usually pursuing apprenticeships, so such activity was closely tied to advancement at work.[73] This desultory interest in further education amongst adolescents was even more pronounced with adults. The cultural critic Raymond Williams recalled that the social character of his WEA classes was 'extremely mixed'.[74] This experience was atypical. In the year 1945–46, 19,570 manual workers enrolled as students in WEA classes across England and Wales. Such people amounted to less than 25 per cent of the total. By 1947–48 the number of manual workers had fallen to 18,112, leaving them forming not much more than 20 per cent of the student body.[75] A survey of those enrolled in University of Manchester extra-mural classes between 1947 and 1949 gives a more detailed picture. This indicated that nearly two-thirds of students came from the lower professions, clerical occupations or the skilled working class. Those in semi- or unskilled occupations accounted for little more than one in ten of the students.[76] To be more specific still, the predominance of the lower middle class in adult education was confirmed by the composition of an adult education social science class held in Dumfries in the early 1950s. Of the fifteen enrolled, there were four housewives, two secretaries, two school teachers, a cycle agent, a nursery assistant, a town planning assistant, a shop manager, an assistant housing manager, a sub-postmaster and a bank manager.[77] Thus, having started the period confident about expansion, educators failed to make a positive impact on popular attitudes. Moreover, they could not explain the decline in the participation of workers in adult education, perhaps unwilling to believe that this was a sign of the proletariat's rejection of 'improving' leisure. This sorry state of affairs was summed up by the forced closure of the BCA in 1951 due to lack of funds.[78]

The failure to transform popular leisure was not confined to the general public: most Labour Party members resisted the appeal of improving pursuits even when they were promoted by their own leaders and activists. Those national bodies which aspired to attract young Labour people were especially noteworthy failures. The Wood Craft Folk's grand objective was to train 'children and young people in the light of modern progressive philosophy for the service of the peoples' movements'. Despite this ambition, the organisation did not prosper, with membership in industrial areas being particularly poor. There were, for example, only three fitfully active branches in the whole of the North-West region. Such was the Folk's parlous financial state that in 1949 it had to make a number of paid officials redundant. As its 1948 Report rather eccentrically stated, 'Our own impact ... upon the society of which we are part, is so often encountered by one in reverse'.[79] Another body which had to embrace disappointment was the Socialist Sunday School movement. This sought to 'train children to be good citizens and [urged] them to play their part in attaining Socialism'. However, in 1949 the movement's National Secretary was forced to admit that his organisation was 'having an uphill struggle'. So low was the movement's national profile that even members of Labour's own Research Department were ignorant of its activities.[80]

The British Workers' Sporting Association was rather more successful in appealing to adults, although its organisation was patchy at best. Under its auspices, in 1946 a darts tournament was arranged in London while inter-factory boxing competitions were held in Cardiff. Perhaps the Birmingham area was the most lively as it held a tennis tournament whilst sustaining thirty cricket teams, a table tennis league and darts tournament. There were enough national members to hold a 'Workers' Wimbledon', an athletic and cycling championship as well as a national bowls championiship in Hyde Park. A few members also played table tennis matches in Paris and lawn tennis in Switzerland. Yet, this success was modest and the Association remained the preserve of a tiny minority.[81]

Unlike many of its European counterparts, the Labour Party did not have its own educational wing. Moreover, apart from the

Transport and General Workers' Union few unions had their own educational programmes. Instead, individual Party members led or participated in the activities of one of two organisations: the National Council of Labour Colleges (NCLC) or the WEA. Individual trade unions also contributed financially to these bodies. The WEA provided a wide-ranging 'liberal' education to all adults without the assumption of a prior political position. In contrast, the NCLC saw its role as explicitly aiding workers' education and playing a direct role in furthering the interests of the labour movement. For these reasons, the two bodies were unwilling to co-ordinate their activities for the wider good.[82]

As noted in Chapter 4, the Labour leadership sought to increase the role of internal Party education. The attempt to introduce Labour discussion groups floundered due to lack of interest in local parties. When Transport House sent out a questionnaire in 1947 on the development of such groups to all 660 district Labour parties well over two-thirds did not bother to even reply.[83] This lack of support in the country was a problem because Morgan Phillips found it difficult enough to finance simple organisation and so little money was available to develop any more thorough-going initiatives.[84] One way around this difficulty was for the Party to take over the NCLC and place it under the direct control of the NEC. However, the NCLC resisted such overtures and nothing came of them.[85]

One example will suffice to indicate the provision of leisure by Labour ward and constituency parties across the country. This is taken from Stockport in Cheshire, an industrial town located just to the south of Manchester.[86] The Stockport party looked on the organisation of recreational activities as predominantly a means of making money to finance electoral work. A secondary role of such events was, however, to 'raise the prestige of the party by the quality of the events its promotes'. Under the direction of a social committee the Party usually held six dances a year at Stockport Town Hall. Apart from that, the committee arranged an annual day trip for members to places such as Stratford and the Lake District and also held a Christmas Draw. Individual ward parties in the town reproduced these same activities on a smaller scale, supplementing them with an apparently unbounded desire for whist drives. In fact, so many ward parties wanted to hold fund-raising dances at the Town Hall that the Stockport party stopped them holding events at weekends and bank holidays: it wanted to reserve such prime times for itself. These modest ambitions did pay off – financially at least. Activities during the year 1948–49 helped the social committee raise the considerable sum of £628. Other than dances and draws, Labour in Stockport was unable to do more. There were attempts to be rather more adventurous, but these led nowhere. For example, in 1948 the propaganda committee thought that a socialist library would be a good idea; nothing more was heard of this suggestion. Similarly, towards the end of 1950 it was felt that the Party should organise a Gala to celebrate May Day the following year. The election of a Labour May Queen was mooted, as was a fire work display and a special day trip for members and children. However, by the spring of 1951 little organisational work had been done. The proposal was abandoned, as was the day trip, due to lack of interest.

If most Labour Party members were not interested in establishing their own leisure activities, except to raise money, then trade unionists were even less concerned. In 1945 the Civil Service Clerical Association Theatre Group claimed to be the only union body of its kind, although the Amalgamated Engineering Union was said to be more active in this field than most.[87] Amongst the miners – where the union movement is often considered to have had its greatest impact outside work – there was little sense that leisure was a 'problem'. In pit villages, drinking and gambling in working men's clubs was the most common way workers enjoyed their spare time. As one study suggested, the miner's pursuit of entertainment was 'vigorous and predominantly frivolous'. Few saw merit in spending time outside work in ways considered appropriate in *Tribune* or the *New Statesman*. Comics rather than books were the popular reading material; those books in demand were devoted to crime and romance. Libraries in welfare institutes that had not been replaced by a games room, were little used except for the procurement of racing tips. After 1945, an increasing number of miners were said to be spurning choirs, dramatic societies and musical clubs in favour of purely commercial pursuits.[88]

The continued success of 'escapist' entertainments and the failure of 'improving' pursuits frustrated Labour's cultural critics. In response, they vainly called on the Government to take further steps to change the situation, especially with regard to cinema and radio. Attitudes to the cinema were mixed. Most saw film as a potentially beneficial means of mass education and entertainment.

As President of the Board of Trade, Stafford Cripps remarked that cinema was 'one of the most important expressions of British culture'.[89] However, the products spawned by the Hollywood-dominated commercial cinema were generally deprecated. The *New Statesman* even advocated increasing censorship to limit the ability of 'an industrial monopoly to control the taste and morality which may work contrary to the aims which enlightened education would seek to achieve'.[90] Such ambivalence was most vividly expressed in J.B. Priestley's first post-war novel, *Bright Day* (1946). This concerned Gregory Dawson, a middle-aged screen writer and Hollywood refugee who had returned to his native Britain to produce films during the war. Priestley had also written film scripts in both Britain and Hollywood. He used Dawson to express his own misgivings about the industry. Thus, Dawson considered that contemporary cinema was 'a wonderful medium ... bitched up by money-lenders and salesmen and second-rate solicitors on the make'. He characterised Hollywood bosses as 'just a bunch of giant parasites, sucking the life out of films, ruining the best medium for communal entertainment that's been invented during the last two thousand years'. Therefore, despite its potential, the film industry was a 'dreamland', a 'gigantic doped jam-puff industry'. As a writer, Dawson's role was to administer anaesthetic to the audience. By the end of the novel, however, the hero had rejected his place in the scheme of things and with a group of trade union-backed idealistic film makers set out to produce work about how 'real people behaved in a real world'.[91]

Tribune frequently gave voice to the left's frustration with film. One correspondent condemned 'the intellectual bankruptcy and dishonesty of the average American script'. Others indicted Hollywood for being an agent of 'capitalist propaganda'.[92] Another wrote:

> I, for one, have ceased to look upon the cinema as a form of entertainment, with its celluloid glamour and manufactured figures of American beauty ... Thank God, America has not yet polluted the legitimate stage of this country, to which we look for our entertainment and recreation.[93]

Yet, not all the journal's contributors and readers thought the situation irretrievable. To this group, British cinema was a frustrated people's art. Few would have disagreed with Ted Willis's comment that films and cinemas 'like public libraries and art galleries, must be regarded as public amenities, not a profit-maker's paradise'.[94] Cinema's potential was constrained by the monopolistic control of those interested only in making profits. Hollywood was seen to be the biggest impediment to development, although J. Arthur Rank's domination of the distribution and production of films in Britain was also severely criticised. Rank was said to threaten 'what, rightly directed, can become one of the nation's most valuable cultural, educational and economic assets'.[95]

Tribune wanted to elevate the public's cinematic taste. It considered that the popular preference for formulaic fantasies was the result of manipulation, not a positive choice. Reflecting the perspective of documentary film makers, the journal predicted that, once given an alternative, audiences would prefer innovative and challenging films to the ones provided by the commercial sector.[96] That choice could only be achieved, it was believed, if the government took action 'to sponsor what the public really wants, instead of what Hollywood and Wardour Street think it wants'.[97] The main purpose of state intervention was to liberate film makers from commercial pressures, enabling them to make 'realistic' films.[98] Thus, it was suggested that in combination with local authorities, government could form a fourth circuit to distribute artistically stimulating works. It was also proposed that the state could purchase studio space and rent it to independent producers.[99] The Board of Trade under Harold Wilson responded to some of these proposals in 1948 by establishing a National Film Finance Corporation to provide low interest loans to independent producers. Wilson also instituted means to ensure that independent films were not excluded by the big circuits: *Chance of a Lifetime* had benefited from this. The Government did not go much further because ministers were reluctant to interfere with an industry that promised to generate much-needed foreign revenue in the United States.[100]

Despite popular discontent with the output of BBC radio, most Labour members supported the Corporation's attempt to improve listeners' tastes. When the BBC's Charter was due for renewal in 1946 the Government expressed its satisfaction with the monopoly and rejected calls for the introduction of commerical competition.[101] The mainstream Labour figure Alderman Wright Robinson, of Manchester City Council, considered that the Corporation was:

the real epitome of what is best in our way of life, in our thoughts,

the arts, science, politics and culture. It embodies more of the elements out of which a modern moral imperative can emerge than
any other social institution.[102]

Both *Tribune* and the *New Statesman* had applauded the creation of
the Third Programme in 1946. *Tribune* described it as 'an intelligent and lively affair, a long way removed from the banalities of
most radio'. It was, in fact, only after the creation of the Third Programme that the journal deigned to appoint a radio critic.[103] In a
similar vein, the *New Statesman* claimed that 'no one who has the
values of civilisation at heart could be other than ... delighted by
the almost incredible prospect' of it.[104]

The main complaint made by Labour activists about the BBC was
that elements within the Corporation were politically biased.
Alleged examples of partiality were found in the 'highbrow' part of
the BBC's output rather than in light entertainment – although the
alleged anti-Labour material of some comedians was noted.[105] The
content of talks and discussions broadcast on the Third Programme
was often criticised. Such sensitivity was because by the late 1940s
the Third's largely middle-class audience was felt to be slipping
from Labour's grasp. This concern motivated Morgan Phillips to
write to Sir William Haley and complain about the discussion programme *Any Questions*, whose chair was said to favour Conservative speakers. The *Daily Herald* even published an editorial on the
matter. During this period the Labour MP George Wigg formed the
Democrats' Listening Association to monitor pro-Conservative sentiments. However, the Party leadership did not think this a damn-
ing indictment of the Corporation. Phillips considered that any
hostility to Labour was due to the narrow social base from which
BBC employees were recruited, rather than deliberate policy.[106]

Whilst the aesthetic content of BBC output was generally praised,
some in the Party considered that it could still be improved.[107] The
pages of *Tribune* frequently contained calls for the termination of
the BBC's monopoly. The case, as with cinema, was that monopoly
led to lack of artistic endeavour. Lack of competition was the cause
of what was described as the Corporation's 'essentially conservative
and unadventurous spirit'. Commercialisation, however, was firmly
rejected: to allow profit-makers into broadcasting would, it was
feared, only enhance the power of capitalist interests. Instead, *Tribune* called for the creation of regionally-based corporations able to

broadcast nationally.[108] In a similar vein, the New Statesman made
a case for municipal authorities or public bodies such as universities to operate stations in order to encourage local educational and
cultural activities. In this way, it suggested, the 'Athenian concept
of democracy' could gain a contemporary manifestation.[109]

This chapter has not focused on Labour critics of popular pastimes because they changed the way people enjoyed their time outside work. They certainly failed in this regard, being unable even
to influence the way many in their own Party acted during their
leisure hours. What the discussion has highlighted is the considerable cultural and political chasm which separated the few who
sought to articulate Labour's wider purpose from the many whose
interests they aspired to represent. The former misunderstood the
role of leisure pursuits in working-class life whilst the latter, male
manual workers especially, resented the attempt to reform their
recreations. Writing in 1946 Mass-Observation's Tom Harrisson
introduced readers of the New Statesman to the term 'wowser'
which he claimed was Australian slang for somebody wishing to
interfere with or limit the pleasures of others. This desire, he said,
often sprang from 'a sincere – if sometimes misguided – urge to
improve other minds, generally those "below" you'. This attitude,
he concluded, had been 'the impetus to much social reform and cultural advance in Britain'.[110] It is tempting to suggest that many of
the comments quoted in this chapter were saturated in 'wowser-
dom'.

Labour activists were amongst those most likely to criticise their
workmates' overwhelming fascination with sport because it
diverted them from more important topics.[111] Such pleasures were
not to be encouraged when socialism was in prospect. It needs to
be stressed that not all Labour activists or thinkers can be seen in
this light. The Rotherhithe MP Bob Mellish spoke for the less critical when he complained that 'Too many people are running
around trying to cure other people's souls and putting them on the
path to righteousness'.[112] However, those who set the tone of internal Party debate often came close to the caricature of the 'wowser'.
Furthermore, Harrisson's main point was that the attempt to
'improve' how people enjoyed their leisure was often misguided as
it was based on an ignorance of working-class culture. In fact, some
regarded workers as lacking anything worthy of the name of 'culture'. As one Tribune correspondent put it, in relation to what was

described as the 'shoddy rubbish' that was contemporary popular music: 'The British working class (the most dispossessed in the world) have to accept it because they have lost what was their own culture and have not yet created another for themselves'.[113]

This misunderstanding underpinned much of the analysis described above. It was possibly at its most acute in the case of attitudes to public houses. The Workers' Temperance League, formed by total abstainers within the labour movement, counted George Tomlinson, Minister of Education, and Stafford Cripps among its members.[114] Although 200 Labour MPs were said to be abstainers, those who had taken the pledge were a small minority within the Party. However, members who thought workers drank too much beer and wanted public houses transformed were rather more numerous.[115] Some considered that pubs had to be controlled by the state in order to turn them into social and cultural centres where drinking would be but one of a number of activities. This lay behind a proposal in the Government's Licensing Bill.[116] Yet, in Harrisson's eyes, the pub was less a den of vice and more an already-existing social centre which sustained the much-vaunted sense of community. While this community was dominated by a masculine ethos that still considered women who drank morally dubious, Harrisson's general point was well made. Despite the fear that such leisure time promoted passivity, the pub was described by Mass-Observation as 'a labyrinth of minor social activities, often requiring the most complete and intelligent participation from the citizen'.[117]

Labour was in danger of appearing as the wowser's party in a number of other respects. In early 1947 the Government placed a ban on mid-week sports meetings as a response to a severe coal shortage so that workers would not be diverted from production. This measure curtailed events which had a great appeal to many male manual workers and by no means all were happy with their enforced sacrifice. One complained that the Government had no right to interfere with the sport of the working man.[118] A number of *Daily Herald* readers protested against the measure; as one stated, 'the Government must give us some light in these days of austerity. Football and the dogs have been some of that light'.[119] Such readers had evidently not been persuaded by Harold Laski's earlier speech in which he baldly declared:

> We cannot afford to luxuriate either in the expensive escapism of
> Hollywood films or the pleasant opiate of Virginia tobbacco.
>   We cannot waste thousands of workers upon pools and dog-racing
> and mid-week football. We have to test workers' demands by work-
> ers' output.[120]

The *Daily Express*, ever ready to project Labour as the killjoy party,
exploited such discontent on behalf of the Conservatives by assum-
ing the mantle of defender of the workers' pleasures. One editorial
thundered: 'People in high places should never forget that the
masses lead humdrum lives of dreary monotony. An occasional
escape does good, not harm'. The ban, it claimed, was an example
of 'austerity for the sake of it', showing that few in the cabinet read
the sports pages.[121] Later in the same year, Labour was again in
difficulties, having to justify increases in cigarette tax, a measure
which the *Daily Herald* spent many valuable column inches defend-
ing, albeit rather uneasily.[122] By the time of the run-up to the 1950
general election, the Conservatives had begun to realise the potential of leisure as a political issue. Central Office placed one adver-
tisement in *Picture Post* which suggested that Labour preferred to
nationalise more industries rather than use revenues to cut tax on
beer or reduce the cost of a football match ticket.[123]
     It is impossible to calculate the electoral impact of criticisms of
popular leisure which emanated from the Labour Party. In Aneurin
Bevan's 1948 speech which famously described Tories as 'lower
than vermin', he predicted that Conservative policies would result
in the building of cinemas, mansions, hotels and theatres but not
homes for the poor. In so doing, Bevan deliberately juxtaposed the
construction of cinemas against the building of homes in order to
make a rhetorical point. Those living in sub-standard housing
would, in all probability, have preferred a new place of abode rather
than a new cinema. However, Bevan came close to suggesting that
Labour in principle favoured the former to the exclusion of the
latter.[124] For reasons outlined above, this reflected the attitude of
numerous Party activists, by whom Bevan was well-liked, but it did
not find an echo in the minds of most voters: they wanted homes
and cinemas.

Notes

1 *New Statesman*, 20 July and 21 December 1946.

2 Manchester City Labour Party, *Manchester To-Morrow. Cultural Facilities for Manchester* (Manchester, 1945), p. 1; J.B. Priestley, *The Arts Under Socialism* (London, 1947), pp. 18–19.

3 F. Zweig, *Labour, Life and Poverty* (London, 1949, 1975 ed.), pp. 77–80.

4 See C. Waters, *British Socialists and the Politics of Popular Culture, 1884–1914* (Manchester, 1990).

5 See for example, H. Durant, *The Problem of Leisure* (London, 1938); C. Day Lewis (ed), *The Mind in Chains. Socialism and the Cultural Revolution* (London, 1938); D. Thompson, 'The Importance of Leisure', *Current Affairs*, 73, 22 January 1949, pp. 2–14.

6 Women's Group on Public Welfare, *Our Towns: A Close-Up* (Oxford, 1944), pp. xix, 101.

7 *Tribune*, 17 August 1945.

8 Priestley, *Arts*, pp. 6–10; *Tribune*, 6 July and 31 August 1945.

9 Unless otherwise stated, the following three paragraphs are based on Labour Party Archive [hereafter LPA], RDR 284/March 1945, P.J. Noel-Baker, 'Facilities for Popular Entertainment and Culture', [n.d.]; RD 35/November 1946, Anon., 'A Policy for Leisure', [n.d.] and RD 43/February 1947, Anon., 'The Enjoyment of Leisure', [n.d.].

10 *Tribune*, 24 August 1945.

11 *Tribune*, 17 August and 7 September 1945. Emphasis added.

12 Unless otherwise stated, the discussion in the following five paragraphs is heavily indebted to H. Ichihashi, 'Working-Class Leisure in English Towns 1945–1960, with Special Reference to Coventry and Bolton' (University of Warwick, Ph.D., 1994), in particular chapters 2 and 5.

13 F.M. Leventhal, '"The Best for the Most": CEMA and State Sponsorship of the Arts in Wartime, 1939–45', *Twentieth Century British History*, 1:3 (1990), 289–317.

14 Quoted in P. Addison, *Now the War Is Over. A Social History of Britain, 1945–51* (London, 1985), p. 134.

15 E.W. White, *The Arts Council of Great Britain* (London, 1975), pp. 17–63.

16 A. Bevan, *In Place of Fear* (London, 1952), pp. 50–1; LPA, RD 222/December 1948, Social Services Sub-Committee, 'Fabian Society Arts Group. Policy for Leisure', [n.d.].

17 P. Crane 'Enterprise in Local Government', *Fabian Research*, 156 (London, 1953), pp. 14–17; N. Tiratsoo, *Reconstruction, Affluence and Labour Politics: Coventry 1945–60* (London, 1990), pp. 28–52.

18 Both quoted in M. Frayn, 'Festival', in M. Sissons and P. French (eds), *Age of Austerity, 1945–51* (Harmondsworth, 1964), pp. 334–7.

19 *Listener*, 10 and 24 May 1951.

20 Zweig, *Poverty*, pp. 62–3, 76–7, 83–4.

21 C. Madge, *War-time Patterns of Saving and Spending* (Cambridge, 1943), pp. 29–32; M. Abrams, *The Home Market. 1950 Edition* (London, 1950), pp. 52–3, 68–9, 70–1.

22 Tom Harrisson Mass-Observation Archive [hereafter THMOA], File Report 3075, 'Present-Day Cost of Living', January 1949, passim.

23 M. Young, 'Distribution of Income within the Family', *British Journal of Sociology*, 3:4 (1952), 305–21.

24 THMOA File Report 3075, 'Cost of Living', passim; F. Zweig, *Men in the Pits* (London, 1948), pp. 95–6.

25 P.G. Allen, 'Evening Activities in the Home', *Sociological Review*, 43, Section 6 (1951), p. 133, Table 3; P. Jephcott, *Rising Twenty. Notes on Some Ordinary Girls* (London, 1948), pp. 143–4.

26 F. Zweig, *Women's Life and Labour* (Harmondsworth, 1952), pp. 141–4; Jephcott, *Rising Twenty*, pp. 143–4.

27 *Lancet*, 4 December 1948.

28 Zweig, *Poverty*, pp. 48–52.

29 Political and Economic Planning [hereafter PEP], *The British Film Industry* (London, 1952), pp. 182–8.

30 See, for example, J.P. Meyer, *British Cinemas and Their Audiences* (London, 1948), pp. 251–75; M. Abrams, 'The British Cinema Audience', *Hollywood Quarterly*, 4:3 (1950), 251–5; Hulton Research, *Patterns of British Life* (London 1950), p. 139; PEP, *British Film*, pp. 182–4.

31 Madge, *Saving and Spending*, p. 113.

32 Jephcott, *Rising Twenty*, pp. 62, 153–6; P. Jephcott, *Some Young People* (London, 1954), p. 63.

33 Jephcott, *Some Young People*, pp. 64–5.

34 *Lancet*, 4 December 1948.

35 Zweig, *Pits*, p. 107.

36 PEP, *British Film*, pp. 203–8.

37 J. Highet, *Dumfries Speaks Out* (Glasgow, 1951), p. 31; British Film Institute, Bernstein Film Questionnaire, 1946–7, p. 6.

38 J. Poole, 'British Cinema Attendance in Wartime: Audience Prefer-

ence at the Majestic, Macclesfield', *Historical Journal of Film, Radio and Television,* 7:1 (1987), 15–34.

39 J. Richards, 'Wartime British Cinema Audiences and the Class System: The Case of "Ships With Wings" (1941)', *Historical Journal of Film, Radio and Television,* 7:2 (1987), 129–41.

40 G. Lambert, 'Film and the Idea of Happiness', in A.G. Weidenfeld (ed), *Good Living* (London, 1948), pp. 61–2.

41 N. Swallow, 'Social Realism in Film and Radio. A Comparative Analysis', *Sight and Sound,* 16:4 (1947/8), 170–1.

42 Mass-Observation, 'Film and the Public: Chance of a Lifetime', *Sight and Sound,* 19:1 (1951), 349–50.

43 *Daily Mirror,* 11 January 1946.

44 J. Coatman, 'Radio and Society', *Social Welfare,* 5:11 (1944), 295–7.

45 F. Williams, *Nothing So Strange* (London, 1970), pp. 271–2.

46 M. Gorham, *Sound and Fury. Twenty-one Years in the BBC* (London, 1948), pp. 161–6, 171–3, 193–6.

47 Allen, 'Evening Activities', 139.

48 Jephcott, *Some Young People,* p. 61.

49 E.L. Packer, 'Backstreet', in A.G. Weidenfeld (ed), *Other People's Lives* (London, 1948), p. 62.

50 Lord Simon, *The BBC From Within* (London, 1953), p. 190.

51 THMOA, File Reports 3105, 'Radio Listening and Attitudes Towards "Rediffusion" in Nottingham and Plymouth', April 1949, passim, and 3162, 'Radio Personalities', September 1949, passim.

52 Simon, *BBC,* pp. 106–8, 188.

53 *Daily Mirror,* 24 January 1946.

54 R.H. Coarse, *British Broadcasting. A Study in Monopoly* (London, 1950), pp. 201–2.

55 Anon., 'Britain's Book Reading Habits' in A.G. Weidenfeld (ed), *Overture* (London, 1945), p. 62.

56 THMOA, File Report 2537, 'Reading in Tottenham', November 1947, passim.

57 *New Statesman,* 20 July 1946; *Picture Post,* 25 March 1944.

58 THMOA, TC Reading Habits 1937–47, Box 6, File C, passim.

59 THMOA, TC Reading Habits 1937–47, Box 8, File K, passim.

60 THMOA, TC Reading Habits 1937–47, Box 13, File A, passim.

61 THMOA, File Report 2537, passim.

62 C. King, *Strictly Personal* (London, 1969), p. 105; H. Cudlipp, *At Your Peril* (London, 1962), pp. 51–2.

63 The following information is derived from Mass-Observation, *The*

Press and its Readers (London, 1949).

64 Hulton, *British Life*, p. 70.

65 P. Slater, *Final Report on the Demand for Holidays in 1946 and 1947* (The Social Survey No. 86, 1947) and P. Slater, *Report on the Demand for Holidays in 1947 and 1948* (The Social Survey No. 118, 1948).

66 THMOA, File Report 2509, 'Holidays', August 1947, passim.

67 L. Blair (ed), *The Butlin Holiday Book, 1949–50* (London, 1949), pp. 59–68; THMOA, TC Holidays 1937–51, Box 2, File H, passim.

68 This account is based on THMOA, TC Holidays 1937–51, Box 2, Files G and H.

69 LPA, RDR 153/November 1942, Anon., 'Adult Education', [n.d.].

70 W.E. Williams, 'Civilian "ABCA"', *Industrial Welfare*, 28:304 (1946), 3.

71 *Listener*, 29 June 1950.

72 Workers' Educational Asociation [hereafter WEA], *Annual Report 1946* (London, 1946), p. 9.

73 T. Ferguson and J. Cunnison, *The Young Wage-Earner. A Study of Glasgow Boys* (Oxford, 1951), pp. 103–4; R.F.L. Logan and E.M. Goldberg, 'Rising Eighteen in a London Suburb. A Study of Some Aspects of the Life and Health of Young Men', *British Journal of Sociology*, 4:4 (1953), 330.

74 R. Williams, *Politics and Letters. Interviews with New Left Review* (London, 1979), pp. 73–4.

75 WEA, *Annual Report 1946*, pp. 34–5, Table 6 and *Annual Report 1948* (London, 1948), pp. 54–5, Table 5.

76 W.E. Styler, *Who Were the Students?* (London, 1950), pp. 6–7, 21; W.E. Styler, 'Manual Workers and the Worker's Education Association', *British Journal of Sociology*, 4:1 (1953), 79–83.

77 Highet, *Dumfries*, p. 4.

78 B. Ford, *The Bureau of Current Affairs, 1946–51* (London, 1951).

79 LPA, Morgan Phillips' Papers, Box 6, GS/Wood/2, 9ii.

80 LPA, Morgan Phillips' Papers, Box 6, GS/SSS/1i, 1ii, 2.

81 LPA, Morgan Phillips' Papers, Box 5, GS/BWSA/3–6, 17.

82 Anon., 'The Education of the Worker', *Industrial Welfare*, 32:5 (1950), 141–4.

83 *Tribune*, 11 January 1946; P.C. Gordon-Walker, 'Party Education: The Next Step', *Labour Forum*, 1:1 (1946), 3–5 and Anon., 'Talk It Over', *Labour Forum*, 1:3 (1947), 17.

84 Lord Wigg, *George Wigg* (London, 1972), p. 117.

85 Gordon-Walker, 'Party Education', *Labour Forum*, 1:1–2 (1946); LPA,

RD 16/December 1950, H. Morrison, 'Party Education', [n.d.] and National Executive Minutes, 24 January 1951, 'Memorandum on the Possibilities of a Closer Working Arrangement Between the Labour Party and the NCLC'.
86 This account is based on Stockport Public Library, B/MM/3/5, Stockport Labour Party Annual Reports 1942, 1946–8, 1950–1; B/MM/12/20, Stockport Labour Party Minutes, 1944–51.
87 *New Statesman*, 21 July and 4 August 1945.
88 N. Dennis, F. Henriques and C. Slaughter, *Coal Is Our Life. An Analysis of a Yorkshire Mining Community* (London, 1956, 1969 ed.), pp. 127–8, 130, 150; M. Benny, *Charity Main. A Coalfield Chronicle* (London, 1946), pp. 52–3; Zweig, *Pits*, pp. 90–3, 97–100, 108–10.
89 H.H. Wollenberg, 'Legislation and Film', *Sight and Sound*, 16:63 (1947), 122.
90 *New Statesman*, 31 August and 14 December 1946.
91 J.B. Priestley, *Bright Day* (London, 1946), pp. 44–5, 238, 246, 253–4, 325, 252
92 *Tribune*, 26 March 1943, 26 July 1946 and 19 March 1948.
93 *Tribune*, 29 March 1946.
94 *Tribune*, 7 January 1949.
95 *Tribune*, 29 October 1943 and 2 August 1945.
96 P. Rotha, 'The Future Outlook', in A.G. Weidenfeld (ed), *The Public's Progress* (London, 1947), pp. 72–3; *Tribune*, 19 March 1948 and 25 March 1949.
97 *Tribune*, 16 November 1945.
98 *Tribune*, 21 July 1944, 24 and 31 August 1945.
99 *Tribune*, 16 July 1943, 16 November 1945 and 25 February 1949.
100 M. Dickinson and S. Street, *Cinema and Society. The Film Industry and Government, 1927–84* (London, 1985), pp. 170–4; Ichihashi, 'Working-Class Leisure', pp. 102–8.
101 Coarse, *British Broadcasting*, pp. 146–78.
102 *Education*, 17 June 1949.
103 *Tribune*, 27 September 1946.
104 *New Statesman*, 5 October 1946.
105 *Tribune*, 19 April 1946.
106 Based on the contents of LPA, Morgan Phillips' Papers, Box 9 GS/BCST/1–155.
107 LPA, RD 310/September 1949, Committee on Broadcasting, 'Draft of Evidence to be Submitted by a Committee set up by the National Executive Committee of the Labour Party', [n.d.].

108 *Tribune*, 23 April 1943 and 28 June 1946.

109 *New Statesman*, 2 March 1946.

110 *New Statesman*, 23 November 1946.

111 Zweig, *Worker*, pp. 124–9.

112 *Daily Mirror*, 22 March 1947.

113 *Tribune*, 17 August 1945.

114 LPA, Morgan Phillips' Papers, Box 13 GS/WTL/1–2.

115 LPA, RD 137/August 1948, Anon., 'The Drink Trade', [n.d.], p. 35;
     Tribune, 27 September and 11 October 1946.

116 *Tribune*, 11 October 1946 and 7 January 1949.

117 THMOA, File Reports 2388, 'Drinking Habits', May 1946, passim,
     2505, 'Mutual Aid and the Pub', August 1947, passim and 3112,
     'Qualitative Aspects of the Drink Survey', April 1949, passim; Mass-
     Observation, 'Saturday Night', in A.G. Weidenfeld (ed), *World Off
     Duty* (London, 1947), p. 6; Zweig, *Worker*, pp. 131–9.

118 THMOA, TC Leisure 1940–47, Box 1, File C, passim and TC, Sport,
     1939–47, Box 1, File F, passim.

119 *Daily Herald*, 18 March 1947.

120 *Daily Herald*, 5 March 1947.

121 *Daily Express*, 8, 10, 12, 13 and 14 March 1947.

122 *Daily Herald*, 22 and 26 April 1947.

123 *Picture Post*, 3 December 1949.

124 *The Times*, 5 July 1948.

7

Labour and electoral politics, 1945–1951

On taking office in 1945, the Labour Government recognised that much of its future general strategy would have to be constructed so as to deal with Britain's parlous economic circumstances. The prime objective must be to boost output and exports, whilst restricting home consumption and imports. The American loan negotiated by Keynes allowed some breathing space, but Labour believed that no long-term solution to the country's problems would be possible without a degree of radical internal change. By early 1946, therefore, it had begun to institute a fairly distinctive set of appropriate policy initiatives. On the production side, there was a strong commitment to industrial modernisation (using selective nationalisation where necessary) and a continuous export drive. Accompanying propaganda campaigns aimed to keep workers toiling at the intensity of the war years. Meanwhile, consumption of many different kinds remained tightly restricted, held down by rationing and a severe (if progressive) tax regime.[1]

This strategy seemed laudable in economic terms but it was obviously not without political risk. Britons had given up much during the war, and there was no certainty that self-sacrifice would continue to be acceptable. Austerity and exhortation to work harder might well be considered a poor reward for past endeavour. However, Labour believed that its chances of success were more favourable than this suggested. All restrictive policies would be administered fairly, as in the war, thereby protecting poorer people's standards of living. Furthermore, while Labour would always have to be most concerned with the economy, it was also pledged to introduce substantial welfare reforms, and these appeared likely to prove very popular. Few working-class electors could fail to be impressed by the projected National Health Service, for example, when they had always previously struggled to obtain adequate medical care. Finally, several other developments in the wider political situation seemed to be running in a broadly favourable direction. Labour believed, as has been shown, that 1945 represented a crushing defeat for the Tories and a sign of the electorate's newly gained maturity. So long as socialists continued to light the path, it was suggested, ordinary people would remain generally loyal. Overall, therefore, the chances of a further Labour success in 1950 appeared reasonably good. Prosperity in conventional terms could not be guaranteed during the next few years, but the important point was that a majority of the electorate seemed in tune with the administration's broader ideals.

As the months of 1946 passed, this optimism seemed to be more and more obviously justified. The Labour Party itself was continuing to grow at an impressive rate, with individual membership increasing as never before.[2] To give an example, Luton Divisional Labour Party had 900 members in December 1944 but nearly 5,000 by the end of 1946.[3] Additionally, local election results were very promising. The Party's gains could be described as 'sweeping'. Labour controlled fifty-two out of the eighty-three county boroughs by the end of 1946, compared to fifteen before the November 1945 local government elections. Gains included Birmingham and Manchester. In London, only five of the twenty-eight councils were left in Tory hands.[4] Journalists and commentators continued to underline the scale of the Labour advance. *Tribune* reported on a variety of constituencies in early 1947 and argued that public support for the Attlee administration was almost universally remarkable. The MP for Northampton believed his town was 'satisfied with the choice made at the last election'. In Camberwell (South London), when 'things ... [did] not go so well as they might', the Government received 'no blame but sympathy'. A similar trend was noticeable in Coatbridge (Scotland), from where the local MP reported: 'So far ... the barometer is steady. It is set fair for ... Labour'.[5] Given such sentiments, it was concluded, the Party might well be becoming unbeatable. John Parker, ex-Fabian General Secretary and MP for Dagenham, felt that the Conservatives had little chance of winning the next election unless Labour handed it 'power on a plate either by splitting or by making serious mistakes'. The academic H.L. Beales largely agreed. Writing in *Political Quarterly*, he asked 'Has

Labour Come to Stay?' and answered in the affirmative: 'It is a safe prediction that the people of this country, having given a decision first in local and then in national politics that Labour has something which the other parties have not got, will renew their mandate'.[6]

However, by the early summer of 1947, the atmosphere had perceptibly changed. The winter months had been amongst the coldest on record, leading to coal shortages, and allegations of Government incompetence. Ministers found themselves embroiled in a further crisis, as sterling first became convertible in line with American wishes, and then had to be withdrawn from markets because of its obvious weakness.[7] Influenced by these events, public opinion appeared to be growing more critical. Hostility was most evident amongst the middle class. J.L. Hodson confided to his diary in January 1947: 'We wonder if the Cabinet is aware of the bitterness and cynicism expressed in clubs and the mood that it's no use making money because you won't be allowed to keep it'.[8] In a wider survey of middle-class attitudes, Maude and Lewis reported that assessments of the Government 'ranged from white fury to hurt bewilderment'. Families felt under siege, heavily taxed, unable to buy luxuries, deprived of traditional cultural pursuits, and deserted by servants and 'helps'. In the minds of the disenchanted middle class, on one side were greedy workers and on the other a new black market plutocracy, made up of unpleasant 'cosmopolitans':

> And who were all these extraordinary people one saw about nowadays, who seemed to have all the money, all the large cars, all the best flats and all the scarce food and drink? Foreigners, of course. The first whispers of anti-semitism (strengthened by events in Palestine) began to go about, even in intelligent middle-class circles.[9]

All told, as Mass-Observation found, the comforts of a pre-war Home Counties' household seemed to have evaporated, so that many were reduced to 'little more than living'.[10]

Nevertheless, antipathy towards Labour was certainly not always confined to the middle class. The Principal of Morley College, E.M. Hubback, produced a survey of grumbling and found that it was 'widespread' across the social spectrum. In ordinary conversation, she noted, there was a common tendency 'to dwell on the hardships which we are being called upon to endure'.[11] The pattern of people's feelings could be studied in data collected by the opinion pollsters.

As predicted, Labour's welfare reforms were generally popular. Gallup asked about attitudes towards the new National Health Service at the beginning of 1948 and found 61 per cent rated it as 'good' and only 13 per cent as 'bad'.[12] On the other hand, the public appeared less certain about the more ideological of the Government's commitments. A majority supported controls in industry and rated the nationalisation of coal favourably, but only a minority felt that steel should be state-owned, as some left-wingers were suggesting.[13] Moreover, most believed that Labour was over-zealous in its desire for change. In a poll of December 1947, 42 per cent described the administration as having been 'too socialistic', 30 per cent 'about right' and only 15 per cent 'not socialist enough'. Five months later, a repeat survey found opinion even more unfavourable to the Government.[14]

However, it was clear that these kinds of questions were far less important to people than the more mundane issues of everyday life. Housing, food shortages and the cost of living were the problems most widely cited and acutely felt.[15] Unfortunately for Labour, judgements on such matters often provided little more reassurance. At the beginning of 1947, more than half of those questioned by Gallup rated the Government's progress with housing as unsatisfactory.[16] Two *Daily Express* polls of March 1947 and March 1948 found that about 60 per cent of respondents believed they were not getting sufficient food to sustain themselves in good health.[17] Even unemployment was returning to haunt the popular mind: in April 1948, one-third of those questioned agreed that Britain was likely 'to have some serious unemployment over the next year or two'.[18] Given these figures, it was inevitable that many would view the Government's first two years in office as largely unsatisfactory. Gallup enquired about Labour's overall record on eight occasions between June 1946 and March 1948, and found a favourable majority only once. By the latter date, though 35 per cent were satisfied with what had been done, some 53 per cent actively disapproved.[19]

These figures were worrying enough for Labour, but by this time the Government also had to contend with a Conservative revival. Many Tories were devastated by the 1945 election defeat, and for a time afterwards the Party appeared to be struggling, 'undecided

... flustered, and divided'.[20] During 1946, however, a new sense of resolve began to emerge, fuelled by the idea that if the Conservatives were to win the next election, they must start preparing immediately. It was generally agreed in Tory circles that the 1945 defeat had occurred partly because of the Party's lack of policy, and so one immediate task was to fill this gap.[21] Additionally, it was recognised that electoral verdicts were no longer determined during the short campaigns before polling day but reflected much longer-term political activity. Labour had learned this lesson, apparently, and triumphed because of a steady flow of propaganda during the war.[22] In future, it was argued, the Conservatives must pursue a similar strategy. As one activist concluded, 'the process of instilling Conservative common sense ... into the minds of the masses must go on all the time and everywhere'; the rank and file would have to continually 'fight with the fervour of crusaders'.[23] Spurred on by such perceptions, Party members of all kinds began an overhaul of ideology, organisation and practical politics.

Much attention was given to the question of articulating a fresh and modern Conservatism.[24] The newly appointed Tory Director of Information Services believed that the very word 'Conservative' conjured up too many negative images, from 'a David Low Blimp' to a 'potbellied ... magnate'. 'At best', he wrote, 'we are believed to be stupid and out of date; at worst wicked ... for ever planning new ways of grinding the faces of the poor'.[25] To distance themselves from this legacy, leading Tories decided that in future they must project very different ideals. There were two strands to the new thinking. Conservatives were keen to contrast the drabness and regulation allegedly rife under Labour's 'state socialism' with their own faith in individual freedom and choice. It was thought that a property-owning democracy, where opportunity was open and virtue rewarded, would prove much more satisfying than alien collectivism.[26] Nevertheless, it was stressed, this did not mean returning to an age of Darwinian laissez-faire. Conservatives had learnt from the past, and now accepted that the state had some role to play in providing welfare and perhaps encouraging economic reform. Indeed, when a much heralded statement of Tory industrial policy finally appeared during 1947, it contained a workers' charter and even a section acknowledging trade unions ('How We Have Helped Them and Count on Them Now'), prompting the *Daily Herald*'s editor to remark that the Conservatives were '"thumbing a lift from the Left"'.[27]

On the organisational front, changes occurred with bewildering speed. The first nine months after the 1945 election saw the revivification of the Party's Research Department under R.A. Butler, the establishment of a Political Centre to disseminate propaganda and stimulate discussion, and the launch of a wholly new Young Conservative organisation.[28] When the ex-Minister of Food, Lord Woolton, became Party chairman in September 1946, there was a further round of reforms. Woolton transformed the Party's methods of collecting finance and encouraged some careful democratisation of its routine practices, inviting participation by ordinary activists on an unprecedented scale. He also instituted a membership drive shortly after his appointment which quickly netted 226,000 new recruits.[29]

Finally, to match all of this, there were various developments in the ways Conservative parties in the constituencies went about everyday politics. Long-standing views about how campaigns should be conducted were closely scrutinised, to be replaced in certain cases by much more imaginative approaches. All Conservatives were instructed to take a full interest in local politics and there was considerable discussion about how propaganda could be spread throughout the community. Some tried to develop 'whispering campaigns', using slogans and rhetoric supplied by head office ('Nationalise. Subsidise. Paralyse'). Others cultivated a 'fifth column' of publicans, shopkeepers and garage proprietors, figures who could be relied upon to spread anti-Labour gossip.[30] Everywhere, the scale of activity was stepped up whenever possible. 'Shipley Conservative Week' in September 1947 included a fete (with choirs, a brass band, a fashion parade and a 'Miss Personality' competition judged by two local speedway stars); over 100 political meetings; numerous 'bring-and-buys' and socials; and the distribution of 30,000 copies of the campaigning *Shipley Unionist*. A membership drive in London earlier the same summer was even more impressive, involving some eight hundred open-air meetings.[31]

Not all of this effort achieved the desired result, but by the autumn of 1947, it was quite clear that Labour had begun to be damaged. Gallup polls assessing the electorate's voting intentions placed the parties on an equal footing in March and June, but by August the Tories had opened up a three point gap.[32] Furthermore, morale amongst Labour activists seemed to be slipping. Individual Party membership in 1947 was 6 per cent below the figure for 1946.[33] More significantly, while some southern constituencies were still recruiting, it was quite obvious that many old Labour strongholds had begun to stagnate.[34] At a meeting of the Stepney Borough Party in mid-1947, the chairman was frank about membership apathy: 'From his observation it appeared that the same half dozen had to do all the jobs while the rest of the movement sat back and criticised'.[35] A few weeks after, a similar complaint was made at a meeting in the Durham coalfield: 'The Chairman's remarks were pointed. He declared that not very much enthusiasm was evident and owing to the poor attendance it was better to find other methods'.[36] Public work on behalf of the Party ran into similar problems. One activist complained: 'I live in an area where if you put up a broomstick they would vote Labour; yet I find great difficulty on the doorstep canvassing for members'.[37]

The scale of Labour's problems was finally fully revealed at the November 1947 local elections. The Party had been increasingly less successful in parliamentary by-elections since 1945, winning contests but losing votes.[38] It now found itself soundly beaten by the Tories, losing 652 seats and 24 councils in England and Wales alone.[39] Labour's vote had held up, but the Conservative turn-out was much increased. Some in Labour's ranks felt that their opponents were better organised than ever before: the 'Tory machine set out to pool the whole Tory vote ... and it did a good job'.[40] For others, there was an uncomfortable ring of truth in the *Economist's* trenchant verdict that 'Austerity has awoken the middle classes from their apathy and made them politically active, while it has quenched the evangelist enthusiasm of the working class for "our Government"'.[41]

Prompted by this defeat, the Labour leadership decided to follow the Tory lead and reassess the Party's policies and bases of electoral support. Herbert Morrison, in charge of co-ordinating Labour's forthcoming general election effort, was the key figure in this project, and at the May 1948 conference outlined how the review would proceed. He stated that a period of discussion over the succeeding few months would guide the National Executive Committee in formulating a new statement of policy. This was to be presented at the 1949 conference and then used as the basis for Labour's next election manifesto. On more substantive issues, Morrison warned that the Party was in a difficult position. Labour had passed legislation on many of the 1945 promises, but Acts of Parliament were the beginning, not the end, of ensuring that reforms really worked. Transferring assets from the private to the public sector, as well as creating a new welfare system, were large and complicated matters. The challenge of the next few years was to ensure that the measures taken were delivering the advantages envisaged. At the same time, the Party would have to be sensitive to popular feelings and criticisms. Talking of the eventual election manifesto, Morrison declared: 'We must make the programme as attractive as we can to ourselves, but we must make it attractive also to public opinion'.[42]

Over the next few months, many in Labour's ranks commented on these basic themes. Morrison continued to lead the discussion. He had long experience of electoral politics at local and national level and was at the time very involved in dealing with the administrative teething problems of the nationalised industries.[43] His central argument was that Labour needed to be more realistic about its position and achievements. He considered that most electors had backed the Party in 1945 for pragmatic reasons; few were convinced socialists. Labour had done much to satisfy the ordinary person's aspirations but it should not pretend that criticism of its reforms was always misplaced. Both main political parties would be able to call upon loyal blocks of voters at the next general election. However, the result was likely to turn upon the judgements of the less partisan. A re-invigorated Tory machine had already begun to court such people, promoting a less ideological and harsh brand of Conservatism, and Labour must respond. 'Consolidation', Morrison argued, should be the new theme. It did not mean 'going backwards in any sense of the term' but rather 'laying firm and secure foundations upon which further progress ... [could] be made'.[44]

Others responded to this analysis in a variety of ways. Some were clearly impressed by Morrison's logic and willing to explore its implications. The MP Woodrow Wyatt argued that too many had indeed mythologised the 1945 election victory. There had been no mass conversion to socialism; most Labour voters felt 'fed up with the war and wanted to make a clean break with it'. There should be no mistaking the fact that the 'great mass of the people' were 'almost entirely non-political'.[45] The editor of the *Women's Co-operative Guild Monthly Bulletin* came to similar conclusions:

THE
PEOPLE OF BRITAIN
FOUGHT FROM 1939 - 1945 FOR
FREEDOM FROM OPPRESSION
• • •

When we are
    parked with relatives
        and
    the kids are hungry,

it helps a bit to know——
*WE own the Bank
    of England.*

Published by Fighting Fund For Freedom Ltd., 1 Dover St., London, W1.
Printed by Becks' Printing Works, London, W.10.
LEAFLET 3

THE
PEOPLE OF BRITAIN
FOUGHT FROM 1939 - 1945 FOR
FREEDOM FROM OPPRESSION
• • • •

When we're sitting
around
FIRELESS GRATES

let us remember
that —
WE OWN THE MINES !

Published by Fighting Fund For Freedom Ltd., 1 Dover St., London, W1.
Printed by Becks' Printing Works, London, W.10.
LEAFLET 4.

8   An alternative view. Two leaflets attacking the record of Attlee's
Government, *c.*1949

The General Election of 1945 was no manifestation of a politically-conscious electorate setting up machinery for a changed order of society. At its best it was no more than a profound distrust of the old political set-up ... at its worst it was a cynical hope that change might, perhaps, be for the better ... a vast body of opinion still looks to Tory politics and Tory politicians for satisfactory government.[46]

With this in mind, it was obviously necessary, as Morrison recommended, to look closely at how Labour might maximise voter appeal. Labour, he suggested, needed to think again about the middle classes. Some richer people were 'plain anti-social' and would never support reform because of their jobs or great wealth. Many others had a more enlightened outlook. They performed 'useful' work, as schoolteachers, doctors and technicians, and believed in helping the national effort. Labour could win their support if it took their problems seriously and addressed them without rancour.[47] A similar re-evaluation might produce gains amongst women voters. Many housewives were experiencing difficulties in keeping their families fed and clothed, and some had been drawn to the Tory critique of state direction. Nevertheless, Labour should not blame women for their grumbling but try to respond positively. What was needed involved imagination and humility, as a corre- spondent to the Scottish socialist weekly *Forward* explained:

> If mother is not to become the cinderella of the Socialist State, as well as a reactionary influence, the rest of us will have to see she gets her chance to develop her own personality, whether it be as amateur actress, town councillor, discussion group leader ... or what she will.
>
> That this may come about we need more of the 'good neighbour' policy we came to know in air-raids. It means more 'baby-sitting' by in-laws and certainly less 'bowling club' or golf course for father. It requires a greater readiness on the part of many husbands to recog- nise the mother's rights as an intelligent member of the community, rather than the 'Mother Macree' who stakes her claim on the chim- ney-corner at far too early an age.[48]

By contrast, many on the left of the Party felt that Morrison was simply mistaken. He had misunderstood the electorate (perhaps deceived by his own experiences as a South London MP) and been over-sensitive to middle-class hysteria. The fact was that most British workers wanted socialism and were ready to make it happen. As Ian Mikardo, a left-wing MP, put it in 1948: 'We are already a nation more amenable to forthright Governmental action than it was three years ago, and by 1950 our people will be still more conscious of their power to will the ends they seek'.[49] In this situation, there was little to be gained from a programme that was 'wishy washy and watered down'; what ordinary people wanted was a 'bold and challenging' declaration of socialist faith.[50]

When the National Executive turned to examine these issues, it was soon apparent that those at the top of the Party also differed about the way to proceed.[51] Morrison and his allies wished the new policy statement to concentrate on the cost of living, food and homes, 'the three questions of greatest concern in the country'. To them, the nationalisation of further industries and services was a lower priority: 'the spiritual results' of public ownership had been disappointing, requiring fresh thinking about current organisation and hierarchies.[52] On the other side were those who demanded a clear statement of 'socialist ideals' and an unambiguous commit- ment to further extensive nationalisation – believers in 'the bicycle theory of socialism', that 'to stop moving forward ... [was] to fall'.[53] In the end, it was the Morrisonians who were able to dominate, though not to the extent that they would have wished. *Labour Believes in Britain*, published in April 1949, began from Morrison's conception that Labour should appeal to all sections of the community (it was 'The Party of the Nation') and contained some innovative thinking on common problems, proposing, for example, a new set of measures to protect the consumer.[54] Nationalisation remained on the agenda, though it was hardly emphasised. On the other hand, though middle-class support was invited and welcomed in a general way, little seemed to have been included so as to make this appeal more specific. The better-off were, in effect, being asked to vote Labour because of the overall advantages of life under socialism.[55]

Rank and file reactions to this programme once again varied. Left-wingers were displeased at what they saw as its insipidness, and there were rumours of trouble at the forthcoming Party conference, with radical amendments allegedly flooding into Labour's head office.[56] However, conditions were not propitious for this kind of rebellion. In April 1948, Labour had again performed badly at local elections, while many were becoming more and more aware that (as the previous chapters have shown) instituting socialist change did not always bring the desired results.[57] When delegates assembled, therefore, they were in a more sober mood than had once been predicted. A total of sixty-four speeches were made on the Executive document but only a few were very critical. The nationalisation issue proved only a minor irritant, especially after Bevan backed moderation and attacked fundamentalism, observing: 'I would point out that in some way or another the conceptions of religious dedication must find concrete expression'.[58] As the *Economist* remarked, though important tensions remained unresolved – for example, between 'the idea of socialism as a way of life, and of Labour as a political party' – the moment largely belonged to the 'consolidators'.[59] Morrison's own speech was well received and dealt, among other things, with his profound belief that Labour must be realistic about the mood of the electorate: 'I would recommend to all orators and to all idealists that they had better go and see the people on the doorstep and find out what sort of people they are. It is important that all that should be done, because it will educate the canvasser no less than the canvassed'.[60]

With the review completed, many delegates left the conference ruminating on the more practical question of how propaganda could be best disseminated amongst the electorate. Some had been critical of recent political campaigns, and felt that both Government and Party lacked a proper appreciation of public relations.[61] In future, all sides agreed, Labour would have to make much better use of the media and spend more money on publicity, issuing an extended range of appropriate literature. However, closer inspection of the practicalities involved demonstrated that this was easier said than done. The Government's hands were tied, because it was under considerable pressure inside and outside Parliament to ensure that official information and public relations services remained strictly non-partisan.[62] The Party could try to influence journalists and provide good copy, but most local and national newspapers were firmly pro-Tory and thus unlikely to be sympathetic.[63] Finance, too, remained a problem. An 'ideal' advertising campaign, similar to that used for some commercial products, was estimated to cost £50,000, or more than one-third of Labour's total income for 1948.[64] In this situation, it was concluded, great responsibility would have to lie with the Party's grass-roots. Head office must provide as much propaganda material as possible, but local activists would be absolutely crucial in establishing an effective public presence. As one experienced party agent explained: 'Labour's canvassers are Labour's salesmen'.[65]

During the months of 1949, therefore, continual pressure was placed on the membership to redouble its efforts. Reports in the Party press highlighted possible options and urged local parties to explore as many as possible. It was considered that an efficient organisation should hold regular business meetings and education classes, with occasional socials (whist drives, dances and sports competitions) to provide funds. Public work might take a number of forms. Parties could attempt to organise regular street-corner and district meetings, as well as canvasses aimed at spreading Labour literature and establishing personal contacts. There were advantages, too, in establishing a weekly surgery, to be attended by local councillors or a 'poor man's lawyer'. Finally, influence might be gained by arranging community events, whether thrift clubs and bazaars, or more ambitious festivals such as May Day carnivals, summer fetes and Christmas Fairs. The idea, on every occasion, was to underline a political message. Nevertheless, as Party strategists emphasised, this always needed to be done with some thought, particularly about local conditions. Morrison had observed that propaganda was 'not a matter of gramophone records' and all Labour organisations were urged to bear this in mind when approaching the public.[66] An instruction pamphlet outlined correct procedure:

> the first step is to discover what you as a ... Party *think* you have to get over to the people who live in your constituency ... That sounds easy, for you will undoubtedly say 'Why! the policy of the Labour Government'. Which, of course, is true: but is by no means the whole truth. Your real job is to interpret that policy in terms of its impact upon the lives of the people around you.[67]

Carrying out such instructions obviously required political acumen as well as energy. Some judged that local parties were generally performing well. The *Daily Express* believed that Labour was building an 'election-fighting machine' of almost unprecedented efficiency, indeed 'one not always in accord with ... [Britain's] traditions of happy-go-lucky sporting contests'.[68] However, the actual situation was less clear-cut. Completely moribund organisations were relatively unusual and general activity levels seemed to be rising. On the other hand, few parties did not suffer from one problem or another, and in many cases these proved quite debilitating.

Labour organisations were usually fairly poor in monetary terms, and so even relatively simple matters could lead to difficulties. Every local party needed somewhere to meet, and some were lucky enough to be able to use long-established Labour or trade union halls. Elsewhere, finding suitable accommodation was difficult and required ingenuity. One outer London ward party finally built its own pre-fabricated headquarters in 1949 at a cost of £3,000, having previously met 'over a stable, behind a fried fish shop, and in the front parlour of members' homes'.[69] Communication with the electorate, too, had its pitfalls. Few Labour members had much training in the relevant skills and many found themselves floundering. Local parties had always been encouraged to publish their own newspapers and about 240 were doing so by 1949. Nevertheless, as a sympathetic journalist observed, few were very readable and most resembled 'parish magazine efforts' which would 'be read by the faithful and nobody else'.[70] Similar problems were evident at outdoor meetings, particularly if speakers were using amplification equipment. A *Daily Herald* reporter regretted the frequent waste of effort: 'I wish we did more to train microphone talkers instead of having unskilled though well-meaning helpers, blasting their heads off, and inviting complaints of "nuisance". There are few areas of the country where our propaganda squads have been trained to achieve skilled mastery over the microphone'.[71]

In addition to these practical difficulties, local Labour parties sometimes found themselves constrained because of their own members' attitudes and prejudices. It was clear, to begin with, that many in Labour's ranks did not want to be very active. The vast majority of the national membership had been automatically enrolled in the Party because of their trade union affiliation. A minority had chosen to join as individuals. Most of the former and some of the latter displayed only a vague commitment to socialism. An official of a Kent party was astonished at the general indifference to politics that existed amongst his fellow members, noting that: 'Incredible as it may sound, it is a difficult task to persuade many of them to exercise their franchise at election times'.[72] In fact, what such people clearly relished most about party life were the opportunities it offered for friendship and recreation. An investigation into Manchester constituencies found that many members were hazy about Labour politics: between elections they attended meetings 'rather as they would go to a club', in order 'to meet their friends and discuss the business of running a club'.[73] Visiting one Tottenham women's section, a Mass-Observer felt it was functioning primarily as a support group: 'they liked to meet together once a week, not only to discuss political matters but to hear news of each other, and ... if a member were away ill they kept in contact with her, so that she might feel a member of the group still and know that the other members were thinking of her'.[74] In other cases, members were attracted by the facilities available. Bethnal Green activists complained that some of their rooms were used by a Labour sports section several times a week and without payment, but those who attended 'gave nothing in return in the way of political activity'.[75] The general preference, indeed, often seemed to be for what Morgan Phillips called 'whist-drive-and-dance Socialism'.[76] Pleasure came first, so that a Tamworth official was by no means exceptional when she complained that political meetings had to be organised with great care because there was 'the very "devil" to pay' if they encroached on members' usual cinema evenings.[77]

All of this meant that most local parties tended to be run by small groups of dedicated activists, 'real socialists' as opposed to 'passengers'.[78] This sometimes allowed advantages: a well organised and highly motivated group could exert an influence out of all proportion to its size. On the other hand, there were clear potential drawbacks. Activists often had a fixed and fairly restricted outlook and, if they dominated, fashioned Labour politics in their own image. The result could be a narrowing of the Party's appeal – the very opposite of what Morrison intended.

As has been demonstrated in Chapter 4, to many of those in Labour's ranks, socialism was, first and foremost, a system of ethics, an overarching set of moral imperatives different from those found in most other ideologies. The point of agitation was to win converts or, in the traditional phrase, 'make socialists'. This raised an important question about who would respond best to proselytising, and here the influence of Marx continued to be strong. Middle-class people of goodwill could be won to the cause, but the greatest potential existed amongst the most economically exploited. The implications for practical politics were obvious. Most effort should be expended on 'our people' and their problems; other issues and groups came a clear second.[79]

The consequences of this thinking could be seen in the way parties functioned. In many, male trade unionists dominated, importing a particular proletarian ethos. Members from other backgrounds had to adapt accordingly. Middle-class socialists often felt out of place, though some colluded in an 'inverted snobbery', adopting popular mannerisms.[80] The young complained of being ignored and there was often trouble if they tried to raise their own concerns.[81] Inevitably, too, women usually occupied subordinate positions. Few attained executive status except in their own all-female sections, and this was commonly attributed to the prejudices of male members.[82] Women argued that they were automatically pigeon-holed as wives and mothers, whatever their occupation, and invariably allotted the most mundane tasks at any public function. 'Why is it the *women* member', one correspondent asked in a Labour journal, 'who is always chosen to wield the mop?'.[83] Even those who believed that there was 'little "man-minded" hindrance' to female progress in the Party nevertheless agreed that unconscious attitudes were still a problem. Home and children might come first for many women, but Labour branches did not help to encourage female participation by rarely organising creches or babysitting rotas.[84] Comment about the way women looked was another irritant. Older female members sometimes felt ignored because of their age, leading one to complain: 'there are a good many men who, with the increase of years and waist measurement, are unable to shed the flattering idea that it is their right, on public occasions, to be surrounded by young and glamorous women'.[85]

Such attitudes inevitably carried over into electoral work. Activists tended to be happiest campaigning in working-class constituencies but anxious when they moved outside these heartlands. It was not unknown for Labour trade unionists to ignore pleas for help from suburban parties because they believed that the better-off would always vote Tory.[86] Similar, though less tangible, inhibitions governed the discussion of issues. Most Labour members were quite confident about debating the problems they saw as dominating working-class life – for example, poor wages, unemployment and inadequate housing. However, other questions could easily raise hackles. As Chapter 6 has shown, frivolity was particularly frowned upon, and denounced in the Labour press. Too many, it was believed, were deceived by 'the capitalist daydream' and so the Party must stand firm, whether the threat be the evil of violent American films, gambling, the sale of contraceptives through automatic vending machines or the fashion industry's 'new look'.[87] Women, some judged, were particularly prone to erratic behaviour because they allegedly lacked political maturity and were thus highly vulnerable to publicity stunts.[88] They needed to be firmly reminded of their real interests. A contributor to *Labour Woman*, discussing meat rationing, demonstrated the right tone:

> I write as a frequent and uncomplaining recipient of thin flank or scrag-end. It happens that I am often out of town towards the end of the week and get back just on closing time at the butchers ... So I take what is left, and it is often not what one would wish. It does not occur to me to write to the Minister, or my M.P., or the *Daily Mail*. What occurs to me is this. 'Here I am with as big a piece of meat for myself as our mother could afford in most weeks of my childhood for five of us.'[89]

In the end, therefore, Labour's period of reassessment brought about less change than its originators intended. The 1949 conference had ratified a restyled programme and formally accepted Morrison's strong recommendation that the Party should widen its appeal whenever possible. However, this had not necessarily altered much at grass-roots level, since many activists continued to be guided by older and far less expansive nostrums. In this situation, coming to firm conclusions about how Labour stood with the electorate appeared difficult. The country was still beset by economic difficulties, not least a new sterling crisis. Would the Party faithful's determination to turn-out the working-class vote be enough? Some in the leadership were doubtful about this, but few completely pessimistic. Much would obviously depend on the Conservatives and this allowed some hope. For while the Tory revival had certainly continued in 1948 and 1949, there were good reasons for believing that it might already have peaked.

The Conservatives would certainly be formidable opponents. The momentum of the early post-war recovery was still in evidence. At head office, policy statements appeared with impressive frequency. Moreover, progress continued to be made with modernising methods and techniques. In 1948, the Conservatives began employing Colman, Prentis and Varley, a leading advertising agency, to help with their public presentation. More care, too, was being taken over preparations for the election. Precise information had been collected about various constituencies and used to construct a list of key marginals. Propaganda campaigns were targeted at groups who were considered 'floating' voters or especially likely to be disenchanted with Labour. The Tories had not neglected women, in fact appealing to the housewife with some regularity.[90]

The Conservative constituency parties also looked in good shape. A recruiting drive during 1948 had added another one million members (bringing the total to 2.4 million) and this allowed formidable levels of activity.[91] Developments at Poplar in East London were typical. In early 1948, the local Conservative organisation was virtually moribund, with no money, no premises and few members. By late 1948, however, the position had been transformed. Membership stood at nearly 2,000 and candidates were contesting all local elections. The party was confident enough to be holding regular outdoor meetings both at the nearby dock gates and in residential streets during the evenings.[92] Where a Tory presence had always been strong, the Party was now sometimes nearly hegemonic. Regular activities usually included the recreational and educational, as well as the political. A correspondent to the *Economist* in December 1949 described the Conservative ascendancy in the suburb where he lived and worked:

The social activities of about 20,000 people are, apart from the local cinema, now largely organised openly or at second-hand by Tory interests. Dances, lectures, outings, sports events and so forth are extremely well organised. The young men and women in their early twenties – those on the electoral register for the first time – are, almost without knowing it, Tory voters. A slick little magazine giving all the details of the social events drops through the letter box each month. It is, of course, strongly supported by local shop advertising.[93]

All of this was very impressive, but probing further revealed that the Tories had weaknesses as well as strengths. There were problems over policy formation. In 1946 and 1947, much emphasis had been placed on generating a 'new Conservatism' and some progress in this direction had been made. However, the process of revising doctrine appeared to have run its course.[94] Churchill was not interested, believing that the international situation deserved his full attention.[95] Moreover, the rank and file had other priorities: the cold war was becoming more pressing and with it the perceived need for vigilant anti-Communism. As a result, Party modernisers found their influence on the wane. A major policy statement of July 1949, *The Right Road for Britain*, illustrated the point. It contained grudging recognition that the state should play a minimal role in social and economic life, but was essentially concerned with emphasising a very traditional Tory vision centred on maximising individual choice. Much play was made with Labour's regulatory approach – 'We have too much planning and control, too much centralisation, too little money in the private hands of individual citizens, and a top-heavy administrative machinery too heavy and costly for the people to carry' – and there was a strong suggestion that Attlee was opening the door to Stalin.[96] The reforming zeal evident two years earlier had largely disappeared. In general terms, as a sympathetic critic noted, the Party's attitude seemed to be becoming increasingly reactionary, shaped more by 'the fear of losing privilege' than 'faith in an alternative and more equitable order of society'.[97]

At headquarters, meanwhile, the new techniques might appear innovative but they were not always having the desired effect. Colman, Prentis and Varley found Conservative strategists difficult to work with and felt much of their research had been wasted.

Dealing with the Tories, according to one advertising executive, 'was more infuriating than talking to a small-minded provincial manufacturer of shoe-laces'.[98] There were complaints, as well, about the sheer volume of material being churned out. An agent wrote of his office being 'flooded with circulars, pamphlets, exhortations on this ... homilies on that; requests for this information, requests for that; promptings to develop one particular side, urgings to increase activity in another'.[99] Even the much vaunted Conservative Political Centre was not above criticism. It had been created, in part, to help train ordinary members, but some felt that the literature disseminated was far too advanced and merely pandered to the Party intelligentsia.[100]

Finally, the position at grass-roots level was also not as healthy as it seemed. Many of the new members were only vaguely committed, prompting one experienced constituency activist to complain: 'The Tories are *not* putting in the effort necessary to make sure that we win the next election; the voluntary worker gives up far too easily when it comes to politics and canvassing, and only really shines in socials, whist drives and dances, very nice, but they don't win elections'.[101] Moreover, prejudices and divisions were just as common in the Tory ranks as elsewhere. Some Conservative women shunned their local parties, describing them as 'the men's organisation', while others would only vote for male candidates.[102] Many Tories shared a distaste for modern trends, criticising long skirts, holiday camps and even women who worked.[103] Most damaging, from the electoral point of view, was the common attitude to the working class. Conservatives were sensitive about accusations of snobbishness, and loud cheers greeted any speaker at conferences 'whose accent was either Cockney or provincial'. Nevertheless, few were prepared to join trade unions or Co-operative societies and a good many even refused to canvass in working-class areas.[104] This situation was obviously irritating for those contesting urban seats, and some appealed for a change of heart. The prospective candidate for Warrington in Lancashire told readers of *Tory Challenge* during 1949: 'You can get the working man's support, but you'll have to get down to him; he's not a biological specimen under a microscope nor a small boy to be patted on the head at election times. He is a living, vital, organism. He holds power. He prefers hoss-sense and good management to pity and flattery'. Whether this was right or not, there could be no doubt-

ing the gravity of the existing position. As another correspondent
to the same paper argued, the Tory approach to the working class
seemed 'psychologically wrong'.[105]

As Labour's term of office came to an end, therefore, few in either
main party appeared totally confident about the health of their
organisations. Levels of activity were impressive; as a visiting
French journalist remarked, the political machines were functioning 'like great industries'.[106] However, each side seemed unsure of
its overall strategy. Both had attempted to reorientate without total
success. In this atmosphere, attention inevitably began to be
focused more and more on the electorate. How were British voters
responding to the massive campaigns for their support?

On the surface, the evidence suggested that the Tory revival was
continuing. Gallup polls in the year to July 1949 gave the Conservatives an average three point lead.[107] The Party was doing well
amongst women – a poll of November 1949 found it held a fourteen point advantage over Labour here – and in terms of some key
target issues.[108] More importantly, its new found strength was again
evident at local elections: the 1949 contests yielded five county
councils, six London boroughs and over one thousand individual
seats.[109]

Nevertheless, as Party managers knew, the real position was
rather less certain. To begin with, the Tory lead, as measured by
Gallup, was not at a consistent level but fluctuated widely. Nor
were the Party's local election performances as significant as they
seemed. The issues at stake were usually parochial whilst turn-outs
tended to be low.[110] The important point, as many recognised, was
that the Conservatives were still not winning by-elections, for all
their improved votes. The result at Hammersmith South in March
1949 was felt to be indicative. The seat was a marginal but
remained in Labour hands, despite enormous efforts from the Conservatives and campaigning from Churchill himself.[111]

Detailed enquiries about attitudes and issues added to the impression of complexity. Opinions about each party differed considerably.
Many felt that Labour, to begin with, had failed on important
domestic policy questions, such as housing.[112] A large minority
remained convinced, too, as in previous years, that the Party was
over-ideological. The nationalisation of steel, now before Parliament, had never been popular, while other projected nationalisa-
tions hardly provoked enthusiasm, even among Labour

supporters.[113] As a general judgement, in both 1948 and 1949, about 45 per cent of electors agreed that the administration was 'too socialist', compared to the 13 or 14 per cent who believed it to be 'not socialist enough'.[114] On the other hand, Labour also evoked some positive responses. Attlee was personally popular, and the public recognised that some of the Government's problems were caused by external and uncontrollable forces.[115] Policy failures had to be balanced against policy successes, such as Labour's handling of both the economy and the continuing food shortages, and, most importantly, its welfare reforms.[116] Indeed, Labour's long-standing identification with social justice for the ordinary person still counted for much. A confidential Conservative head office evaluation of early 1949 concluded:

[Labour] ... draws its main strengths out of the following beliefs:
i   The working man must keep faith with his own class.
ii Labour alone is responsible for full employment, shorter hours and better social services.
iii All restrictions are simply to ensure fair shares all round.[117]

Assessments of the Tories were equally varied. Many women had concluded that the Conservatives genuinely cared about their everyday difficulties with shopping and housekeeping.[118] The Party inevitably benefited, too, from a pervasive feeling amongst the better-off that they had been especially badly treated by Labour, in fact 'subjected to a cold class-war'.[119] On the other hand, it was by no means certain what such judgements would mean when it came to voting. Working-class women, it was commonly believed, would be subject to much pressure from their Labour-supporting husbands, with unforeseeable results.[120] Nor was middle-class support necessarily guaranteed: dislike of Labour was balanced in some quarters by suspicion that the Conservatives remained a 'party of privilege'.[121] A further important element in the whole equation was the legacy of the interwar years. The Tories had tried hard to distance themselves from any association with the long depression, but many workers of both sexes and all ages remained unconvinced. As a party document of early 1949 candidly admitted, 'unemployment' was 'the universal one-word indictment of Conservative policy between the wars', with all that this implied for current voting intentions.[122]

One final factor added to the unpredictability of the situation.

Those in politics tended to assume that the public shared their ways of thinking and basic enthusiasms. However, such a view was somewhat unrealistic. Many ordinary people certainly had opinions about politics and believed the party battle to be significant,[123] but this did not mean that they were necessarily doing much hard thinking about these subjects. Indeed, judgements were frequently based on observations about politicians' personality or style, with issues disregarded entirely. A Mass-Observation study of newspaper reading habits was very indicative about the character of popular preferences:

> *On the whole, although the majority of people look at the political news, it is only to glance at it.* Relatively few ignore it completely, but on the other hand equally few show signs of any real interest in it. And though most of people's reading time, in so far as dailies are concerned, is devoted to news, it is largely the sort of home news that is partly gossip, and that has an easy personal appeal.[124]

Moreover, politics, even in these terms, was only one of many matters that troubled people, and so could easily be accorded a low priority. Pearl Jephcott reported in the *New Statesman* that her fellow employees in a light engineering factory rarely discussed current affairs:

> The girls' talk hardly ranged beyond two themes, personal appearance and personal relations. The latter means fellows – mine, yours, hers. Even among the older women the only public event in the last three months which has fished folk out of the sea of personal and domestic affairs has been the Derby.[125]

Zweig made a similar observation about male workers, concluding that 'the average working man' was 'far more interested in sport than politics'.[126] In fact, from the workbench or parlour, the antics of politicians could seem very distant and not particularly relevant. The editor of *Woman* was challenged about why so few 'really intelligent' letters appeared in her weekly – letters dealing with 'conditions and circumstances in the world *outside* the home'. In reply, she spelt out what many of her three million readers probably felt instinctively when such matters were raised:

> At first we were puzzled by your use of 'intelligent', until we realized that what you really mean is 'political'.

It is true that we rarely print political letters; like most women, we usually find politics oddly out of touch with real life.

Our contribution to international affairs is not given in a viewpoint but in practical help for each other. No fine feminine phrases will influence the cows but a milk stretching recipe will make it easier for a million or more British households to manage with less pints.

Most women have no time to talk or write about the political aspect of modern life; they are busy living it in every trip to market, in every creditable child.[127]

In these circumstances, it was very hard to make any authoritative assessment about how the country would finally vote. One Tory source suggested that each main party had about ten million convinced supporters, while the Liberals and other organisations might poll about three million. The outcome, therefore, depended upon five million waverers or floaters.[128] Some Conservatives were confident about their prospects with this group, but by the end of 1949, a mood of 'defeatism and despondency' was said to be spreading in the Party's ranks, not helped by London Stock Exchange brokers offering odds of eleven to eight against a change of government.[129] R.B. McCallum, who had written a study of the 1945 election, felt that neither Attlee or Churchill could be hopeful. He told the *Observer* in early January 1950:

although on the Labour shore the tide may be ebbing, it is not at all obviously rising to the same degree on the other side. Of positive new support for the Conservatives there are, indeed, remarkably few signs. The upshot is that a large part of the country is facing the election disillusioned with Socialism but unconverted to Conservatism.[130]

On 11 January 1950, Attlee finally announced that his Government was leaving office and that an election would be held on 23 February. A few days later, the main political parties launched their campaigns. The central points raised in manifestos and speeches echoed themes that had been repeated many times over the previous few years. Labour made little reference to nationalisation and emphasised its record on fair shares, welfare reform and full employment. The post-war years, it argued, had seen real social and economic progress which was in stark contrast to the waste and misery of the 1930s. Nowhere was the Party's message clearer than in relation to jobs: as one observer noted, 'Full employment and unemployment were a sunshine and shadow pair that Labour put in the forefront of their morality play'.[131] The Tories attacked high government spending, nationalisation and 'the big state' generally, asserting that Britain would only finally prosper if individual initiative was once again allowed to reign free. This latter point was stressed again and again. Questioned about the fundamental division between the two parties, the Conservatives' Deputy Chairman replied: 'I would say, from the ordinary voters' point of view, the difference is between living one's own life and having it planned for one'. Churchill provided further elaboration in a keynote speech:

> The British nation now has to make one of the most momentous choices in its history. The choice is between two ways of life – between individual liberty and State domination; between concentration of ownership in the hands of the State and the extension of a property-owning democracy; between a policy of increasing restraint and a policy of liberating energy and ingenuity; between a policy of levelling down and a policy of finding opportunity for all to rise upwards from a basic standard.[132]

To publicise their ideas, both parties used the techniques that had been steadily introduced since 1945. Each made use of radio broadcasts and newspaper coverage, but both placed most emphasis on what was termed 'planned electioneering' at local level. Teams of canvassers toured areas, street by street, visiting each house in order to compile a picture of preferences. Subsequent attention was then concentrated on 'doubtfuls'. The local campaigns were accompanied by a massive outpouring of literature, with the Labour Party alone distributing 15.3 million leaflets, 2.4 million broadsheets, 749,000 pamphlets, 420,000 window cards or strips, and 174,000 posters.[133]

All of this activity inevitably attracted intense media interest. Most newspapers were fairly partisan and forecast victory for their favourites, but more detached observers remained unsure about the probable result. A boundary revision enacted in 1948 was thought likely to benefit the Conservatives, possibly by as many as thirty seats.[134] Furthermore, the Tory electoral machine seemed to be in better order; 'Admiral Woolton', the *Economist* noted, commanded 'a fleet of well-run ships', very different from Labour's 'tramp steamers, in need of paint and repair'.[135] On the other hand, Labour would almost certainly gain from the fact that the electoral register was 'probably the most efficient yet compiled', because on previous occasions non-registration had been most prevalent amongst the poor.[136] A further complication was introduced by the record number of candidates who were standing. This meant fewer straight fights – 112 compared to 274 in 1945 – and a potentially bigger role for the small parties. The Liberals appeared most likely to gain: they were fielding 475 candidates (168 more than in 1945) and had a strong presence in the South West, Wales and parts of Lancashire.[137]

Nevertheless, as before, the biggest unknown in the situation was how ordinary people would react to the two main parties' campaigning. Polls and enquiries provided only a degree of clarification. It was evident that few in the electorate were much interested in foreign affairs or abstract ideologies. What people wanted were answers to everyday problems – more housing, lower prices and taxes, and a guarantee of continued full employment. However, there was no certain link between this and political preferences. Both parties were judged competent on some issues, but there was also a considerable degree of scepticism present. People listened to politicians' promises without necessarily believing them.[138]

Indeed, if the popular mood was taken as a whole, it could probably best be described as resolutely downbeat. In mid-January, *Public Opinion* reported that 'the political temperature' was 'low' and described 'the great majority of voters' as 'not enthusiastic'. Three weeks later, the *Economist* believed little had changed, and suggested that the election might well prove 'the most private ... of modern times'.[139] Detailed research pointed in a similar direction. Only about one-third of the electorate regularly listened to party political broadcasts.[140] A study of 600 voters in six London constituencies found that, one week before polling day, 86 per cent of the sample had not attended a political meeting and 44 per cent had not read an election leaflet. Over 60 per cent were unable to name all the candidates standing in their area.[141] Mass-Observation, too, was struck by the absence of mass political engagement. One of its panel toured East Ham on the 18 February and recorded: 'In all the afternoon I could not discover a single remark with any bearing on the election – on the streets, outside shops, in cafés – the people were shopping and that's all'.[142] Even on polling day itself, there was apparently little sense of excitement. The scene in

Trafalgar Square during the evening was typical:

> The atmosphere throughout the night was extremely good natured.
> There seemed no real bitterness, nor any great anxiety about the
> results. The teenagers and younger people seemed to regard the
> whole thing as a rag – the older people ... were quieter and although
> there seemed to be tremendous interest and absorption in the results
> there was no evidence of very deep personal feeling or concern
> except in a minority of cases.[143]

The upshot of the election surprised many but pleased few. The
turn-out had been an enormous 84 per cent – 10.5 per cent bigger
than five years earlier. Labour was the winner in terms of voters,
though its percentage of the poll had fallen by about 2.5 points,
producing a much reduced number of seats and an overall majority of a mere five in the Commons. The smaller parties had performed badly, returning only twelve MPs between them, so that in
effect the country was polarised between Labour and the Conservatives. Some saw this as reflecting a cleavage between industrial
and suburban Britain, but the reality was more complex. Many
constituencies were fairly evenly divided and even the heartland
areas of both parties had large 'deviant' minorities. As the *Economist* commented: 'It is a remarkable thing that very nearly one
voter in three in South Wales is a Tory and on the south coast is a
Socialist'.[144]

Reaction to these results varied. The left-wing press welcomed
Labour's return and argued that its victory, won despite difficult
circumstances, demonstrated the popular will for more change.
Newspapers and journals sympathetic to the Tories expressed relief
that the socialist adventure had been ended. The *Financial Times*
was typical in celebrating the fact that the new administration's
power of action would be 'severely and mercifully limited'.[145] The
less partisan tended to agree with the *Economist*'s wry assessment
that Labour had 'suffered a Pyrrhic victory'. The most striking point
was that the Party had failed to rouse all of those who might be
considered its 'natural' supporters. *Public Opinion*, for example,
observed: 'In the most critical and exciting peace-time years in
Britain, with the social ideas of the Welfare State being applied with
such effect that nowhere in the world is the available wealth more
fairly shared, the majority of the people are dully disinterested or
drearily resentful'. Accordingly, the future for Labour appeared

bleak. The second Attlee administration would have to call an election sooner rather than later, which the Conservatives were very likely to win.[146]

In the Party itself, the new position reopened the debates of 1948 and 1949. Initial attention focused on the pattern of voting. All sides generally agreed that Labour had not polled to its full potential. The Party had lost ground amongst the middle class and failed to prevent 29 per cent of the working class from voting Tory.[147] Two groups appeared to present particular difficulties. Working-class women had been increasingly drawn to Labour since 1945 but were still significantly less likely to vote for the Party than their male counterparts.[148] In addition, support had clearly declined amongst black-coated workers of both sexes. The latter often lived in 'the non-community conscious dormitory areas', it was said, and perhaps saw themselves as having joined the middle class. They commonly aspired to be freeholders, and had been particularly impressed by the Tory conception of a property-owning democracy.[149] None of this augured very well for the future, but there was a further worrying dimension to the problem. The Liberals had stood in most constituencies at the 1950 election and polled 2.6 million votes (compared to Labour's 13.3 million). They were now in financial difficulties and did not envisage presenting such a full slate for some time to come. It was hazardous to predict how existing Liberal voters would behave in the future but the opinion polls seemed to show that the majority currently saw the Conservatives as their second preference. Unless the problem was addressed, therefore, Labour might find itself starting the next election with an inbuilt disadvantage.[150]

While these facts were largely incontrovertible, there was considerable argument when it came to deciding what they meant for future strategy. Those sympathetic to Morrison believed that the psephological data were of fundamental significance. Labour would always be based on the blue-collar working class but it must in future look very seriously at securing wider support. Phillip Williams, writing in *Socialist Commentary*, clarified the argument: 'Industrial England alone, it is now obvious, can give the Labour Party office but not power; and if the stalemate is to be broken, other groups must be won over. This need not necessarily mean a watered-down policy, but some shifts in policy may and some changes of attitude will be required'.[151] Put differently, Labour must transform itself from a class organisation into a national party moving in a socialist direction.[152]

On the left of the Party, the perspectives were very different. The core belief here was that working-class people of all types would always respond to a clear radical message. Current petty snobberies and political confusions, whatever research or polls indicated, were essentially ephemeral. Their prevalence, in fact, partly reflected Labour's recent tendency to conceal central arguments 'shame-facedly in the wings'.[153] If the Party was to progress, therefore, it must cease trimming and return to articulating real socialist values. The record of government policy since 1945, particularly over nationalisation, made this comparatively easy, as the editor of *Tribune* indicated:

> The Labour Party is a Socialist Party, and Socialism is the dream of
> a new society and a new moral order for mankind. The great advan-
> tage in preaching that doctrine which we have over the pioneers ...
> is that in the past few years socialist principles have started to be
> applied in practice. And they work. The proof is there. It only needs
> to be argued and told.[154]

The converse of this was that far less attention should be given to the problem of the middle-class vote. Attempting to target measures at the better-off could only impede Labour's fundamental purpose; as one left-wing MP declared, 'The suggestion that a party pro-gramme should be a patchwork quilt of varied promises would give to political progress the gait and speed of an inebriated crab'. The middle class should be dealt with firmly, and told that 'in the inter-ests of social justice' they would be 'called on to make sacrifices'.[155]

In May 1950, Labour's National Executive, the Cabinet and rep-resentatives from the TUC and the Co-operative Societies met in an attempt to resolve these differences. Morrison dominated the dis-cussions though he was once again unable to secure a complete victory. Much of the debate remained inconclusive, and there was no real consensus about how Labour might increase its support. As the discussion on the middle-class vote revealed, there was still an unbridgeable gap between those who wanted an alliance of 'all the useful people' and those who clung to a belief in the efficacy of socialist slogans.[156] The final outcome was a distinct lack of fresh thinking: the leadership backed 'a more dynamic form of consoli-dation' – a formula designed to preserve unity – but this encompassed few new policy alternatives. The only significant departure was organisational: a decision to concentrate resources wherever possible on marginal constituencies.[157]

The Conservative discussion of the 1950 result in some ways followed a parallel trajectory. Activists were very dispirited by their defeat and there was a brief period of recrimination. Some wanted a more distinct statement of traditional Tory values while others called for the further elaboration of recent reformist ideas.[158] Nevertheless, by the time of the autumn conference, such debate had largely petered out. In fact, the occasion was most notable for its 'careful and cautious' resolutions and rehearsal of long-standing prejudices, with one journalist observing: 'The hardy annuals of Imperial Preference and free enterprise performed their functions of stimulating unity and enthusiasm'. The only notable moment came during the housing debate, when an apparent rebellion from the floor pledged the Party to build 300,000 homes per year (about one-third more that Labour was currently managing) if it won the election.[159]

Public reaction to these developments remained difficult to gauge. There were certainly reasons for believing that Labour was losing popularity. Britain had become embroiled in the Korean war during mid-1950 and this was obviously causing widespread anxiety. No-one could be sure, given the tension with the Communist bloc, that the fighting would not spread. Moreover, the successive rearmaments programmes of September 1950 and January 1951 threatened a sharp rise in prices. The Labour Government's discomfort was magnified further by a split about how to pay for the new commitments, which eventually led to the resignation of Bevan and two other left-wing ministers. Meanwhile, the Tory initiative on housing seemed to be producing results. Indeed, one regional official claimed: 'Although economists may frown, the promise of a 300,000 a year housing programme has done more to ease the path of the doorstep canvasser than any charter, however profound, far-seeing and progressive'.[160] In these circumstances, support for the Conservatives inevitably surged: the Party had opened up a 14 point lead in the polls by February 1951 and it maintained this position well into the summer.[161]

Nevertheless, Labour was not without hope. In working-class areas, old fears about the Tories – that they would 'bring unemployment, cut the Social Services, and drive us into war ' – continued to be common and offered a considerable opportunity for effective propaganda.[162] In addition, Labour's performance at the spring 1951 local government elections was broadly reassuring, for while the Conservatives won seats, most of these were at the expense of independents.[163] In fact, the Party's biggest problem appeared to be its internal difficulties. Bevan was extremely popular with activists and his departure from the Government provoked much soul searching. Certainly, reports from the constituencies indicated that many lacked enthusiasm when it came to canvassing.[164] However, even this situation had a positive side: after all, it was certain that most stalwart members would return to the fray once a national contest begun.

In late September 1951, Attlee finally announced that a general election would be held on 25 October. The campaign started with each party launching its manifesto. The Labour document contained four sections – on peace, full employment and production, the cost of living and social justice – and ended with a warning in bold type:

> Welfare at home, peace abroad, with a constant striving for international Co-operation – this is Labour's [way]. The Tories with their dark past, full of bitter memories for so many of our people, promise no light for the future. They would take us backward into poverty and insecurity at home and grave peril abroad.[165]

The Conservatives also relied on some familiar themes. The Party once again attacked big government in all its forms and suggested that most of Britain's problems were the result of state interference. Housing was given a priority second only to defence, with the emphasis on maximising owner-occupation. The key theme, repeated in many speeches, was the promise to revive personal initiative. As Churchill explained during an election broadcast, 'the difference between the Conservative and Socialist outlook was the difference between the ladder and the queue – on the one hand a chance for everyone to rise (with the finest social ambulance service in the world should they fall off), and on the other the flat monotony of each in his turn'.[166]

Over the following few weeks, each party settled into a definitive strategy. Labour stressed its achievements and implied that the Tories could not be trusted, particularly over full employment and foreign policy. The Conservative campaign, meanwhile, was shaped

by the fact that the Liberals were standing 366 fewer candidates
than in 1950. Thus, issues focused upon included not only 'the
need for rearmament', 'the Commonwealth and Empire' and
'socialist extravagance' but also 'the maintenance of full employment', 'the need for increased production' and 'the need for a
review of pension rates'.[167] The practical consequences of this pattern could be seen in the constituencies. Both parties believed that,
as before, the election would be won or lost because of local campaigning, and consequently each put enormous effort into maximising traditional activities like canvassing. Indeed, the *Economist*
reported: 'As a struggle between party machines, the election was
more intense than ever'.[168] However, the Conservatives everywhere
made great efforts to woo the Liberal vote, and in seven of the eight
cases where no Tory was standing, they actually went so far as to
provide practical help for the Liberal candidates' campaigns.[169]

The public's reaction to all this activity remained mixed. The
majority of voters were, as in 1950, most concerned with practical
issues, particularly rising prices. Each party was judged to have different competencies, with the Conservatives being favoured on
inflation and housing, and Labour on employment and the maintenance of peace.[170] Nevertheless, the election again produced relatively little passion. Many voters were not particularly convinced by
any of the politicians; as one opinion poll organisation discovered,
'My party right or wrong, may be the battle cry, but only one-half
are firmly convinced they are right'.[171] Moreover, though few completely ignored the campaigning, most took a passive rather than
active interest. A detailed enquiry found that public participation
could be ranked in the following way:[172]

	%
Listened to radio speeches	82
Read election addresses	52
Went to indoor meetings	24
Listened to television speakers	12
Went to outdoor meetings	10
Canvassed for candidate	3
Did other work for candidate	3

In fact, it appeared that much of the political effort had less than the desired impact. Altogether about half of Britain's homes were visited by party workers in the weeks before polling day and this often strengthened people's will to vote. However, only about 1 per cent of those canvassed reported that the activity had actually changed their allegiances.[173] The general lack of interest was widely remarked upon by journalists. Writing in the *Spectator* on 19 October, Edward Hodgkin reported that the electorate was 'in an advanced state of catalepsy'. He added: 'Any visitor who landed in London last week-end would have found it hard to discover from external evidence which of the two forthcoming attractions – the General Election and Christmas – was due first'.[174] Even at the end of the campaign, levels of engagement remained low, as another report indicated: 'On election night one half of the public went to bed and did not bother to wait up and learn the fortunes of the parties. Five per cent were content to hear the first one or two results, going to bed at 11 p.m. Another 15 per cent waited till midnight, whilst a sturdy 9 per cent were still about at 3 a.m.'.[175]

When the election results were announced, it was immediately obvious that Labour's six year term of office had come to an end. The turn-out figure was a large 82.5 per cent, allowing Labour to poll the record number of votes for a single party ever. However, there had been a 1.1 per cent swing to the Tories and this was enough to give them twenty-two new seats and thus a small over-all majority in the Commons. Much of the change could be explained in terms of the absence of Liberal candidates: between eight and eighteen seats had fallen to the Tories for this reason.[176] Morgan Phillips concluded that the result could hardly be seen as indicating any great sea-change in British politics:

> It is difficult to pinpoint any particular issue as having had a deci-
> sive influence on the minds of the electorate, although the cost of
> living and the war danger appeared to be well ahead of other ques-
> tions in many areas. Fear may have been the dominant element in
> many people's minds – fear of the consequences of a Tory victory on
> the one hand and irrationally fostered fears of the consequences of a
> Labour victory on the other.

The Party could be pleased with its level of support, he added, though there was no reason for complacency: 'we cannot overlook the fact that Labour's poll of 48.7 per cent of all votes cast, only represents 40 per cent of the electorate'.[177]

Notes

1 See A. Cairncross, *Years of Recovery* (London, 1985) and N. Tiratsoo and J. Tomlinson, *Industrial Efficiency and State Intervention: Labour 1939–51* (London, 1993).
2 A.L. Williams, 'What's Behind the Membership Figures', *Labour Organiser*, 26:299 (1947), 4–5.
3 *Tribune*, 11 April 1947.
4 W.A. Robson, 'Post-War Municipal Elections in Great Britain', *American Political Science Review*, 61:2 (1947), 294–306.
5 *Tribune*, 7 February, 14 February, and 7 March 1947.
6 J. Parker, *Labour Marches On* (Harmondsworth, 1947), p. 190, and H.L. Beales, 'Has Labour Come to Stay?', *Political Quarterly*, 18:1 (1947), 59–60.
7 See A. Robertson, *The Bleak Midwinter, 1947* (Manchester, 1987) and K.O. Morgan, *Labour in Power 1945–51* (Oxford, 1984), esp. pp. 330–58.
8 J.H. Hodson, *The Way Things Are* (London, 1947), p. 309.
9 R. Lewis and A. Maude, *The English Middle Classes* (London, 1949), pp. 94–5.
10 Anon., '"Little More Than Living"', *Mass-Observation Bulletin*, 17 (1948), 1–4.
11 E.M. Hubback, 'Any Time for Grumbling?', *Current Affairs*, 49 (1948), 6 and 7.
12 *News Chronicle*, 18 March 1948.
13 G.H. Gallup, *The Gallup International Public Opinion Polls. Great Britain 1937–1975, Volume One* (New York, 1976), pp. 173 and 168.
14 *Public Opinion Quarterly*, (Winter 1947–48), 650, and Gallup, *Opinion Polls*, p. 173.
15 Gallup, *Opinion Polls*, pp. 126, 136, 148, 160, 165 and 175.
16 *Ibid.*, p. 148.
17 *Daily Express*, 12 April 1948.
18 Gallup, *Opinion Polls*, pp. 173–4.
19 *Ibid.*, pp. 135, 136, 152, 157, 160, 166, 167, and 171.
20 N. Nicholson, 'His Majesty's Opposition', in A.G. Weidenfeld (ed), *The Public's' Progress* (London, 1947), p. 33.
21 W.W. Astor, 'The Conservative Party in Opposition', *New English Review*, 12:4 (1946), 344–8.
22 *Ibid.* and E.D. O'Brien, 'The Three "Ps"', *New English Review*, 11:5 (1945), 458–9.

23 'D.S.', 'Why the Pendulum Swings', *Onlooker*, (May 1947), 2.

24 The following paragraphs are partly based on J.D. Hoffman, *The Conservative Party in Opposition*, (London, 1964) and J. Ramsden, '"A Party for Owners or a Party for Earners?" How Far Did the British Conservative Party Really Change after 1945?', *Transactions of the Royal Historical Society*, 5:37 (1987), 49–63.

25 Conservative Party, *'Trust The People' Exhibition. Souvenir Programme and Guide* (London, 1947), p. 5.

26 *Ibid.* p. 3 and Anthony Eden reported in *Onlooker*, (November 1946), 5.

27 Hoffman, *Conservative Party in Opposition*, pp. 133–66 and editorial comment, *Labour Forum*, 1:4 (1947), 1.

28 Hoffman, *Conservative Party in Opposition*, pp. 68–70 and 83–4.

29 *Ibid.*, pp. 81–127.

30 R. Kisch, *The Private Life of Public Relations* (London, 1964), pp. 32–3; *Weekly News Letter*, 28 August 1948; and 'Contributed', 'The Fifth Column', *Conservative Agents' Journal*, 327 (1948), 44–5.

31 J.D. Goldsworthy, 'The Shipley Conservative Week', *Conservative Agents' Journal*, 324 (1947), 245–9, and P. Crawforth Smith, 'Operation London', *Tory Challenge*, 1:10 (1948), 5.

32 Gallup, *Opinion Polls*, pp. 152, 158 and 161.

33 Labour Party, *Report of the Forty-Ninth Annual Conference of the Labour Party* (London, 1950), p. 35.

34 Editorial, *Labour Organiser*, 26:299 (1947), 3.

35 Tower Hamlets Local History Library, T.H. 8488, Box 17 (1), Stepney Labour Party minute book, entry for 25 June, 1947.

36 Durham Record Office, D/X 1871/1, Boldon Colliery Labour Party minute book, entry for 29 September 1947.

37 Labour Party, *Report of the Forty-Seventh Annual Conference of the Labour Party* (London, 1948), p. 115.

38 *Economist*, 27 November 1948.

39 Anon., 'Political Stocktaking', *Socialist Commentary*, 3 (1947), 51–2, and G.D.H. Cole, *A History of the Labour Party from 1914* (London, 1948), pp. 457–9.

40 Editor's letter, *Labour Woman*, 35:11 (1947), 252–3.

41 *Economist*, 8 November 1947.

42 Labour, *Forty-Seventh Conference*, pp. 121–2.

43 See B. Donoughue and G.W. Jones, *Herbert Morrison. Portrait of a Politician* (London, 1973).

44 Anon., 'Let Us Face 1950. An Interview with Rt. Hon. Herbert Mor-

rison', *Labour Forum*, 1:8 (1948), 6–9. See also Labour Party Archive, Manchester [hereafter LPA], R.D. 173/Oct. 1948, H. Morrison, 'Some Considerations As To The Next General Election', 18 October 1948.

45 W. Wyatt, 'Let Us Face 1950', *Labour Forum*, 1:6 (1948), 6–7.
46 Editorial, *Women's Co-operative Guild Monthly Bulletin*, 10:5 (1949), 1–2.
47 G. Green, 'Counting the Middle Classes', *Socialist Commentary*, (1947), 705–8 and *Listener*, 11 March 1948.
48 *Forward*, 30 April 1949.
49 I. Mikardo, 'The Second Five Years', *Fabian Research*, 124, (London, 1948), p. 21.
50 Labour, *Forty-Seventh Conference*, p. 123.
51 See Donoughue and Jones, *Herbert Morrison*, pp. 442–7.
52 LPA, Policy and Publicity Committee, Minutes (7), 17 January 1949, 4.
53 *Economist*, 16 April 1949.
54 Labour Party, *Labour Believes in Britain* (London,1949), pp. 16–17.
55 *Ibid.*, p. 18.
56 *Economist*, 2 April 1949.
57 *Tribune*, 9 April 1948.
58 Labour Party, *Report of the Forty-Eighth Annual Conference of the Labour Party* (London, 1949), p. 172.
59 *Economist*, 11 June 1949.
60 Labour, *Forty-Eighth Conference*, p. 211.
61 For example, see *Tribune*, 14 February 1947.
62 W. Crofts, *Coercion or Persuasion* (London, 1989), passim.
63 J. Margach, *The Abuse of Power* (London, 1979), p. 86.
64 *Tribune*, 2 January 1948.
65 F. Shepherd, 'Problems Facing Us in "Suburbia"', *Labour Organiser*, 28:326 (1948), 11.
66 *Forward*, 12 February 1949.
67 Socialist Publicity Service, *Putting It Over* (London, n.d.), p. 11.
68 *Daily Express*, 1 March 1949.
69 Anon., 'Building a Labour Hall', *Labour Organiser*, 28:326 (1949), 8.
70 F. Barber, 'Some Faults in Labour Papers', *Labour Organiser*, 26:300 (1947), 11.
71 A.J. McWhinnie, 'A Journalist Looks at the Party Machine', *Labour Organiser*, 26:302, (1947), 5.
72 S.C. Terry, 'Do We Make Membership Too Easy?', *Labour Organiser*, 26:305 (1947), 9.

73 W. Fienburgh *et al.*, 'Put Policy on the Agenda', *Fabian Journal*, 6 (1952), 32.

74 Tom Harrisson Mass-Observation Archive, the University of Sussex [hereafter THMOA], TC Beveridge Report surveys 1942–7, Box 2, File E, Report by K.B., 'Colerain's Labour Party Women's Section. Weekly Meeting', 30 July 1947.

75 Modern Records Centre, University of Warwick, MSS 9/3/12/60, A.D.O., 'Meeting with Officers of the Sports Section of the Bethnal Green Labour Party ...', 12 August 1948.

76 *Forward*, 4 March 1950.

77 J.A. Roberts, 'Tamworth – Apathy and Athletics', *Socialist Advance*, (1951), 13.

78 F. Moxley, 'Let Us Organise for Victory', *Labour Organiser*, 28:323 (1949), 16.

79 See S. Fielding, 'Labourism in the 1940s', *Twentieth Century British History*, 3:2 (1992), 138–53; and N. Tiratsoo, 'Popular Politics, Affluence and the Labour Party in the 1950s', in A. Gorst *et al.* (eds), *Contemporary British History 1931–1961* (London 1991), pp. 56–8.

80 J.A. Yates, *Pioneers To Power* (Coventry, 1950), p. 122.

81 LPA, Morgan Phillips Papers, Box 6, File GS/ys/1–75, M. Windsor *et al.*, 'The Labour Party and Youth', September 1950, pp. 6–7; and 'A Section Secretary', 'Do You Want the Young Member?', *Labour Woman*, 34:12 (1946), 266–7.

82 M. Morris, 'Give the Women Their Chance', *Labour Organiser*, 27:310 (1948), 16–17.

83 V. Pearce, 'Our Women: Are We Making the Best Use of Their Ability', *Labour Organiser*, 26:301 (1947), 11.

84 P. Crane, 'The Real Problems for Women Party Workers', *Labour Organiser*, 27:312 (1948), 12.

85 J. Geddes, 'Mainly for Men ...', *Labour Woman*, 37:11 (1949), 244.

86 Shepherd, 'Problems', *Labour Organiser*, 12.

87 *Forward*, 5 August 1950; Labour Party, *Report of the Twenty-Sixth National Conference of Labour Women, 1948* (London, 1948), p. 21; *Forward*, 25 June 1949; *Women's Co-operative Guild Monthly Bulletin*, 10:11 (1949), 6–7; and J. Worley 'Is the New Look for the Likes of Us?', *Young Socialist*, 1:20 (1948), 5.

88 *Forward*, 8 December 1947; Labour Party, *Report of the Twenty-Seventh National Conference of Labour Women, 1949* (London, 1949), pp. 25–7.

89 'M.E.S.', 'Pity the Poor Housewife – Why?', *Labour Woman*, 37:2

(1949), 30–1.

90 Hoffman, *Conservative Party in Opposition*, pp. 172–95 and I. Zweiniger-Bargielowska, 'Rationing, Austerity and the Conservative Party Recovery after 1945', *Historical Journal*, 37:1 (1994), 173–97.

91 Hoffman, *Conservative Party in Opposition*, p. 90.

92 Conservative Party Archive, Bodleian Library, Oxford, [hereafter CPA], CCO 1/7/31, Borough of Poplar Conservative and Unionist Association, 'Agenda and Annual Report for year ended 30 December 1949'.

93 *Economist*, 10 December 1949.

94 E. Willenz, 'The Conservative Party in Britain since 1945', *Social Research*, 16:1 (1949), 28–30.

95 *Economist*, 5 March 1949 and P. Addison, *Churchill on the Home Front* (London, 1992), pp. 386–407.

96 Conservative Party, *The Right Road for Britain* (London, 1949), pp. 7–8.

97 *Spectator*, 15 October 1948.

98 M. Abrams, 'Public Opinion Polls and Political Parties', *Public Opinion Quarterly*, 27:1 (1963), 11.

99 Anon., 'Clear the Decks', *Conservative Agents' Journal*, 329 (1948), 77–8.

100 Letter in *Objective*, 6 (1950), 7.

101 Letter to *Tory Challenge*, 2:8 (1949), 10.

102 M. Maxse, 'The Conservative Party Organisation 1922–1951', *Tory Challenge*, 4:11 (1951), 1, and E. Hodder, *Hats Off! to Conservative Women* (London, 1990), pp. 24–5.

103 Feature article in *Tory Challenge*, 1:5 (1947), 6–7; R. Pole and J. Seymour, 'Holiday Camps', *Tory Challenge*, 2:2 (1948), 6–7; and Hodder, *Hats Off!*, p. 22.

104 Nicholson, 'Opposition', p. 34; and letter in *Tory Challenge*, 3:1 (1949), 10.

105 Letters in *Tory Challenge*, 2:12 (1949), 10 and 2:10 (1949), 10.

106 P. Treves, *England, the Mysterious Island* (London, 1948), p. 70.

107 Gallup, *Opinion Polls*, pp. 178, 180, 182, 184, 187, 190, 193, 195, 196–7, 199, 200 and 202.

108 *Economist*, 7 January 1950.

109 P. Williams, '1949 Elections Analysed', *Socialist Commentary*, 13:7 (1949), 163–5.

110 *Economist*, 7 May 1949.

111 *Economist*, 5 March 1949.

112 Gallup, *Opinion Polls*, pp. 158, 191, 206 and 212.

113 *Ibid.*, pp. 168, 191, 206 and 213; *Picture Post*, 21 May 1949 and 12 November 1949.

114 Gallup, *Opinion Polls*, pp. 173, 190–1, 206 and 212–13.

115 *Ibid.*, pp. 189 and 207; *Picture Post*, 12 December 1949.

116 Gallup, *Opinion Polls*, pp. 170 and 215; *Public Opinion Quarterly*, 176 (1950), 176.

117 CPA, CCO 4/3/249, Public Opinion Summary No. 1, January 1949, p. 2.

118 *Ibid.*, p. 6.

119 *Spectator*, 27 January 1950.

120 CPA, CCO 4/3/249, Public Opinion Summary No. 12, December 1949, p. 7.

121 *Economist*, 31 January 1948.

122 CPA, CCO 4/3/249, Public Opinion Summary No. 1, January 1949, p. 4.

123 Gallup, *Opinion Polls*, pp. 187, 197 and 212.

124 Mass-Observation, *The Press and Its Readers* (London, 1949), p. 23.

125 *New Statesman*, 11 September 1948.

126 F. Zweig, *The British Worker*, (Harmondsworth, 1952), p. 189.

127 *Woman*, 1 October 1949.

128 CPA, CCO 4/3/249, Public Opinion Summary No. 10, October 1949, p. 1.

129 CPA, CCO 4/3/249, P.O.R.D. Confidential Supplement to Public Opinion Summary No. 12, December 1949, p. 1.

130 *Observer*, 15 January 1950.

131 H.G. Nicholas, *The British General Election of 1950* (London, 1951), p. 97.

132 *Illustrated*, 11 February 1950 and the *Barking and East Ham Express*, 3 February 1950.

133 LPA, NEC Minutes, 22 March 1950, Morgan Phillips, 'General Election Campaign. Head Office Service', [n.d.], p. 2.

134 *Economist*, 7 January 1950.

135 *Economist*, 4 February 1950.

136 *Economist*, 7 January 1950.

137 A.H. Booth, *British Hustings 1924–50* (London, 1956), p. 251; Nicholas, *General Election*, passim.

138 S.J. Eldersveld, 'British Polls and the 1950 General Election', *Public Opinion Quarterly*, 15 (1951), 130–1; Mass-Observation, *The Voters' Choice* (London, 1950), pp. 8–9.

139 *Public Opinion*, 20 January 1950 and *Economist*, 11 February 1950.

140 Mass-Observation, *Voters' Choice*, p. 13 and 'Newsman', 'Broadcasting the Election', *Fortnightly*, 1000 (1950), 251–7.

141 Mass-Observation, *Voters' Choice*, pp. 5–6. See also S.B. Chrimes (ed), *The General Election in Glasgow, February 1950* (Glasgow, 1950), pp. 83–4.

142 THMOA, TC General Elections 1944–55, Box 4, File C, Report dated 18 February 1950.

143 *Ibid.*, Box 4, File J. Report by E. Cornhill, 'Trafalgar Sq. – Election Night', 23 February 1950, p. 5.

144 Nicholas, *General Election*, pp. 283–305; *Economist*, 4 March 1950 and 11 March 1950.

145 *Financial Times*, 25 February 1950.

146 *Economist*, 4 March 1950 and *Public Opinion*, 26 May 1950.

147 LPA, R.D. 350/April 1950, R. Plant, 'General Election 1950. Notes on the Findings of the Public Opinion Polls', [n.d.], p. 3.

148 *Ibid.*, pp. 3–5.

149 Editorial and feature article 'General Election Reports from around The Regions', *Labour Organiser*, 29:336 (1950), pp. 1, 4–7, and 15; and LPA, NEC Minutes, 22 March 1950, 'General Election Campaign Report. Personal Observations by the General Secretary', [n.d.], pp. 6–7.

150 LPA, R.D. 350/April 1950, R. Plant, 'General Election', p. 10.

151 P. Williams, 'Election Analysis', *Socialist Commentary*, 14:4 (1950), 90.

152 *New Statesman*, 11 March 1950.

153 Editorial, *Tribune*, 3 March 1950.

154 *Ibid.*

155 *Tribune*, 17 March 1950 and *Forward*, 6 May 1950.

156 LPA, NEC Minutes, 28 June 1950, R./3 June 1950, 'Summary of Discussions at the Conference Held at Beatrice Webb House, Dorking, 19–21 May, 1950', p. 4.

157 Morgan, *Labour in Power* p. 415; Donoughue and Jones, *Herbert Morrison*, pp. 457–8. and 465; Labour Party, *Report of the Fiftieth Annual Conference of the Labour Party* (London, 1951), p. 12.

158 Editorial, *English Review*, 4:4 (1950), 222; W.L. Burn, 'The Two Nations', *Nineteenth Century And After*, (April 1950), 211–20.

159 Hoffman, *Conservative Party in Opposition*, p. 202; *Economist*, 21 October 1950.

160 CPA, P.O.R.D. Confidential Supplement to Public Opinion Summary

No. 22, November 1950.

161 News Chronicle, *Behind the Gallup Poll* (London, 1951), pp. 15–17.

162 CPA, P.O.S. No. 28, May 1951, p. 2.

163 'Commentator', 'Eye on Events', *Socialist Commentary*, 15:6 (1951), 132.

164 *Economist*, 30 June 1951; LPA, NEC Minutes, 27 June 1951, N.A.D., 'Report on the Municipal Elections', [n.d.], pp. 1–6.

165 Labour Party, *Labour Party Election Manifesto, 1951* (London, 1951), p. 2.

166 D.E. Butler, *The British General Election of 1951* (London, 1952), p. 66.

167 *Ibid.*, pp. 55–6 and 105–28.

168 *Economist*, 27 October 1951.

169 T.P. Jenkin, 'The British General Election of 1951', *Western Political Quarterly*, 5:1 (1952), 57–8.

170 News Chronicle, *Gallup Poll*, p. 19.

171 *Ibid.*, p. 22.

172 *Ibid.*, p. 22

173 *Ibid.*, p. 25.

174 *Spectator*, 19 October 1951.

175 News Chronicle, *Gallup Poll*, p. 25.

176 Butler, *The British General Election of 1951*, p. 242.

177 LPA, NEC Minutes, 7 November 1951, Morgan Phillips, 'General Election Campaign. General Secretary's Report', [n.d.], p. 6.

8

Conclusion

Despite losing the 1951 general election Labour left office in a sanguine mood. What was described as the Party's 'Victory in votes' gave members considerable comfort; it led Morgan Phillips to declare that they could be 'confident that final victory for democratic socialism' was 'assured'.[1] Others echoed this optimistic interpretation: Attlee was cheered not jeered by Labour MPs in the wake of his defeat.[2] This reaction was partly due to relief that Labour had suffered nothing like the electoral rout some had once feared. More fundamentally, as Phillips's comment makes plain, it reflected the continued belief that Labour's vision of the responsible society would eventually prevail. Initially, some even considered the Party's period in opposition to be a welcome respite which would allow Labour to regain its vitality before resuming the second stage of the journey to socialism. It was widely assumed that Churchill would not remain in power for long.

Subsequent events proved the Party to have been mistaken. The Conservatives went on to secure victory at a further two general elections in 1955 and 1959, each time winning a larger share of the vote. In contrast, Labour's support consistently declined. Voices, already present in the late 1940s, questioned ever more insistently some of the assumptions that had underpinned Labour's vision of socialism. As the Attlee Government had not led to the Socialist Commonwealth, such critics called for the revision of the Party's ideology.[3] Aspects of this point of view were appropriated by Hugh Gaitskell who became Labour leader in 1955. He used 'revisionism' to justify distancing the Party from increasing state control of the economy in the hope that this would enhance its electoral appeal. In contrast, others considered that, if Labour was to revive its fortunes, the Party simply had to extend the boundaries of the state.[4] Those who followed the disenchanted Aneurin Bevan, after his resignation from Attlee's Cabinet in April 1951, asserted that the Labour Government would have retained office had it boldly enhanced its nationalisation programme after 1948. This difference of opinion underpinned the 'Bevanite' revolt of the first half of the 1950s and continued to fuel much of the antipathy which existed between Gaitskell and Party conference delegates thereafter. Thus, by the late 1950s, many ordinary Labour members considered socialism to be largely a matter of implementing Clause IV of Labour's constitution. For those in agreement with the leadership, however, electoral success depended upon dispensing with the commitment. Both sides had separated themselves from an emphasis on ethical transformation, so much to the fore in the 1940s.

By the beginning of the 1960s memories of 1945 had been clouded by the internal struggle over nationalisation and Labour's repeated electoral failures. Writing at this time, the journalist Anthony Howard reflected Party attitudes to the Attlee Government:

> Occasionally late at night at a Labour Party conference – or in the small hours of the morning at the more strenuous gatherings of the T.U.C. – the cry can still be heard. 'Where', a plaintive, maudlin voice will ask, 'did it go wrong?'.[5]

Most historians of the 1945–51 Labour Governments have tried to answer this question. In so doing, they have often assumed one or other of the embattled positions adopted within the Party during the 1950s. Consequently, many accounts of the Attlee years suggest that if only ministers had acted in a different manner – a bit more or less nationalisation here, a more rigorous or flexible set of controls there – then electoral success would have been guaranteed. Thus, failure can be reduced to an examination of the Labour leadership and Cabinet decision-making. One important corollary of this approach has been the widespread, but barely substantiated, belief amongst historians that wartime public sentiment was conducive to the implementation of radical policies.[6] There is, in fact, little difference in the way defenders and critics of the Labour Party have interpreted popular politics during this period. Whereas the former have considered that Labour reflected the people's mood, the latter have stated that the Party was much the more conservative

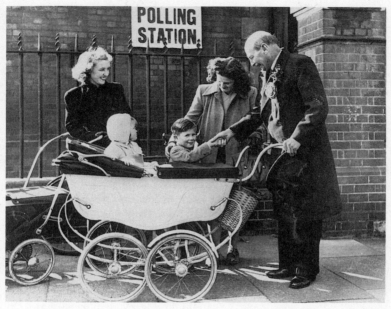

9 Canvassing the youth vote. Clement Attlee during the 1951 general election

force.[7] That the people's politics may have inhibited Labour's attempt to build socialism has never been seriously countenanced.

It should be clear by now that this study is critical of accounts which view Labour's time in office exclusively through Cabinet minutes, Commons debates and Trades Union Congress reports. Any complete history of the period has to take account of such matters. However, to exclude other subjects from view seriously distorts our understanding of politics in the 1940s. Evidence derived from a range of sources, in particular Mass-Observation, opinion polls and social surveys also needs to be given adequate weight. These take us beyond the charmed circle of enlightened civil servants and the politically engaged and allow some assessment to be made of the actions and opinions of the vast majority of the British people. Such an approach has been adopted in this work because it is quite clear that, as has been emphasised in the preceding chapters, the context in which Labour operated was much more influential on the Party's fortunes than has hitherto been granted. Moreover, given Labour's belief that individual moral transformation was one of socialism's two prerequisites, the investigation of popular attitudes is especially pertinent to an account of 1940s politics.

In order to emphasise the case made in this work it is now appropriate to recapitulate its argument. The war's impact was widely misconstrued both by many influential contemporaries and later historians. Whilst the conflict promoted the desire for social harmony and a new political settlement in the minds of a minority, in others this was clearly not the case. First, though the evacuation of working-class children to the homes of the more fortunate may have temporarily bridged social differences in some households, in others, it actually reinforced pre-existing class antagonisms. Similarly, German bombing of Britain's urban centres often failed to bridge status distinctions within the working class, let alone overcome those more profound differences which divided the classes. Second, the political radicalisation, much commented on at the time and subsequently, has been greatly exaggerated. The Army Bureau of Current Affairs appears to have helped those few already interested in contemporary events to gain a greater insight into the world in which they lived. Yet, it did little to excite curiosity in such matters amongst the rest. As some pessimists noted at the time, the experience of the Second World War – whether it was spent in the factory or at the Front – did not imbue most people with a new conception of public affairs.

Analysis of Labour's 1945 victory, still in terms of constituencies won the Party's greatest triumph, confirms this conclusion. Invariably interpreted as evidence of the public's radicalisation, Labour's achievement in fact relied upon a number of other, more mundane factors. The Party clearly won the positive support of a large number of voters who wished to see the implementation of substantial reforms. Labour exploited this advantage to the full because, as Conservatives alleged, Transport House's organisation was, perhaps uniquely, better than their own. The Party also benefited from the support of those more disenchanted with the Conservatives than enthused by Labour's promise of socialism. As a consequence, Attlee's Commons majority gave the impression of a landslide which, on the basis of the popular vote, was not merited.

Many of those who considered that Dunkirk and the Blitz had fundamentally changed social and political attitudes were Labour-inclined writers who viewed the war in the light of their own hopes for the future. This version of events was also embraced, a few doubters apart, by the majority of Labour leaders and members. To interpret the war as an ethical breakthrough suited their conception of socialism. Thus, the Second World War was seen as supplying the missing sense of purpose that had barred Labour's route to power before 1939. The social solidarity and political engagement believed to define the wartime mood were thought to be the means by which socialism would emerge after the war. Labour's 1945 victory was presented as proof of this view. Once installed in office, it was Labour's peacetime task to promote the consummation of wartime developments.

Labour in power encouraged further change in popular attitudes through a combination of exhortation and legislation. The Government introduced a number of measures to sustain a sense of community. It was hoped that these would build on wartime solidarity and transform people from private individuals uninterested in wider events into active citizens seeking to influence public affairs. Unfortunately, most people remained preoccupied with their private spheres and rejected initiatives to make them community-spirited. Labour was also unable to make much of an impact on popular leisure patterns. It was believed that the war had caused people to be favourably disposed to 'improving' pastimes which promoted values necessary for the building of socialism. Yet, the vast majority continued to patronise 'escapist' entertainments thought to promote attitudes inimical to the responsible society.

Labour's inability to make socialists on the scale anticipated in 1945 demonstrated the extent to which the effect of the Second World War had been misinterpreted. Whilst Labour's promise of full employment and social security encouraged voters to support the Party in unprecedented numbers few were willing to embrace its ethical vision. Thus, institutions which emerged during the course of the conflict, such as British Restaurants, interpreted by some Party members as the germ of the new moral order, were viewed by the majority as undesirable after the defeat of Germany.

Pressing electoral considerations forced the Labour leadership to come to terms with this popular indifference. Problems raised by the implementation of the Government's nationalisation programme also had to be addressed. For both practical and political reasons, Labour decided in 1948 not to push the boundaries of the state ever forward. In any case, this was considered a pointless exercise if the people were not 'in spirit' socialists. Moreover, Labour had to contend with a revived Conservative Party. The Tories' impressive recovery proved that they had not been the wasted political force many thought in 1945. This led to competition for the political middle ground which forced Labour to further temper its wider ambitions. Even so, Labour lost the battle for middle-class votes, conceding a number of vital suburban constituencies to Churchill and, thereby, its slim 1950 Commons majority.

This study argues, therefore, that something did go 'wrong' during 1945–51. The basic problem, however, was not Party policy. Instead, the answer to the question 'what went wrong?' lies in the more fundamental issue of Labour's flawed perception of the electorate. Due to the effects of the Second World War, many Labour leaders and activists believed that the British people had become uniquely responsive to ethical socialism. Yet, in 1945 most voters simply wanted to return to pre-war conditions, albeit without the insecurity induced by high unemployment and inadequate public welfare. Consequently, they approved of the practical reforms outlined in *Let Us Face the Future*. However, whilst Labour members saw this programme as merely the first step towards the responsible society, even a majority of Labour supporters had no wish to embrace ethical change. The electorate's fundamental indifference to Labour's wider vision was only recognised by a few in the Party. Inheritors of a nineteenth century political tradition predicated on a forward march to an ineluctable end, Labour activists in particular refused to accept the legitimacy of popular feeling. After the crisis of 1947 the leadership responded to Labour's electoral unpopularity and lack of support for ethical transformation by proposing to temporarily 'consolidate' the Government's achievements. This was opposed by those in the Party who remained confident that votes would eventually be forthcoming. They wanted to advance further down the road to socialism without regard to public opinion. If Labour was losing support, they argued, this was because too little, not too much, socialist legislation had been passed. Thus, the battle lines for the policy disputes of the 1950s were set.

Two important general observations can be made on the basis of this account of Labour's fraught relationship with popular politics in the 1940s. The first relates to conceptions of the working class and the second to the nature of the Labour Party. These both have implications for how contemporary political history has been normally understood.

Labour's victory in 1945 is often considered to mark the end of the long march of the British working class. Having endured a General Strike, mass unemployment and the Second World War, the proletariat had finally matured socially, industrially and politically. Thus, the 1940s are generally seen to be the zenith of what Eric Hobsbawm has described as 'traditional' working-class culture.[8] Embracing nearly two-thirds of the occupied population such a way of life is said to have encompassed attendance at football matches and the cinema, eating fish and chips as well as going on Blackpool holidays. This social world clearly marked out workers from those drawn from other classes. As Richard Hoggart famously pointed out, manual workers came to see the world as divided between 'us' and 'them'.[9] As a result, members of the working class voted Labour; indeed Hobsbawm has described them as giving the Party 'natural' and 'instinctive' support. It was only during the 1950s that sturdy working-class values such as collectivism were, along with the Labour vote, undermined by the superficial individualism promoted by mass affluence.

This study reinforces the contrasting view that 'traditional' working-class culture was not homogeneous.[10] Even the Blitz failed to make collectivism predominant. Thus, it can be no surprise to discover that the opinion 'Decent people should not mix with slum people' was general amongst residents of one Wolverhampton municipal housing estate in the later 1940s.[11] More importantly, the preceding chapters have also indicated that the working class did not supply Labour with universal or unquestioning support. The number of workers voting Conservative was of great concern even during this decade. Indeed, at a conference held in 1950, some Labour leaders conceded that they had been guilty of overestimating workers' 'instinctive class loyalty' to the Party.[12] This account has further revealed the extent to which the vision of socialism enunciated by activists and leaders found little resonance within the working class. By 1950 that point had also been acknowledged by elements in the Labour leadership.[13] Even amongst working-class men – the Party's most loyal cohort – there was little evidence of support for Labour's stress on ethics. Many

apparently unquestioning working-class Labour voters criticised
the Attlee Government, deploying Conservative arguments against
'their' Party. Such people voted Labour because, as one asked,
'"how else would a working man vote?"'.[14]

One reason for the misrepresentation of Labour's relationship
with the working class is the means by which the Labour Party
itself is usually understood. The emphasis has been mainly on the
mechanics of power within the institutions of the Party; the
thoughts and actions of its leaders; and the formulation and implementation of policy. This has led to Labour being characterised as
a party preoccupied with pragmatic and immediate reforms. It has
also caused innumerable critics to declare that Labour has never
been, in any serious sense, committed to socialism. Instead, they
suggest, the Party has been mainly concerned to defend the trade
union interest within capitalism.[15] Even those broadly sympathetic
to the Party's purpose have emphasised Labour's 'materialism'.
Indeed, according to Stephen Brooke, during the Second World
War Labour was in the grip of 'an obsession with materialism'
which led to a 'bloodlessness' in its approach.[16]

In contrast to such a view, this account has emphasised the
significance of Labour members' belief that their socialism meant
transcending capitalism through both material and moral change.
This preoccupation had origins in an indigenous radical political
tradition which integrated idealism with aspects of Marx's historical materialism. In an autobiography written in the 1960s, the
doggedly mainstream figure of James Griffiths, Minister of National
Insurance in the 1945 Government, approvingly quoted the late
nineteenth century socialist James Bruce Glazier's definition that,

> 'Socialism means not only the socialization of wealth, but of our
> lives, our hearts, ourselves. Socialism consists not in getting but in
> giving, not in being served but in serving.' This was the socialism
> which inspired our service and enriched our lives in fellowship.[17]

Herbert Morrison has been quoted on numerous occasions in this
study in order to underline the influence of the ethical vision. This
is because he is usually presented by Labour Party historians as the
epitome of a machine politician. There is at least some truth in this
charge. Morrison tried to ensure that Labour won elections by
avoiding policies which he believed unnecessarily alienated voters.
Yet, even after Labour's 1951 defeat and the disappointments

which had preceded it, he continued to believe in the necessity of moral transformation.[18] Thus, an overtly pragmatic politician such as Morrison remained the captive of a vision that was, in a number of important respects, electorally disabling.

By concentrating on how ethical considerations determined many Labour members' appreciation of their wider purpose, this study has questioned the conventional characterisation of the Party's ethos. David Marquand has been only one of the more notable advocates of the belief that Labour's relationship with the working class has been its defining element.[19] It is certainly true that, even in 1945, Labour relied heavily on the votes of manual workers who disproportionately, if not universally, supported the Party. Yet, Labour members did not see the sole purpose of power as rewarding such voters with material comfort. Instead, the achievement of a genuinely classless society was one of Labour's basic aims and its leaders were keen to promote alliances between the 'useful people', a category which embraced manual workers, bank clerks, factory managers and even owners of industrial capital. Class co-operation rather than conflict defined Labour's purpose. This was why the likes of Morrison took so much heart from the social solidarity allegedly promoted by the Second World War. Despite such hopes, however, class difference remained a matter which complicated and ultimately defeated the Party's task. Thus, class, according to one post-war investigation into socially mixed housing, was a subject 'hedged about with prudery and taboo'. This led respondents to state that whilst they thought streets which intermingled the classes were desirable in principle they were not practical. One Labour voter even replied: 'Following my political views, I ought to say "mixed"; but you've got to think of the children'.[20] The electoral significance of continued class division was revealed in 1951. Whilst Labour won more working-class votes than ever before, the Conservatives succeeded in detaching sufficient middle-class voters to win a Commons majority and thereby lay the basis for fourteen uninterrupted years in power.

A sceptical reader might consider that the preceding chapters have been unduly negative. It has been argued that the war did *not* transform social and political attitudes to the extent once thought; that Labour members *failed* to accurately interpret the moment; that the Party was *unable* to fully connect with popular concerns. This would not be an entirely accurate impression. The Labour

Government, after all, implemented a reform programme without
precedent in spite of this. In fact, in the light of the social and political context outlined in this account, such an achievement appears
all the more remarkable. Yet, Labour's hopes for a socialist transformation were never fulfilled. Overlooking the Party's appeal for a
new morality, voters were, instead, attracted by the prospect of a
welfare state and full employment. This was only half of what was
on offer in 1945.

Labour is often blamed for the shortcomings of the post-war settlement because according to one account 'it put on its model of
socialism a stamp of authoritarian bleakness and unfeeling bureaucracy'.[21] Yet, the state-centred and bureaucratic outcome of
Labour's period in office was not intended. Labour's vision of socialism was inimical to it. Indeed, in attempting to foster the responsible society Morrison, amongst many others, was concerned to avoid
such a conclusion. Thus, if guilt for the subsequent character of the
years of 'consensus' is to be apportioned, then Labour should not
be alone in the dock. The Party might, in fact, find itself in the role
of the prosecuting counsel. The Labour Party had always aspired to
create something greater than a welfare state and a mixed economy. In 1949 Transport House issued *You and Tomorrow* which
summed up the Party's intentions during the period covered by this
study.

> It is our ambition that historians of the future will look back upon
> our endeavour and say of this generation:
>   'They did not build in marble. The stuff out of which they con-
>   structed the great monument of their time was simple human
>   decency and kindness ...
>   In this way, they built a community in which people were united
>   instead of obstructive; contented instead of passive; enterprising
>   instead of frightened – a society in which man's finest qualities,
>   instead of his worst, were evoked by the very nature of the com-
>   munity in which he lived.'[22]

There were many more responsible than the Labour Party for
ensuring that this exemplary ambition was never achieved.

Notes

1   Labour Party Archive [hereafter LPA], National Executive Committee

Minutes, 7 November 1951, Morgan Phillips, 'General Election Campaign 1951. General Secretary's Report' [n.d.], passim.

2   P. Williams, 'What Happened on 25th October', *Socialist Commentary*, 15:12 (1951) 280–3; *Tribune*, 28 December 1951; B. Pimlott (ed), *The Political Diary of Hugh Dalton, 1918–40, 1945–60* (London, 1986), pp. 567–70.

3   See especially the contributions of R.H.S. Crossman and C.A.R Crosland in R.H.S. Crossman (ed), *New Fabian Essays* (London, 1952).

4   Labour Party, *Report of the Fifty-Eighth Annual Conference of the Labour Party* (London, 1959), pp. 105–27.

5   A. Howard, '"We Are the Masters Now"', in M. Sissons and P. French (eds), *Age of Austerity, 1945–51* (Harmondsworth, 1964), p. 15.

6   S. Fielding, 'What Did "The People" Want?: The Meaning of the 1945 General Election', *Historical Journal*, 35:3 (1992), 626–7.

7   K.O. Morgan, *Labour in Power 1945–51* (Oxford, 1984), p. 285; R. Miliband, *Parliamentary Socialism* (London, 1961, 1972 ed.), pp. 272–4.

8   This view is most clearly expressed in E. Hobsbawm, 'The Formation of British Working-Class Culture' and 'The Making of the Working Class 1870–1914' in his *Worlds of Labour: Further Studies in the History of Labour* (London, 1984) and 'The Forward March of Labour Halted?', in M. Jacques and F. Mulhern (eds), *The Forward March of Labour Halted?* (London, 1981). See also R. Samuel, 'The Lost World of British Communism', *New Left Review*, 152 (1985), pp. 3–14.

9   R. Hoggart, *The Uses of Literacy* (Harmondsworth, 1958), pp. 72–101.

10   For work which takes this view, see J. Benson, *The Working Class in Britain, 1850–1939* (London, 1989); A. Davies and S. Fielding (eds), *Workers' Worlds. Cultures and Communities in Manchester and Salford, 1880–1939* (Manchester, 1992) and J. Bourke, *Working-Class Cultures in Britain 1890–1960* (London, 1994).

11   T. Brennan, *Midland City. Wolverhampton Social and Industrial Survey* (London, 1948), p. 70.

12   LPA, National Executive Committee Minutes, 28 June 1950, 'Summary of Discussion at the Conference held at Beatrice Webb House, Dorking, 19–21 May 1950', p. 4.

13   *Ibid.*, p. 2.

14   J.H. Robb, *Working-class Anti-semite. A Psychological Study in a London borough* (London, 1954), p. 187.

15   See, for example, G. Foote, *A History of the Labour Party's Political*

Thought (London, 1985).

16 S. Brooke, *Labour's War. The Labour Party during the Second World War* (Oxford, 1992), pp. 285, 340.

17 J. Griffiths, *Pages from Memory* (London, 1969), pp. 122–3.

18 LPA, National Executive Minutes, 12 December 1951, H. Morrison, 'Considerations Arising out of the General Election 1951'.

19 D. Marquand, 'The Paradox of British Democracy' in his *The Progressive Dilemma* (London, 1991), pp. 22–5.

20 B. Hutchison, *Willesden and the New Towns* (The Social Survey, No. 88, 1947), pp. 39–40.

21 W. Thompson, *The Long Death of British Labourism* (London, 1993), p. 17.

22 Harvester Press, *The Archive of the British Labour Party. Series II. Pamphlets and Leaflets. Part III. 1940–52* (Brighton, 1981), 1949/45.

Select bibliography

1   **Party papers**

Harvester Press, *The Archive of the British Labour Party. Series II. Pamphlets and Leaflets. Part III. 1940–52* (Brighton, 1981)

At the Labour Party Archive, National Musuem of Labour History, Manchester

National Executive Committee Minutes, 1938–51
Research Department Memoranda, 1942–50
1945 General Election Addresses
Herbert Morrison News Cuttings, 1938–44
Michael Foot Papers, 1945
Morgan Phillips Papers, 1945–50
Mary Sutherland Papers, 1937

British Library of Political and Economic Science, London School of Economics

Merton and Morden Labour Party Papers, 1939–45
Anthony Crosland Papers, 1941

Cambridgeshire Record Office

Cambridgeshire Divisional Labour Party Papers, 1940

Durham County Records Office

Bishop Auckland Labour Party Minute Book, 1940–42
Boldon Colliery Labour Party Minute Book, 1947

Manchester Central Reference Library, Local Studies Unit

Wright Robinson Papers, 1944–49

Openshaw Ward Women's Section Minute Book, 1947–50

Modern Records Centre, University of Warwick
East Midlands Region of the Labour Party Papers

National Library of Scotland
Dalkeith Labour Party Minute Book, 1935–51

Stockport Public Library
Stockport Labour Party, Annual Reports, 1942–51,
Stockport Labour Party, Minute Book, 1944–51

Tower Hamlets Local History Library
Stepney Labour Party Minute Book, 1947

Fabian Society Archive, Nuffield College, Oxford
Miscellaneous Files, 1936–37

Conservative Party Archive, Bodleian Library, Oxford
Circulars and Correspondence on the Role and Organisation of the Party
   in Wartime, 1939–42
National Union of Conservative and Unionist Associations, Eastern Provin-
   cial Area Minute Book, 1941
National Union of Conservative and Unionist Associations, North Western
   Area, Area Council Minute Book, 1943
Local Party Files, 1949
Public Opinion Summaries, 1949–51
P. Cohen, 'Disraeli's Child. A History of the Conservative and Unionist
   Party' (unpublished manuscript)

Westminster City Library Archives Department
National Society of Conservative Agents Minute Book, 1947–9

2   **Papers of other organisations**

British Film Institute, London
Bernstein Film Questionairre 1946–7

Modern Records Centre, University of Warwick
Confederation of British Industry Papers

Newham Local Studies Library

West Ham County Borough Council Committee Reports, Education Committee, 1949

Tom Harrisson Mass Observation Archive, University of Sussex

File Reports, 1939–51

Topic collections:

Beveridge Report surveys, 1942–47
Coal Mining, 1938–48
Forces, 1939–56
General Elections, 1945–55
Holidays, 1937–51
Leisure, 1940–47
Political Attitudes and Behaviour, 1938–56
Reading Habits, 1937–47
Reconstruction, 1941–43
Sport, 1939–47

3   Official papers

Command papers

Cmd 6348, *Report of the Committee on Amenities and Welfare Conditions in the three Women's Services* (London, 1942)

Cmd 8204, Ministry of Local Government and Planning, *Town and Country Planning 1943–51* (London, 1951)

The Social Survey

D. Chapman, *A Social Survey of Middlesbrough* (No. 50, 1946)

B. Hutchison, *Willesden and the New Towns* (No. 88, 1947)

L. Moss, *Education and the People* (No. 46, 1945)

P. Slater, *Final Report on the Demand for Holidays in 1946 and 1947* (No. 86, 1947)

P. Slater, *Report on the Demand for Holidays in 1947 and 1948* (No. 118, 1948)

Public Records Office, Kew

CAB 117/209
COAL 30/46
INF 1/282

LAB 10/445, 446, 534, 553
MAF 99/1734, 1736, 1737, 1738, 1760
PREM 4/64
POWE 37/7, 77, 81, 233, 234

4   Newspapers, periodicals and journals

American Political Science Review
Architectural Design & Construction
Architects' Journal
Army Education Corps Quarterly Bulletin
Barking and East Ham Express
British Housing and Planning Review
British Journal of Sociology
Caterer and Hotel Keeper
Chemical Worker
Citizen
Conservative Agents' Journal
Co-op News
Co-operative Review
Coventry Evening Telegraph
Coventry Standard
Current Affairs
Daily Dispatch
Daily Express
Daily Herald
Daily Mail
Daily Mirror
Daily Telegraph
Economist
Education
English Review
Fabian Journal
Fabian Quarterly
Fact
Financial Times
Fortnightly
Forward
Future
Good Neighbour

The Highway
Hollywood Quarterly
House-Builder
Illustrated
Independent
Industrial Welfare
Journal of Abnormal and Social Psychology
Journal of the Institute of Personnel Management
Journal of Politics
Journal of the Royal Statistical Society
Labour
Labour Discussion Notes
Labour Forum
Labour League of Youth Organizational Bulletin
Labour Organiser
Labour Woman
Lancet
Listener
Local Government Chronicle
Local Government Service
Mass-Observation Bulletin
Municipal Review
New English Review
New Society
New Statesman
News Chronicle
News Letter
Nineteenth Century and After
Objective
Observer
Onlooker
Public Administration
Public Opinion
Public Opinion Quarterly
Picture Post
Pilot Papers
Planning
Political Quarterly
Quarterly Review
Review of Economic Studies

Sight and Sound
Social Research
Social Welfare
Social Work
Socialist Advance
Socialist Commentary
Socialist Leader
Sociological Review
South Atlantic Quarterly
Spectator
The Times
Times Education Supplement
Tory Challenge
Town and Country Planning
Town Planning Review
The Townswoman
Tribune
Us. Mass-Observation's Weekly Intelligence Service
Virginia Quarterly Review
Weekly News Letter
Western Political Quarterly
Wimbledon Borough News
Woman
Women's Co-operative Guild Monthly Bulletin
Women in Council Newsletter
Yorkshire Bulletin
Young Socialist

5 Published reports

Hansard, 1945–49
Labour Party, *Annual Conference Reports*, 1939–51, 1959
Labour Party, *National Conference of Labour Women Reports*, 1943–9
Trades Union Congress, *Annual Conference Reports*, 1948–50
Workers' Education Association, *Annual Reports*, 1946–48

6 Published biographies, memoirs and diaries

Tony Benn, *Years of Hope. Diaries, Papers and Letters 1940–1962* (London, 1994)

Lord Beveridge, *Power and Influence* (London, 1953)
Lord Butler, *The Art of the Possible* (Harmondsworth, 1973)
H. Cudlipp, *At Your Peril* (London, 1962)
H. Dalton, *The Fateful Years. Memoirs, 1931–1945* (London, 1957)
B. Donoughue and G. Jones, *Herbert Morrison. Portrait of a Politician* (London, 1973)
P. Duff, *Left, Left, Left. A Personal Account of Six Protest Campaigns, 1945–65* (London, 1971)
M. Gorham, *Sound and Fury. Twenty One Years in the BBC* (London, 1948)
J. Griffiths, *Pages from Memory* (London, 1969)
W. Hamilton, *Blood on the Walls* (London, 1992)
J.C. Heenan, *Not the Whole Truth* (London, 1971)
V. Hodgson, *Few Eggs and No Oranges* (London, 1976)
R. Hoggart, *The Uses of Literacy* (Harmondsworth, 1958)
D. Hyde, *I Believed* (London, 1951)
C. King, *Strictly Personal* (London, 1969)
B. Kops, *The World is a Wedding* (London, 1973)
O. Lyttleton, *The Memoirs of Lord Chandos* (London, 1962)
L. Manning, *A Life for Education. An Autobiography* (London, 1970)
I. Mikardo, *Back Bencher* (London, 1988)
B. Pimlott (ed), *The Political Diary of Hugh Dalton, 1918–40, 1945–60* (London, 1986)
M.L. Settle, *All the Brave Promises* (London, 1984)
E. Shinwell, *I've Lived Through it All* (London, 1973)
B. Sokoloff, *Edith and Stepney. The Life of Edith Ramsay* (London, 1987)
A.J.P. Taylor, *A Personal History* (London, 1983)
Lord Wigg, *George Wigg* (London, 1972)
F. Williams, *Nothing So Strange* (London, 1970)
R. Williams, *Politics and Letters. Interviews with New Left Review* (London, 1979)

7   Contemporary published works

M. Abrams, *The Home Market. 1950 Edition* (London, 1950)
M. Abrams, *Social Surveys and Social Action* (London, 1951)
R. Acland, *Unser Kampf* (Harmondsworth, 1940)
Acton Society Trust, *Training and Promotion in Nationalised Industry* (London, 1951)
Acton Society Trust, *The Framework of Joint Consultation* (London, 1952)
Acton Society Trust, *The Worker's Point of View* (London, 1952)

Anon., 'Britain's Book Reading Habits', in A.G. Weidenfeld (ed), *Overture* (London, 1945)

Anon., *Your Inheritance. The Land: An Uncomic Strip* (Cheam, Surrey, n.d.)

C.R. Attlee, *The Labour Party in Perspective* (London, 1937)

C.R. Attlee, *Purpose and Policy* (London, 1947)

G.B. Baldwin, *Beyond Nationalization. The Labour Problems of British Coal* (Cambridge, Mass., 1955)

Barnett House Study Group, *London Children in Wartime Oxford* (London, 1947)

N. Barou, 'Whither Cooperation?', in N. Barou (ed), *The Co-operative Movement in Labour Britain* (London, 1948)

M. Benny, *Charity Main. A Coalfield Chronicle* (London, 1946)

M. Benny, 'Under New Management', in A.G. Weidenfeld (ed), *Other People's Lives* (London, 1948)

A. Bevan, *Why Not Trust the Tories?* (London, 1944)

A. Bevan, *In Place of Fear* (London, 1952)

Lord Beveridge, *Voluntary Action* (London, 1948)

L. Blair (ed), *The Butlin Holiday Book, 1949–50* (London, 1949)

J. Bonham, *The Middle Class Vote* (London, 1954)

W. Boyd (ed), *Evacuation in Scotland. A Record of Events and Experiments* (Bickley, 1944)

T. Brennan, *Midland City. Wolverhampton Social and Industrial Survey* (London, 1948)

British Institute of Public Opinion, *The Beveridge Report and the Public* (London, n.d. but 1943)

D.E. Butler, *The British General Election of 1951* (London, 1952)

C. Cameron, A. Lush and G. Meara, *Preliminary Report on the 18+ Age Group Enquiry* (Edinburgh, 1940)

H. Cantril (ed), *Public Opinion 1935–46* (Princeton, New Jersey, 1951)

T. Cauter and J.S. Downham, *The Communication of Ideas* (London, 1954)

S.B. Chrimes (ed), *The General Election in Glasgow, February 1950* (Glasgow, 1950)

R.H. Coarse, *British Broadcasting. A Study in Monopoly* (London, 1950)

G.D.H. Cole, 'The War on the Home Front', *Fabian Tracts*, 247 (London, 1940)

G.D.H. Cole, *Fabian Socialism* (London, 1943)

G.D.H Cole, 'Plan for Living', in G.D.H. Cole *et al.*, *Plan for Living* (London, 1943)

G.D.H. Cole, *A History of the Labour Party from 1914* (London, 1948)

G.D.H. Cole, 'The Socialisation Programme for Industry', in D. Munro (ed),

Socialism. The British Way (London, 1948)

G.D.H. and M.I. Cole, *The Condition of Britain* (London, 1937)

M. Cole, 'General Effects: Billeting', in R. Padley and M. Cole (eds), *Evacuation Survey. A Report to the Fabian Society* (London, 1940)

M. Cole, 'Wartime Billeting', *Fabian Research*, 55 (London, 1941)

M. Cole, 'Miners and the Board', *Fabian Research*, 134 (London, 1949)

Conservative Party, *'Trust the People' Exhibition. Souvenir Programme and Guide* (London, 1947)

Conservative Party, *The Right Road for Britain* (London, 1949)

P. Crane 'Enterprise in Local Government', *Fabian Research*, 156 (London, 1953)

S. Cripps, *Democracy Alive* (London, 1946)

R.H.S. Crossman (ed), *New Fabian Essays* (London, 1952)

J. Dahir, *The Neighbourhood Unit Plan* (New York, 1947)

H. Dalton, *Hitler's War. Before and After* (Harmondsworth, 1940)

C. Day Lewis (ed), *The Mind in Chains. Socialism and the Cultural Revolution* (London, 1938)

N. Dennis, F. Henriques and C. Slaughter, *Coal is Our Life. An Analysis of a Yorkshire Mining Community* (London, 1956)

H.C. Dent, *Education in Transition* (London, 1944)

The Directorate of Army Education, *The British Way and Purpose* (London, 1944)

B. Drake, 'Communal Feeding in Wartime', *Fabian Research*, 64 (London, 1942)

H. Durant, *The Problem of Leisure* (London, 1938)

H.W. Durant, *Political Opinion. Four General Election Results* (London, 1949)

R. Durant, *Watling. A Survey of Life on a New Housing Estate* (London, 1939)

Fabian Society, 'A Word on the Future to British Socialists', *Fabian Tracts*, 256 (London, 1942)

S. Ferguson and H. Fitzgerald, *Studies in the Social Services* (London, 1954)

T. Ferguson and J. Cunnison, *The Young Wage Earner. A Study of Glasgow Boys* (Oxford, 1951)

A. Flanders, 'Great Britain', in W. Galenson (ed), *Comparative Labour Movements* (New York, 1952)

B. Ford, *The Bureau of Current Affairs, 1946–51* (London, 1951)

G.H. Gallup, *The Gallup International Public Opinion Polls. Great Britain, 1937–75, Volume One* (New York, 1976)

R. Glass and M. Frenkel, *A Profile of Bethnal Green* (London, 1946)

D.M. Goodfellow, *Tyneside. The Social Facts* (Newcastle, 1942)

G. Gorer, *Exploring English Character* (London, 1955)

G. Gorer, *Modern Types* (London, 1955)

A. Greenwood, *Why We Fight. Labour's Case* (London, 1940)

W. Greenwood, *How the Other Man Lives* (London, n.d. but 1939)

F. Le Gros Clark and R.W. Toms, 'Evacuation – Failure or Reform?', *Fabian Tract*, 249 (London, 1940)

M.A. Hamilton, *The Labour Party To-Day* (London, n.d. but 1939)

R.J. Hammond, *Food. Volume Two. Studies in Control and Administration* (London, 1956)

J. Highet, *Dumfries Speaks Out* (Glasgow, 1951)

J. Hilton, *English Ways* (London, 1940)

O.R. Hobson, *A Hundred Years of the Halifax* (London, 1953)

J.L. Hodson, *The Way Things Are* (London, 1947)

Hulton Research, *Patterns of British Life* (London, 1950)

E.D. Idle, *War Over West Ham* (London, 1943)

S. Isaacs (ed), *The Cambridge Evacuation Survey* (London, 1941)

P. Jephcott, *Rising Twenty. Notes on Some Ordinary Girls* (London, 1948)

P. Jephcott, *Some Young People* (London, 1954)

Labour Party, *The Old World and the New Society* (London, 1942)

Labour Party, *Full Employment and Financial Policy* (London, 1944)

Labour Party, *Let Us Face the Future* (London, 1945)

Labour Party, *Labour Believes in Britain* (London, 1949)

G. Lambert, 'Film and the Idea of Happiness', in A.G. Weidenfeld (ed), *Good Living* (London, 1948)

H.J. Laski, 'Marx and Today', *Fabian Research*, 73 (London, 1943)

R. Lewis and A. Maude, *The English Middle Classes* (London, 1949)

'Licinius', *Vote Labour? Why?* (London, 1945)

Lord Lindsay, 'The Philosophy of the British Labour Governments', in F.S.C. Northrop (ed), *Ideological Difference and World Order* (London, 1949)

Liverpool University, Department of Social Science, *Social Aspects of a Town Development Plan* (Liverpool, 1951)

University of Liverpool, *Neighbourhood and Community* (Liverpool, 1954)

A. Lush, *The Young Adult* (Cardiff, 1941)

R.B. McCallum and A. Readman, *The British General Election of 1945* (Oxford, 1947)

Sir A.S. MacNalty, 'Influence of War on Family Life', in Lord Horder (ed), *Rebuilding Family Life in the Post-War World* (London, n.d.)

C. Madge, *Wartime Patterns of Saving and Spending* (Cambridge, 1943)

Manchester City Labour Party, *Manchester To-Morrow. Cultural Facilities for*

Manchester (Manchester, 1945)

E.R. Manley, *Meet the Miner* (Lofthouse, 1947)

Mass-Observation, *War Begins at Home* (London, 1940)

Mass-Observation, *An Enquiry into British War Production Part 1. People in Production* (London, 1942)

Mass-Observation, *Peoples's Homes* (London, 1943)

Mass-Observation, *The Pub and the People* (London, 1943)

Mass-Observation, *The Journey Home* (London, 1944)

Mass-Observation, 'Saturday Night', in A.G. Weidenfeld (ed), *World Off Duty* (London, 1947)

Mass-Observation, *Puzzled People* (London, 1947)

Mass-Observation, *The Press and Its Readers* (London, 1949)

Mass-Observation, *The Voters' Choice* (London, 1950)

J.P. Meyer, *British Cinemas and Their Audiences* (London, 1948)

I. Mikardo, 'The Second Five Years', *Fabian Research*, 124 (London, 1948)

H. Morrison, 'Man: The Master or the Slave of Material Things?', *Barnett House Papers*, 18 (London, 1935)

H. Morrison, *The Peaceful Revolution* (London, 1949)

H.V. Morton, *Our Fellow Men* (London, 1936)

National Coal Board, *Films on Coal* (London, 1961)

National Council of Social Service, *British Restaurants* (London, 1946)

National Council of Social Service, *For the Common Good* (London, 1949)

National Council of Social Service, *Our Neighbourhood* (London, 1950)

National Institute of Industrial Psychology, *Joint Consultation in British Industry* (London, 1952)

B. Newman, *British Journey* (London, 1945)

News Chronicle and the British Institute of Public Opinion, *What Britain Thinks* (London, 1939)

News Chronicle, *Behind the Gallup Poll* (London, 1951)

H.G. Nicholas, *The British General Election of 1950* (London, 1951)

N. Nicholson, 'His Majesty's Opposition', in A.G. Weidenfeld (ed), *The Public's Progress* (London, 1947)

Odhams Press, *Ourselves in Wartime* (London, n.d.)

H. Orlans, *Stevenage. A Sociological Study of a New Town* (London, 1952)

G. Orwell, *The English People* (London, 1947)

E.L. Packer, 'Backstreet', in A.G. Weidenfeld (ed), *Other People's Lives* (London, 1948)

J. Parker, *Labour Marches On* (Harmondsworth, 1947)

Political and Economic Planning, *The British Film Industry* (London, 1952)

J.B. Priestley, 'Introduction', in I. Brown, *The Heart of England* (London,

1935)

J.B. Priestley, *Bright Day* (London, 1946)

J.B. Priestley, *The Arts Under Socialism* (London, 1947)

J.B. Priestley, *Festival at Farbridge* (London, 1951)

J.H. Robb, *Working-class Anti-semite. A Psychological Study in a London Borough* (London, 1954)

W.A. Robson, *The War and the Planning Outlook* (London, 1941)

P. Rotha, 'The Future Outlook', in A.G. Weidenfeld (ed), *The Public's Progress* (London, 1947)

N. Scarlyn Wilson, *Education in the Forces 1939–46* (London, 1948)

Scottish Housing Advisory Commitee, *Planning Our New Homes* (Edinburgh, 1944)

E. Sewell Harris and P.N. Molloy, *The Watling Community Association. The First Twenty One Years* (Edgware, 1949)

E. Shinwell, *When the Men Come Home* (London, 1944)

J. Simeon Clarke, 'Family Life', in R. Padley and M. Cole (eds), *Evacuation Survey. A Report to the Fabian Society* (London, 1940)

Lord Simon, *The BBC From Within* (London, 1953)

R. Sinclair, *Metropolitan Man* (London, 1937)

E. Slater and M. Woodside, *Patterns of Marriage* (London, 1951)

Socialist Publicity Society, *Putting It Over* (London, n.d.)

Standing Joint Committee of Working Women's Organisations, *Working Women Discuss Population, Equal Pay, Domestic Work* (London, 1946)

T. Stevens, 'Army Education', *Fabian Research*, 53 (London, 1940)

J. Strachey, *Why You Should Be a Socialist* (London, 1944)

W. Styler, *Who Were the Students?* (London, 1950)

L. Thompson, *Portrait of England: News from Somewhere* (London, 1952)

N. Tiptaft, *I Saw a City* (London, 1945)

P. Treves, *England: The Mysterious Island* (London, 1948)

W.J. Turner, *Exmoor Village* (London, 1947)

L.E. White, *Tenement Town* (London, 1946)

L.E. White, *Community or Chaos* (London, 1950)

F. Williams, *Ten Angels Swearing ... Or Tomorrow's Politics* (London, 1941)

F. Williams, *Fifty Years March* (London, 1951)

J.C. Wilson, *An Inquiry into Communal Laundry Facilities* (London, 1949)

L. Wolfe, *The Reilly Plan* (London, 1945)

Women's Group on Public Welfare, *Our Towns: A Close Up* (Oxford, 1943)

J.A. Yates, *Pioneers to Power* (Coventry, 1950)

M. Young, *Labour's Plan for Plenty* (London, 1947)

F. Zweig, *Men in the Pits* (London, 1948)

F. Zweig, *Labour, Life and Poverty* (London, 1949)

F. Zweig, *The British Worker* (Harmondsworth, 1952)

F. Zweig, *Women's Life and Labour* (Harmondsworth, 1952)

8 Published historical accounts

M. Abrams, 'Public Opinion Polls and Political Parties', *Public Opinion Quarterly*, 27:1, 1963

P. Addison, 'By-Elections of the Second World War', in C. Cook and J. Ramsden (eds), *By-Elections in British Politics* (London, 1973)

P. Addison, *The Road to 1945* (London, 1975)

P. Addison, *Now the War Is Over. A Social History of Britain, 1945–51* (London, 1985)

P. Addison, *Churchill on the Home Front* (London, 1992)

P. Ayers, *Women at War* (Birkenhead, 1988)

R. Bacon, G.S. Bain and J. Pimlott, 'The Labour Force', in A.H. Halsey (ed), *Trends in British Society Since 1900* (London, 1972)

M. Banton, *The Coloured Quarter* (London, 1955)

J. Benson, *The Working Class in Britain, 1850–1939* (London, 1989)

A.H. Booth, *British Hustings, 1924–50* (London, 1956)

J. Bourke, *Working-Class Cultures in Britain 1890–1960* (London, 1994)

S. Brooke, *Labour's War. The Labour Party during the Second World War* (Oxford, 1992)

S. Burgess, '1945 Observed. A History of the Histories', *Contemporary Record*, 5:1 (1991)

A. Cairncross, *Years of Recovery* (London, 1985)

A. Calder, *The People's War. Britain, 1939–1945* (London, 1971)

A. Calder, 'Labour and the Second World War', in D. Rubinstein (ed), *People for the People* (London, 1973)

A. Calder, *The Myth of the Blitz* (London, 1991)

B. Campbell, *The Iron Ladies* (London, 1987)

R. Clarke (ed), *Enterprising Neighbours* (London, 1990)

H.A. Clegg, *A History of British Trade Unions since 1889. Volume III 1934–51* (Oxford, 1994)

W. Crofts, *Coercion or Persuasion?* (London, 1989)

R. Croucher, *Engineers at War* (London, 1982)

A. Davies and S. Fielding (eds), *Workers' Worlds. Cultures and Communities in Manchester and Salford, 1880–1939* (Manchester, 1992)

M. Dickinson and S. Street, *Cinema and Society. The Film Industry and Government, 1927–84* (London, 1985)

G. Elliott, *Labourism and the English Genius* (London, 1993)

G. Field, 'Perspectives on the Working-Class Family in Wartime Britain, 1939–45', *International Labor and Working-Class History*, 38 (1990)

S. Fielding, 'What Did "The People" Want?: The Meaning of the 1945 General Election', *Historical Journal*, 35:3 (1992)

S. Fielding, 'Labourism in the 1940s', *Twentieth Century British History*, 3:2 (1992)

S. Fielding, 'The Second World War and Popular Radicalism: the Significance of the "Movement away from Party"', *History*, 80:1 (1995)

G. Foote, *A History of the Labour Party's Political Thought* (London, 1985)

M. Frayn, 'Festival', in M. Sissons and P. French (eds), *Age of Austerity, 1945–51* (Harmondsworth, 1964)

M. Freeden, *The New Liberalism. An Ideology of Social Reform* (Oxford, 1978)

J. Fyrth (ed), *Labour's High Noon* (London, 1993)

P. Grafton, *You! You! and You!* (London, 1981)

P. Graves, *Labour Women. Women in British Working-Class Politics, 1918–1939* (Cambridge, 1994)

J. Harris, 'Did British Workers Want the Welfare State? G.D.H. Cole's Survey of 1942', in J. Winter (ed), *The Working Class in Modern British History* (Cambridge, 1983)

J. Harris, 'Poiltical ideas and the debate on State welfare' in H.L. Smith (ed), *War and Social Change. British Society in the Second World War* (Manchester, 1986)

W. Harrington and P. Young, *The 1945 Revolution* (London, 1978)

T. Harrisson, *Living through the Blitz* (Harmondsworth, 1978)

C. Harvie, 'Labour in Scotland during the Second World War', *Historical Journal*, 26:4 (1983)

J. Hasegawa, *Replanning the Blitzed City Centre* (Buckingham, 1992)

P. Hennessey, *Never Again. Britain, 1945–51* (London, 1992)

F.H. Hinsley and C.A.G. Simkins, *British Intelligence in the Second World War. Volume 4 Security and Counter-Intelligence* (London, 1990)

J. Hinton, 'Coventry Communism: a Study of Factory Politics in the Second World War', *History Workshop Journal*, 10 (1980)

E. Hobsbawm, 'The Foward March of Labour Halted?' and 'Observations on the Debate', in M. Jaques and F. Mulhern (eds), *The Forward March of Labour Halted?* (London, 1981)

E. Hobsbawm, 'The Formation of British Working-Class Culture' and 'The Making of the Working Class 1870–1914', in his *Worlds of Labour: Further Studies in the History of Labour* (London, 1984)

E. Hodder, *Hats Off! to Conservative Women* (London, 1990)

J.D. Hoffman, *The Conservative Party in Opposition* (London, 1964)

A. Howard, '"We Are the Masters Now"', in M. Sissons and P. French (eds), *Age of Austerity, 1945–51* (Harmondsworth, 1964)

P. Inman, *Labour in the Munitions Industries* (London, 1957)

J. Jacobs, 'December 1942: Beveridge Observed. Mass-Observation and the Beveridge Report', in J. Jacobs (ed), *Beveridge 1942–1992* (Brighton, 1992)

K. Jefferys, 'British Politics and Social Policy during the Second World War', *Historical Journal*, 30:1 (1987)

K. Jefferys, *The Churchill Coalition and Wartime Politics, 1940–45* (Manchester, 1991)

R. Kisch, *The Private Life of Public Relations* (London, 1964)

F.M. Leventhal, '"The Best for the Most": CEMA and State Sponsorship of the Arts in Wartime, 1939–45', *Twentieth Century British History*, 1:3 (1990)

S. P. Mackenzie, *Politics and Military Morale* (Oxford, 1992)

J. Macnicol, 'The Effect of the Evacuation of Schoolchildren on Official Attitudes to State Intervention', in H.L. Smith (ed) *War and Social Change. British Society in the Second World War* (Manchester, 1986)

J. Margach, *The Abuse of Power* (London, 1979)

D. Marquand, 'The Paradox of British Democracy', in his *The Progressive Dilemma* (London, 1991)

T. Mason and P. Thompson, '"Reflections on a Revolution"? The Political Mood in Wartime Britain', in N. Tiratsoo (ed), *The Attlee Years* (London, 1991)

R. Miliband, *Parliamentary Socialism* (London, 1961)

K.O. Morgan, *Labour in Power 1945–51* (Oxford, 1984)

K. Newton, *The Sociology of British Communism* (London, 1969)

T.H. O'Brien, *Civil Defence* (London, 1955)

H.M.D. Parker, *Manpower* (London, 1957)

H. Pelling, 'The 1945 General Election Reconsidered', *Historical Journal*, 23:2 (1980)

H. Pelling, 'The Impact of the War on the Labour Party', in H.L. Smith (ed), *War and Social Change. British Society in the Second World War* (Manchester, 1986)

B. Pimlott, *Labour and the Left in the 1930s* (London, 1977)

J. Poole, 'British Cinema Attendance in Wartime: Audience Preference at the Majestic, Macclesfield', *Historical Journal of Film, Radio and Television*, 7:1 (1987)

D.L. Prynn, 'Common Wealth – a British "Third Party" of the 1940s', *Jour-*

nal of Contemporary History, 7:12 (1972)

J. Ramsden, *The Making of Conservative Party Policy. The Conservative Research Department since 1929* (London, 1980)

J. Ramsden, '"A Party of Owners or a Party for Earners?" How Far Did the British Conservative Party Really Change after 1945?' *Transactions of the Royal Historical Society*, 5:37 (1987)

J. Richards, 'Wartime British Cinema Audiences and the Class System: The Case of "Ships With Wings" (1941)', *Historical Journal of Film, Radio and Television*, 7:2 (1987)

B. Roberts, 'A Mining Town in Wartime: the Fears for the Future', *Llafur*, 6:1 (1992)

A. Robertson, *The Bleak Midwinter, 1947* (Manchester, 1987)

R. Samuel, 'The Lost World of British Communism', *New Left Review*, 154 (1985)

J. Saville, *The Labour Movement in Britain* (London, 1988)

H.L. Smith (ed), *War and Social Change. British Society in the Second World War* (Manchester, 1986)

P. Summerfield, 'Education and Politics in the British Armed Forces in the Second World War', *International Review of Social History*, 26 (1981)

P. Summerfield, 'Mass-Observation: Social History or Social Movement?', *Journal of Contemporary History*, 20:3 (1985)

A. Sutcliffe and R. Smith, *Birmingham 1939–1970* (Oxford, 1974)

A.J.P. Taylor, *English History, 1914–45* (Oxford, 1965)

I. Taylor, 'Labour and the Impact of War, 1939–45', in N. Tiratsoo (ed), *The Attlee Years* (London, 1991)

W. Thompson, *The Long Death of British Labourism* (London, 1993)

A. Thorpe, 'The Consolidation of a Labour Stronghold 1926–1951', in C. Binfield *et al.* (eds), *The History of the City of Sheffield 1843–1993. Volume 1: Politics* (Sheffield, 1993)

N. Tiratsoo, *Reconstruction, Affluence and Labour Politics: Coventry 1945–60* (London, 1990)

N. Tiratsoo, 'Popular Politics, Affluence and the Labour Party in the 1950s', in A. Gorst *et al.* (eds), *Contemporary British History, 1931–61* (London, 1991)

N. Tiratsoo, 'The Reconstruction of Blitzed British Cities 1940–55: A General Introduction', in J. Hasegawa (ed), *The Reconstruction of British and Japanese Cities* (Tokyo, 1995)

N. Tiratsoo and J. Tomlinson, *Industrial Efficiency and State Intervention: Labour, 1939–51* (London, 1993)

R. Titmuss, *Problems of Social Policy* (London, 1950)

L. Verrill-Rhys and D. Beddoe, *Parachutes and Petticoats. Welsh Women Writing on the Second World War* (Dinas Powys, South Glamorgan, 1992)

C. Waters, *British Socialists and the Politics of Popular Culture, 1884–1914* (Manchester, 1990)

E.W. White, *The Arts Council of Great Britain* (London, 1975)

F. Williams, *Dangerous Estate. The Anatomy of Newspapers* (London, 1959)

R. Worcester, *British Public Opinion. A Guide to the History and Methodology of Political Opinion Polling* (London, 1991)

I. Zweiniger-Bargielowska, 'Rationing, Austerity and the Conservative Party Recovery after 1945', *Historical Journal*, 37:1 (1994)

9 Unpublished historical accounts

A.L.R. Calder, 'The Common Wealth Party 1942–45' (University of Sussex D.Phil., 1968)

H. Ichihashi, 'Working-Class Leisure in English Towns 1945–1960, with Special Reference to Coventry and Bolton' (University of Warwick Ph.D., 1994)

S.R. Parsons, 'Communism in the Professions. The Organisation of the British Communist Party among Professional Workers, 1933–1956' (University of Warwick Ph.D., 1990)

P. Thompson, 'Citizen Soldiers: The Resettlement of Ex-Sevice Men and Women in Britain, 1939–51' (University of Warwick Ph.D., forthcoming)

T. Tsubaki, 'Postwar Reconstruction and the Question of Popular Housing Provision, 1939–1951' (University of Warwick Ph.D., 1993)

Index